ภาษาและวัฒนธรรมไทยสำหร

Thai Language and Culture for Beginners

2

Yuphaphann Hoonchamlong

ยุพาพรรณ หุ่นจำลอง

THAI LANGUAGE PROGRAM

UNIVERSITY OF HAWAI'I AT MANOA

2007

Thai Language and Culture for Beginners Book 2
ภาษาและวัฒนธรรมไทยสำหรับผู้เริ่มเรียน เล่ม ๒
ISBN 978-974-7512-26-7

Yuphaphann Hoonchamlong
e-mail: **yuphapha@hawaii.edu**
Website: **www.yhoonchamlong.net**

พิมพ์ครั้งที่ 1: สิงหาคม 2550 | จำนวน 500 เล่ม
1st printing: August 2007 | 500 copies

Designed by: Dream Catcher Graphic Co., Ltd.
Tel. +662 455 3995 Fax. +662 454 4266

Printed in Thailand.

Preface

Thai Language and Culture for Beginners aims to provide a basic foundation in conversational Standard Thai for beginning learners. It focuses on developing the learners' listening and speaking skills.

Designed primarily for use in Thai as a Foreign Language classes in U.S. universities, this course book uses a proficiency-based approach to learning Thai and covers the daily real life topics and situations that a student might encounter. The materials in this volume (Book 2) will provide students with a foundation in Thai language proficiency for listening and speaking skills at the Intermediate Low/Mid level, as defined by American Council on the Teaching of Foreign Languages (ACTFL). Completion of these materials through classroom study and self practice will prepare students for further study of Thai.

The **Thai Language and Culture for Beginners** coursebook set (Book 1 and Book 2) consists of 31 lessons and appendix sections providing samples of songs and poems from Thailand, as well as an index to structural patterns introduced in the text and a vocabulary index in both Thai to English and English to Thai order, providing both IPA transcription and Thai script.

This volume (Book 2) consists of 11 lessons, grouped into five units. Each lesson provides the learners with a presentation of the language points or skills to be practiced by providing key terms, structures and expressions relating to the skills indicated and contextualizing them in dialogs based on the theme of the lesson.

The content of each lesson also provides relevant cultural explanations and grammar notes for the learners, so that the classroom time can be spent on language practice and language interaction for communication between teachers and students and among students.

The language material in this text is presented both in Romanized transcription based on the International Phonetic Alphabet (IPA) and Thai script, with English explanation.

For this volume (Book 2), the vocabulary index also includes the vocabulary items that appear in Book 1.

The accompanying audio-CD provides the reading of the terms and expressions introduced in each lesson. The video-DVD provides video-clips of the enactment of the contextualized dialogs as audio-visual samples of language usage.

The course book, along with the audio-CD and video-DVD, can also be used as a reference material for beginning learners to prepare and review language points practiced in class.

This textbooks and the accompanying audiovisual materials should be used in conjunction with the study of the Thai writing system. The recommended resource for Thai script instruction is J. Marvin Brown's AUA Language Center Thai Course Reading and Writing (text and workbook), published by the AUA Language Center.

Despite our effort in checking, editing and proofreading, I am certain that there are errors and inconsistencies that remain in this edition. I welcome comments, feedback and suggestions to improve this textbook.

Please send them to **yuphapha@hawaii.edu**

Description of Proficiency Thai Proficiency Guidelines

(adapted from ACTFL 1986 and Revised 1999)

Speaking

Intermediate-Low

Able to handle successfully a limited number of interactive, task-oriented, and social situations. Can ask and answer questions, initiate and respond to simple statements, and maintain face-to-face conversation, although in a highly restricted manner and with much linguistic inaccuracy. Within these limitations, can perform such tasks as introducing self, ordering a meal, asking directions, and making purchases. Vocabulary is adequate to express only the most elementary needs. Strong interference from native language may occur. Misunderstandings frequently arise, but with repetition, the Intermediate-Low speaker can generally be understood by sympathetic interlocutors.

Intermediate-Mid

Able to handle successfully a variety of uncomplicated, basic, and communicative tasks and social situations. Can talk simply about self and family members. Can ask and answer questions and participate in simple conversations on topics beyond the most immediate needs; e.g., personal history and leisure time activities. Utterance length increases slightly, but speech may continue to be characterized by frequent long pauses, since the smooth incorporation of even basic conversational strategies is often hindered as the speaker struggles to create appropriate language forms. Pronunciation may continue to be strongly influenced by first language and fluency may still be strained. Although misunderstandings still arise, the Intermediate-Mid speaker can generally be understood by sympathetic interlocutors.

Listening

Intermediate-Low

Able to understand sentence-length utterances that consist of recombinations of learned elements in a limited number of content areas, particularly if strongly supported by the situational context. Content refers to basic personal background and needs, social conventions and routine tasks, such as getting meals and receiving simple instructions and directions. Listening tasks pertain primarily to spontaneous face-to-face conversations. Understanding is often uneven; repetition and rewording may be necessary. Misunderstandings in both main ideas and details arise frequently.

Intermediate-Mid

Able to understand sentence-length utterances that consist of recombinations of learned utterances on a variety of topics. Content continues to refer primarily to basic personal background and needs, social conventions and somewhat more complex tasks, such as lodging, transportation, and shopping. Additional content areas include some personal interests and activities, and a greater diversity of instructions and directions. Listening tasks pertain not only to spontaneous face-to-face conversations but also to short routine telephone conversations and some deliberate speech, such as simple announcements and media reports. Understanding continues to be uneven.

Acknowledgments

The **Thai Language and Culture for Beginners** course book and the accompanying audio-CD and video-DVD were developed during 2003-2006 with funding from the U.S. Department of Education (International Research and Studies Program Grant Award No. P017A030070).

I also would like to acknowledge the influence and guidance of the following predecessor Thai textbooks: J. Marvin Brown's *A.U.A. Language Center Thai Course* Books 1 and 2, Adrian Palmer's *Small Talk*, Preecha Juntanamalaga and Tony Diller's *Beginning Thai*, Wilaiwan Khanittanan's *An Introductory Course in Thai Language and Culture* and Manas Chitakasem and David Smyth's *Linguaphone Thai*. For the presentational format, I am also particularly inspired and influenced by Cynthia Ning's *Communicating in Chinese*.

My special thanks to Yudthaphon "Noom" Vichianin, my technical assistant, whose technical expertise is instrumental in the preparation and production of the text manuscript and the audio-visual materials. He also contributed as one of the readers of lists of words and phrases for the audio CD, and he served as a sounding board for the realistic quality of the language used in the dialogs.

I would like to thank my English language editors, Liam Kelley and Carol Compton, who not only took time from their busy schedules to help improve the English explanations but also provided useful comments and suggestions on the overall content, format and organization of the book. I also thank Michael Snook, who edited the English translation of the dialogs in the first draft. For the audio-visual material production, I would like to thank Rugchanok Janevarakul for her assistance with the audio materials production, Weerin Chaiariyakul and Kanjana Thepboriruk for their assistance in the final compilation of the audio CD, Suthida Kalayanarooj for her advice on the video production, and Yi Yong Huang for his technical assistance. I am also grateful to the National Foreign Language Resource Center of the University of Hawaii for permission to use their language instruction graphics and clip-art collection. My thanks also go to John Hartmann, Prawet Jantharat, Chintana Takahashi and to my other Thai Language teaching colleagues in the United States and Thailand for providing moral support over the years. Lastly, I thank the University of Hawaii's Department of Indo Pacific Languages and the College of Languages, Linguistics and Literatures for administrative support during this project.

Pictures & Graphics

ABOUT THE LANGUAGE

- Map of Thailand: from CIA World Factbook 2002, public domain https://www.cia.gov/cia/publications/factbook/geos/th.html

UNIT 6.1

- Clip art graphics of clothing items: UH-NFLRC and UVic's Language Teaching Clipart Library http://web.uvic.ca/hcmc/clipart/
- Thai boy and girl wearing Thai costume: www.siamweb.org

UNIT 6.3

- face shapes and eyeglasses frame: Kaiser Permanente Brochure: Lens Choices
- Thai fruit pictures from: http://www.yummytaste.com/ingeneral/fruits.htm

UNIT 7.1

- Clip art graphics (in color): UH-NFLRC and clipart.com
- Clip art graphics (black and white): Purdue's Royalty-Free Clip Art Collection for Foreign/Second Language Instruction: http://tell.fll.purdue.edu/JapanProj/ /FLClipart/
- Takraw game: http://www.a2xtreme.com/art/0012d.jpg
- surf-girl: http://www.sunsetsuzy.com/waikikisl.htm
- web-surf: http://www.caos.deanza.fhda.edu/misc/weblinks.htm
- play-computer: http://users.telenet.be/a141174/afdelingen/rak.htm
- chatroom: http://www.lindamoran.net/imageteens/chatroom.jpg
- waterfall: http://www.mtviewresort.com/picture/narok.jpg

UNIT 8.1

- Man and body parts: กรมการศึกษานอกโรงเรียน (2545) *แบบฝึกอ่านหนังสือไทย กศน.* พิมพ์ครั้งที่ 2 กรุงเทพฯ: กองพัฒนาการศึกษานอกโรงเรียน. หน้า 54
- Clip art graphics (in color): UH-NFLRC and clipart.com
- Clip art graphics (black and white): Purdue's Royalty-Free Clip Art Collection for Foreign/Second Language Instruction http://tell.fll.purdue.edu/JapanProj/ /FLClipart/

UNIT 8.2

- Clip art graphics: clipart.com

UNIT 10.1

- Clip art graphics: clipart.com and UVic's Language Teaching Clipart Library http://web.uvic.ca/hcmc/clipart/

UNIT 10.2

- Special express, 2nd class (rail) train: http://www.seat61.com/Thailand.htm

APPENDIX 2.1

- Loy Krathong poster: http://www.loikrathong.net/TH/download.php (Tourist Authority of Thailand)

APPENDIX 2.4

- Jit's picture: http://www.geocities.com/thaifreeman/jit/jit.html

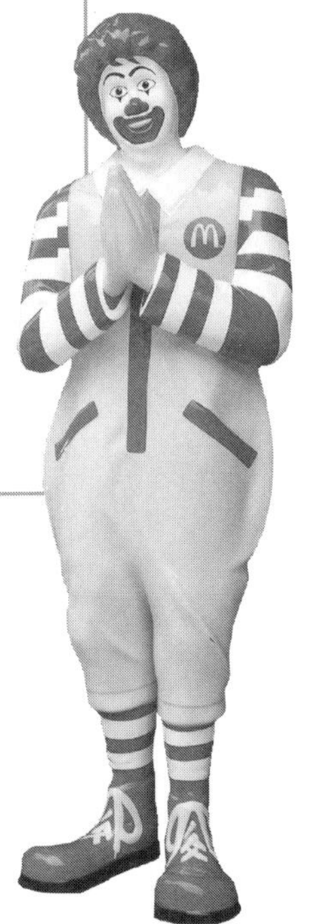

The remaining graphics and pictures were created/taken by the author.

Music & Songs

UNIT 10.2

- ผู้ใหญ่ลี (Village Chief Lee)
  Music and vocal by: ต่อพงศ์ วรรณวาที (Torpong Wannawati)

APPENDIX 2.3

- Loy Krathong karaoke: http://www.loikrathong.net/TH/download.php
  (Tourist Authority of Thailand)

There are instances where we have been unable to trace or contact the copyright holder before our printing deadline. We apologize for this apparent negligence. If notified, we will be pleased to rectify any errors or omissions at the earliest opportunity.

Table of Contents

UNIT 10

APPENDICES

REFERENCES

Abbreviations

The following abreviations are used to indicate the "part of speech" or "grammatical category."

n.	**noun**
num.	**numeral**
clf.	**classifier**
d.a.	**demonstrative adjective**
d.p.	**demonstrative pronoun**
pron.	**pronoun**
conj.	**conjunction**
prt.	**particle**
excl.	**exclamation**
aux.	**auxiliary**
neg.	**negation**
prep.	**prepositon**
adv.	**adverb (degree, manner, duration, frequency, time)**
quant.	**quantifier**
v.	**verb**
name	**name**
mod.	**noun modifier**
q.	**question word**

About the Thai Language & Transcription Guide

Thai, also known as **Siamese** or **Standard Thai**, is the official national language of Thailand, a country located in the center of Southeast Asia sharing common borders with Malaysia, Myanmar, Laos and Cambodia. It is spoken by about 60 million people in Thailand.

Thai is a tonal language belonging to the **Tai language family**, which includes languages spoken in Assam, northern Burma, all of Thailand including the peninsula, Laos, Northern Vietnam and the Chinese provinces of Yunnan, Guizhou (Kweichow) and Guangxi (Kwangsi).

A Thai sentence may contain a subject, a verb, and an object in that order, similar to English. Thai does not make use of inflections or verb conjugation. Tense distinctions in the sentences are either determined by context or by adverbs and expressions of time.

Thai has its own script, which is basically alphabetic in nature, i.e., the script corresponds with the pronunciation.

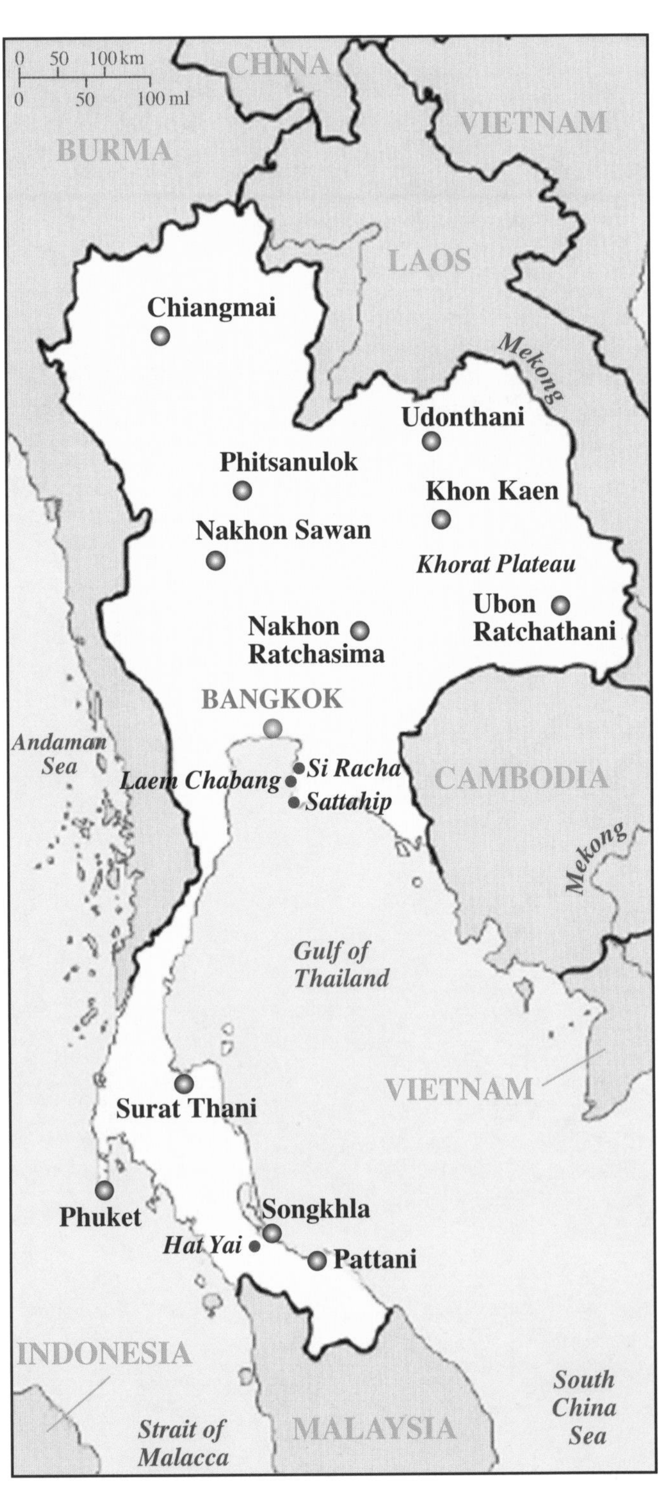

Standard Thai is only one of four major regional Thai dialects spoken in Thailand. It is based on the Central Thai dialect as spoken in Bangkok. Other major regional dialects are: Kham Muang spoken in Northern Thailand, Isan or Lao, spoken in the Northeast region and Pak Tai or Southern Thai, spoken in Southern Thailand.

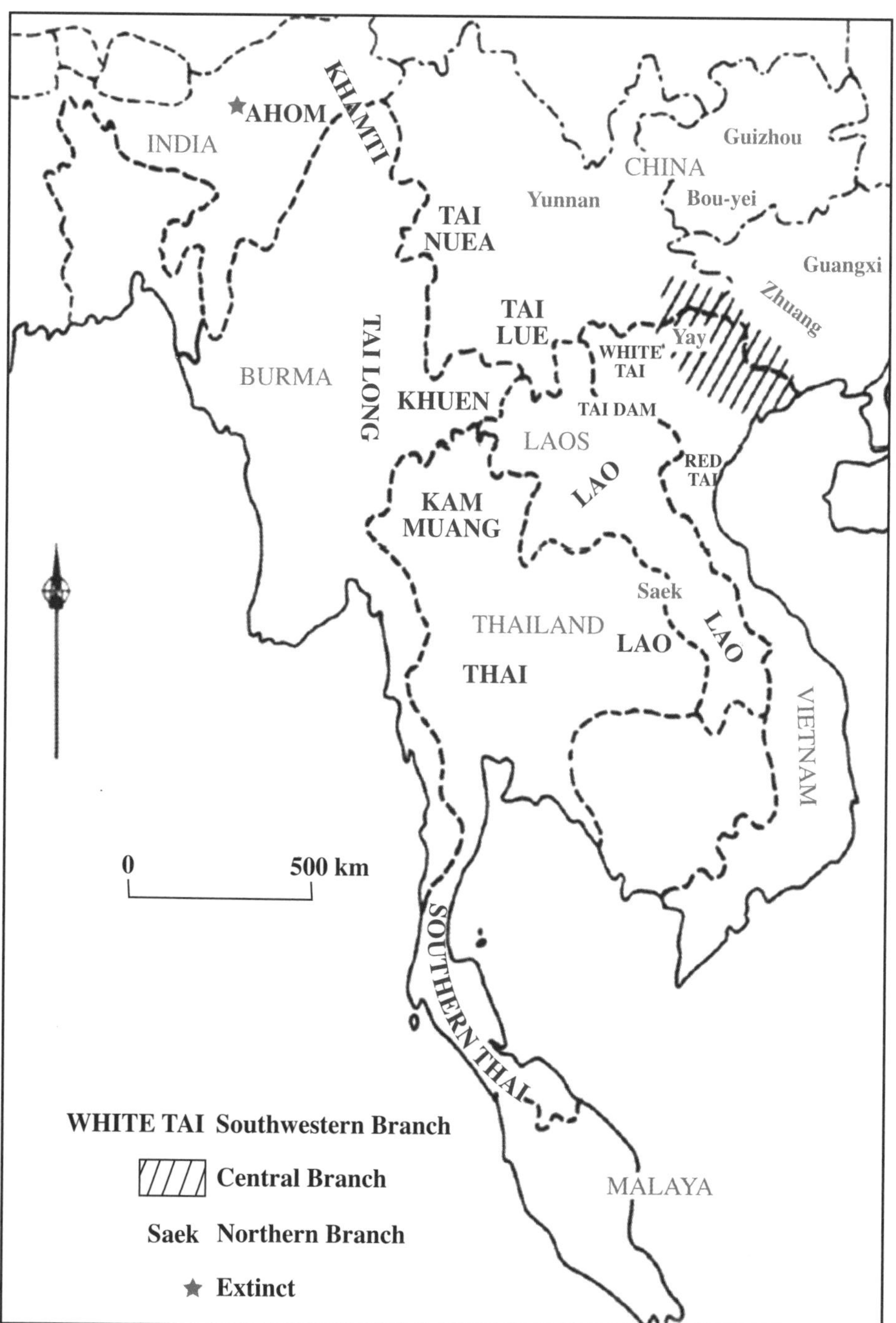

Map: Approximate General Location of Some Tai Language (From Comrie, Bernard (ed). ***The World's Major Languages*****. New York: Oxford University Press, 1990.)**

Standard Thai Sound System and Transcription Guide

In this book, the lessons are presented in Thai script and in transcription symbols marked by /.... /, representing the pronunciation. A syllable break within a multi-syllable word is indicated by the marker -.

The transcription symbol set used in this book follows the transcription convention used in Brown 1967, which is based on the International Phonetic Association (IPA) Symbols.

Consonant Sounds

There are 20 consonant sounds in Standard Thai.

The following chart presents IPA consonant symbols matched with the corresponding Thai consonants that are pronounced in a similar way or the same way as the sounds of their English consonant counterparts.

b	d	f	h	l	m	n	r	s	w	y
บ	ด, ฎ	ฟ	ห, ฮ	ล, ฬ	ม	น, ณ	ร	ส, ศ, ษ	ว	ย, ญ

The following chart of symbols presents those consonants that are pronounced a bit differently from the sounds as pronounced in English. The closest pronunciation of a sound as it occurs in an English word is provided as a guide.

Note: The h combination in the following symbols means that a sound is pronounced with a puff of air.

Symbol	Approximate pronunciation	Thai Consonants	Thai word Example
p	as in s**p**in	ป	ปา /paa/ *to throw*
ph	as in **p**in	พ, ภ, ผ	พา /phaa/ *to bring along*
t	as in s**t**ill	ต, ฏ	ตา /taa/ *eye*
th	as in **t**ill	ท, ฑ, ถ	ทา /thaa/ *to spread on*
k	as in s**k**in	ก	กา /kaa/ *crow*
kh	as in **k**in	ค, ฆ, ข	คา /khaa/ *to be lodged in*
c	as in Spanish **c**incilla:	จ	จาน /caan/ *plate*
ch	as in **ch**urch:	ช, ฌ, ฉ	ชา /chaa/ *tea*
ʔ	as in the beginning sound in the second syllable of "uh-uh" (meaning "no")	อ	อา /ʔaa/ *younger sibling of father*
ŋ	as in si**ng**	ง	งาน /ŋaan/ *work*

Vowel Sounds

There are 18 single vowels in Standard Thai: a set of nine short vowels, and a set of their nine long counterparts. There are also three diphthongs. The following charts show the place of articulation and tongue height in pronunciation. The long vowels are indicated by double vowel symbols.

Short Vowels

	Front	Central	Back
High	i	ʉ	u
Mid	e	ə	o
Low	ɛ	a	ɔ

Long Vowels

	Front	Central	Back
High	ii	ʉʉ	uu
Mid	ee	əə	oo
Low	ɛɛ	aa	ɔɔ

Diphthongs

ia	ʉa	ua

The following are approximate pronunciations in English words that each vowel transcription symbol represents, along with an example of a Thai word with the vowel.

Short and Long Vowels

i	as in h**i**t ติ /tìʔ/ *to scold*	ii	as in b**ea**t ตี /tii/ *to hit*
e	as in g**e**t เอ็น /ʔen/ *tendon*	ee	as in g**a**te เอน /ʔeen/ *to lean*
ɛ	as in c**a**t แกะ /kɛʔ/ *sheep*	ɛɛ	as in b**a**d แก /kɛɛ/ *you*

u	as in co**u**ld ยุง /yuŋ/ *mosquito*
o	as in log**o** สด /sòt/ *to be fresh*
ɔ	as in b**o**ttom* เกาะ /kɔ̀ʔ/ *island*
a	as in b**u**tter วัง /waŋ/ *palace*
ə	– เถอะ /thə̀ʔ/ *a final particle*
ʉ	as in **u**h-**u**h ขึง /khʉ̌ŋ/ *to stretch*

uu	as in t**oo** ยูง /yuuŋ/ *peacock*
oo	as in s**o** โสด /sòot/ *to be single*
ɔɔ	as in P**au**l* ก่อ /kɔ̀ɔ/ *to create*
aa	as in f**a**r วาง /waaŋ/ *to put*
əə	as in b**ir**d เธอ /thəə/ *she*
ʉʉ	as in h**mm** ขืน /khʉ̌ʉn/ *to resist, defy*

*Please note that in some dialects of American English, the ɔ sound and the ɔɔ sound may not occur in these words.

Diphthongs

ia	as in b**eer**	เมีย /mia/ 'wife'
ʉa	-	เรือ /rʉa/ 'boat'
ua	as in t**our**	ทั่ว /thûa/ 'throughout'

Note that for the diphthongs, the vowels in the English examples only approximate the Thai sounds; they are not exact equivalents.

Tones

Thai is a tonal language. This means pitches are meaningful. A syllable pronounced with a different pitch will carry a different meaning.

There are five distinctive tones (pitches) in Standard Thai. They are

1. mid level tone (no tone mark in the transcription)
   for example: คา /khaa/ *to be lodged in*

2. low level tone (marked with the symbol ` in the transcription)
   for example: ข่า /khàa/ *Galanga, an aromatic root*

3. falling tone (marked with the symbol ˆ in the transcription)
   for example: ข้า /khâa/ *I, slave, servant*

4. high level tone (marked with the symbol ´ in the transcription)
   for example: ค้า /kháa/ *to sell*

5. rising tone (marked with the symbol ˇ in the transcription)
   for example: ขา /khǎa/ *leg*

Mid	**Low**	**Falling**	**High**	**Rising**
คา /khaa/ 'to be lodged in'	ข่า /khàa/ 'Galanga, an aromatic root'	ข้า /khâa/ 'I, slave, servant'	ค้า /kháa/ 'to sell'	ขา /khǎa/ 'leg'

The following is a chart of average fundamental frequency contours for tones adapted from the chart given in Jackson Gandour (1976).

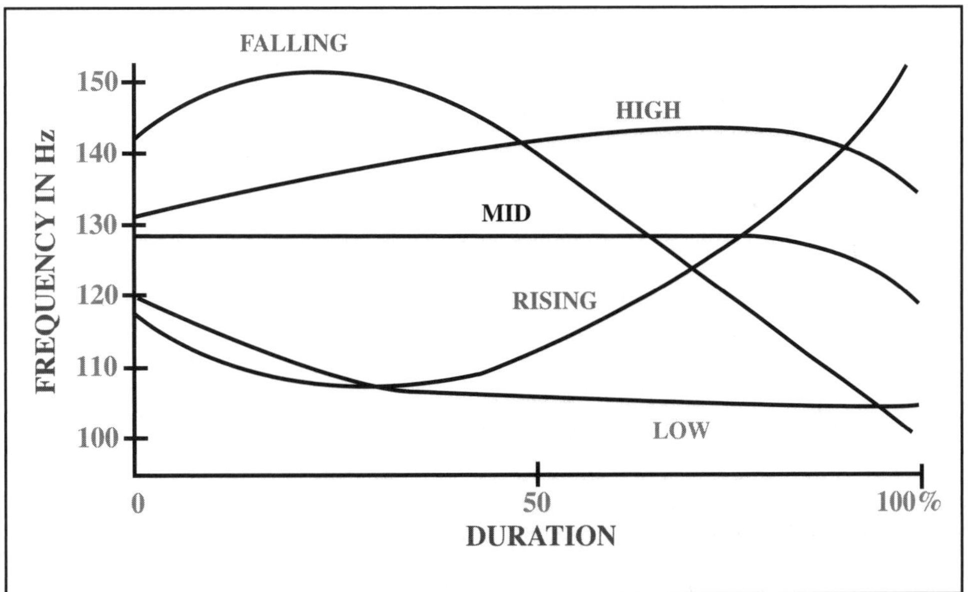

References

Comrie, Bernard (ed.). *The World's Major Languages.* New York: Oxford University Press, 1990.

Gandour, Jackson. 1996. *Aspects of Thai Tones. Doctoral Dissertation.* University of California, Los Angeles. Ph.D.Dissertation, 1996.

A Note on Transcription, Pronunciation and Orthography.

The transcription in this textbook reflects the pronunciation of the words used in careful connected speech in conversational Standard Thai, to serve as a guide for pronunciation for learners. It is a compromise between the "authoritative" pronunciation of words in citation form (i.e. said in isolation) which reflects the written form (in Thai script) and the actual pronunciation in colloquial Thai in everyday natural speech.

There can be some discrepancy between the transcription and the recorded pronunciation in the accompanying audio files. This serves as an example of the variation in pronunciation in natural speech of Thai speakers.

The following are some of the prevalent and noticeable variations in spoken Thai that you might encounter in natural conversational speech of Thai speakers.

- Vowels in unstressed syllables (typically the first syllable in a multi-syllable word) tend to be shortened, and the tone in such shortened syllables tends to be neutralized to mid tone
- The substitution of the sound /r/ with /l/, for example, เรา /raw/ is pronounced as เลา /law/
- The omission of the sound /r/ or /l/ in initial consonant clusters, for example, อังกฤษ /ʔaŋ-krìt/ is pronounced as /ʔaŋ-kìt/, เปล่า /plàaw/ is pronounced as /pàaw/
- For speakers in their twenties or younger, there are slight change in the ending pitch of the falling tone and the rising tone; i.e., the falling tone does not quite "fall" and the rising tone does not quite "rise"

หน่วยที่ ๖

lesson 1
Talk about clothing and colors

lesson 2
Talk about size and fittings, and request specific items of clothing

lesson 3
Talk about shapes and colors; describe objects; learn about Thai fruits; and review the names of months

บทที่ ๑

Lesson 1

Skill: To talk about clothing and colors

Clothes ...เสื้อผ้า /sʉ̂a-phâa/

เสื้อ /sʉ̂a/
• upper garment (clf. ตัว /tua/)

เสื้อแขนยาว
/sʉ̂a khɛ̌ɛn yaaw/
long-sleeved top

เสื้อแขนสั้น
/sʉ̂a khɛ̌ɛn sân/
short-sleeved top

เสื้อแขนกุด
/sʉ̂a khɛ̌ɛn kùt/
sleeveless blouse

เสื้อยืด
/sʉ̂a-yʉ̂ʉt/
T-shirt, tee-shirt

เสื้อเชิ้ต
/sʉ̂a-chə́ət/
shirt

เสื้อฮาวาย
/sʉ̂a haa-waay/
aloha shirt

เสื้อโปโล
/sʉ̂a poo-loo/
polo shirt

เสื้อกล้าม
/sʉ̂a-klâam/
men's undershirt

กางเกง /kaaŋ-keeŋ, kaŋ-keeŋ/
• trousers (clf. ตัว /tua/)

กางเกงขายาว
/kaŋ-keeŋ khǎa-yaaw/
long pants, trousers

กางเกงขาสั้น
/kaŋ-keeŋ khǎa-sân/
shorts, short pants

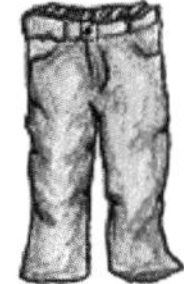

กางเกงยีน
/kaŋ-keeŋ yiin/
jeans

กระโปรง
/krà-prooŋ/, /kra-prooŋ/
• skirt

กระโปรงชุด
/krà-prooŋ chút/
• dress

สูท
/sùut/
• suit

เสื้อนอก
/sɯ̂a-nɔ̂ɔk/
• suitcoat, jacket

รองเท้า /rɔɔŋ-tháaw, rɔŋ-tháaw/
• footware (clf. คู่ /khûu/ for a pair; ข้าง /khâaŋ/ for in a pair)

รองเท้าแตะ
/rɔɔŋ-tháaw-tɛ̀/
• slippers, sandals

รองเท้ากีฬา
/rɔɔŋ-tháaw kii-laa/
• sports shoes

รองเท้าผ้าใบ
/rɔɔŋ-tháaw phâa-bay/
• canvas shoes, tennis shoes, sneakers

ถุงเท้า
/thǔŋ-tháaw/
• socks, stockings, hose

เข็มขัด
/khěm-khàt/
• belt (clf. เส้น /sên/)

หมวก
/mùak/
• hat, cap (clf. ใบ /bay/)

เนคไท
/nék-thay/
• necktie (clf. เส้น /sên/)

เสื้อชั้นใน /sɯ̂a chán nay/
• upper undergarment
(Lit. inner layer upper-garment)

กางเกงชั้นใน /kaŋ-keeŋ chán nay/
กางเกงใน /kaŋ-keeŋ nay/
• lower undergarment (Lit. inner layer pants)

เขาใส่อะไร kháw sày ʔa-ray	s/he + to wear + what	What is s/he wearing?
เขาแต่งตัวยังไง kháw tὲŋ-tua yaŋ-ŋay	s/he + to dress + how	What is s/he wearing?
เขาใส่ ______ kháw sày ______	s/he + to wear ______	S/he wears/puts on ______.
เขาสวม ______ kháw sǔam ______	s/he + to wear ______	S/he wears/puts on ______.
เขานุ่งกางเกง kháw nûŋ kaŋ-keeŋ	s/he + to wear lower garment + pants	S/he wears/puts on pants.
เขานุ่งกระโปรง kháw nûŋ kra-prooŋ	she + to wear lower garment + skirt	She wears/puts on a skirt.
เขาคาดเข็มขัด kháw khâat khěm-khàt	s/he + to put around + belt	S/he wears/puts on a belt.
เขาผูกเน็คไท kháw phùuk nék-thay	he + to tie + necktie	He wears/puts on a necktie.
เขาลองเสื้อผ้า kháw lɔɔŋ sʉ̂a-phâa	s/he + to try + clothes	S/he tries on clothes.
เขาลองใส่เสื้อผ้า kháw lɔɔŋ sày sʉ̂a-phâa	s/he + to try + to put on + clothes	S/he tries on clothes.
เขาเปลี่ยนเสื้อผ้า kháw plìan sʉ̂a-phâa	s/he + to change + clothes	He changes clothes.
เขาถอดเสื้อผ้า kháw thɔ̀ɔt sʉ̂a-phâa	s/he + to take off + clothes	S/he takes off clothes.

/kà-rú-naa
thɔ̀ɔt rɔɔŋ-tháaw/

Colors ...สี /sǐi/

สีอะไร? /sǐi ʔa-ray/

สีขาว	sǐi khǎaw	white
สีน้ำเงิน	sǐi nám-ŋən	dark blue
สีน้ำตาล	sǐi nám-taan	brown
สีเขียว	sǐi khǐaw	green
สีส้ม	sǐi sôm	orange
สีม่วง	sǐi mûaŋ	purple

สีดำ	sǐi dam	black
สีฟ้า	sǐi fáa	sky blue
สีแดง	sǐi dɛɛŋ	red
สีเหลือง	sǐi lɨ̌aŋ	yellow
สีชมพู	sǐi chom-phuu	pink
สีเทา	sǐi thaw	grey

Color of the day

สีประจำวัน /sǐi pra-cam wan/

วันจันทร์ สีเหลือง	wan can sǐi lɨ̌aŋ
วันอังคาร สีชมพู	wan ʔaŋ-khaan sǐi chom-phuu
วันพุธ สีเขียว	wan phút sǐi khǐaw
วันพฤหัส สีส้ม	wan phá-rɨ́-hàt sǐi sôm
วันศุกร์ สีฟ้า	wan sùk sǐi fáa
วันเสาร์ สีม่วง	wan sǎw sǐi mûaŋ
วันอาทิตย์ สีแดง	wan ʔaa-thít sǐi dɛɛŋ

Patterns ...ลาย /laay/

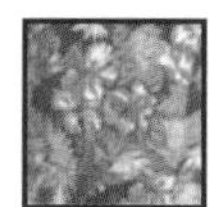

ลายดอก
/laay-dɔ̀ɔk/
• **flower pattern**

ลายจุด
/laay-cùt/
• **dot pattern**

ลายทาง
/laay-thaaŋ/
• **stripe pattern**

ลายสก็อต
/laay-sa-kɔ́t/
• **Scottish plaid pattern**

Listening Practice ...ฝึกหัด ฟัง /fʉ̀k-hàt faŋ/

Uniform
เครื่องแบบ /khrʉ̂aŋ-bɛ̀ɛp/

ที่มหาวิทยาลัยเมืองไทย นักศึกษาส่วนมากใส่เครื่องแบบนักศึกษา
นักศึกษาชายใส่กางเกงขายาวสีดำหรือสีน้ำเงิน เสื้อเชิ้ตแขนสั้น
หรือแขนยาวสีขาว ผูกเนคไทสีน้ำเงิน และคาดเข็มขัด
นักศึกษาหญิงใส่กระโปรงสีดำ หรือสีน้ำเงิน หรือสีกรมท่า
ใส่เสื้อสีขาว และคาดเข็มขัด

thîi ma-hǎa-wít-tha-ya-lay mʉaŋ thay nák-sʉ̀k-sǎa
sùan-mâak sày khrʉ̂aŋ-bɛ̀ɛp nák-sʉ̀k-sǎa.
nák-sʉ̀k-sǎa chaay sày kaaŋ-keeŋ khǎa yaaw sǐi dam rʉ̌ʉ sǐi nám-ŋən sʉ̂a-chə́ət
khɛ̌ɛn sân rʉ̌ʉ khɛ̌ɛn yaaw sǐi khǎaw. phùuk nék-thay sǐi nám-ŋən lɛ́ khâat khěm-khàt.
nák-sʉ̀k-sǎa yǐŋ sày kra-prooŋ sǐi dam rʉ̌ʉ sǐi nám-ŋən rʉ̌ʉ sǐi krom-ma-thâa.
sày sʉ̂a sǐi khǎaw lɛ́ khâat khěm-khàt.

- **At Thai universities, most of the students wear a uniform. Male students wear black or dark blue trousers, a short-sleeved or long-sleeved white shirt, and a dark blue or black neck tie. They also wear a belt. Female students wear a black or dark blue skirt, a white blouse, and wear a belt.**

Vocabulary ...ศัพท์ /sàp/

แขน	khɛ̌ɛn	n. arm, sleeve (clf. ข้าง /khâaŋ/)
กุด	kùt	v. to cut off, to be truncated
ยืด	yʉ̂ʉt	v. to stretch, extend, lengthen
กล้าม	klâam	n. muscle
ขา	khǎa	n. leg (of the body, of a piece of furniture, of a journey) (clf. ข้าง /khâaŋ/)
ชุด	chút	clf. for a suit, dress (e.g. of clothing)
เท้า	tháaw	n. foot (clf. ข้าง /khâaŋ/)
ผ้าใบ	phâa-bay	n. canvas, sailcloth (clf. ผืน /phʉ̌ʉn/)
ชั้น	chán	n. layer

ใส่	sày	v. to put on, to put in, insert
แต่ง	tɛ̀ŋ	v. to ornament, decorate, adorn
แต่งตัว	tɛ̀ŋ-tua	v. to dress, get dressed, be dressed
สวม	sǔam	v. to put on, wear
นุ่ง	nûŋ	v. to dress, put on, wear (lower garment, e.g. trousers, the phanung, etc.)
คาด	khâat	v. to put around, to tie around, to belt, to strap
ผูก	phùuk	v. tie, bind, fasten
เปลี่ยน	plìan	v. to change, vary, alter
ถอด	thɔ̀ɔt	v. to remove, take off (as an article of clothing)
กรุณา	kà-rú-naa, ka-ru-naa	v. to be so kind as to, please (do such and such)
ประจำ	pra-cam	v. constantly, regularly, habitually
ประจำวัน	pra-cam wan	daily; everyday, routine
ดอก	dɔ̀ɔk	clf. classifier for flowers of all kinds
จุด	cùt	n. spot, speck, dot, point
สก็อต	sa-kɔ́t	n. Scotch, Scottish, Scotland (from English Scot)
ส่วนมาก	sùan-mâak	adv. mostly, the greater part
กรมท่า	krom-ma-thâa	n. navy blue

Dialogs ...บทสนทนา /bòt sǒn-tha-naa/

Dialog 6.1.1

Chai (A) and Amy (C) compliment Suda (B) on her clothes.

A	โอ้โฮ วันนี้ตุ๊กแต่งตัวสวยจัง มีนัดกับแฟนเหรอ	ʔôo-hoo. wan-níi túk tɛ̀ŋ-tua sǔay caŋ. mii nát kàp fɛɛn rɤ̌ɤ.	Wow! You're wearing such a nice outfit today. Do you have a date with your boyfriend?
B	ขอบใจจ้ะ ตุ๊กไม่ได้มีนัดกับใครหรอก นี่เสื้อใหม่จ้ะ ซื้อเมื่ออาทิตย์ที่แล้ว	khɔ̀ɔp-cay câ. túk mây-dây mii nát kàp khray rɔ̀k. nîi sʉ̂a mày câ. sʉ́ʉ mʉ̂a ʔaa-thít thîi lɛ́ɛw.	Thanks. I don't a have a date with anyone. This is my new blouse. I just bought it last week.
C	เสื้อสวยจริงๆ ค่ะ ซื้อที่ไหนคะ	sʉ̂a sǔay ciŋ-ciŋ khâ. sʉ́ʉ thîi-nǎy khá.	It's a real pretty blouse! Where did you buy it?
B	ซื้อที่จตุจักรค่ะ	sʉ́ʉ thîi cà-tu-càk khâ.	I bought it at Chatuchak.
C	แพงไหมคะ	phɛɛŋ máy khá.	Was it expensive?

B	ไม่แพงหรอกค่ะ 200 บาทเท่านั้น ที่จตุจักรมีเสื้อผ้าสวยๆ ราคาไม่แพง ถ้าเอมี่สนใจ ตุ๊กจะพาไปซื้อเสาร์อาทิตย์นี้ ดีไหม	mây phɛɛŋ rɔ̀k khâ. sɔ̌ɔŋ rɔ́ɔy bàat thâw-nán. thîi cà-tu-càk mii sʉ̂a-phâa sǔay-sǔay raa-khaa mây phɛɛŋ. thâa ʔee-mîi sǒn-cay túk ca phaa pay sʉ́ʉ sǎw ʔaa-thít níi dii máy	Not at all. Only 200 Baht. At Chatuchak, there are lots of pretty but inexpensive clothes. If you are interested, I can take you shopping there this weekend. What do you think?
C	ตกลงค่ะ	tòk-loŋ khâ.	OK.

Dialog 6.1.2

Suda (A), Amy (B) and Dan (C) discuss students' clothing.

สถาบันการศึกษา
โปรดแต่งกายสุภาพ

/sa-thǎa-ban kaan-sʉ̀k-sǎa pròot tɛ̀ŋ-kaay sù-phâap/

A เอมี่ กับ แดน ที่อเมริกา นักศึกษาต้องใส่เครื่องแบบไหม

ʔee-mîi kàp dɛɛn thîi ʔa-mee-ri-kaa nák-sʉ̀k-sǎa tɔ̂ŋ sày khrʉ̂aŋ-bɛ̀ɛp máy.

- Amy and Dan, in America do students have to wear a uniform?

B ไม่ต้อง นักเรียนบางโรงเรียนเท่านั้นที่ต้องใส่เครื่องแบบ

mây-tɔ̂ŋ. nák-rian baaŋ rooŋ-rian thâw-nán thîi tɔ̂ŋ sày khrʉ̂aŋ-bɛ̀ɛp.

- No. Only some school students need to wear a uniform.

A ถ้ายังงั้น ที่อเมริกานักศึกษาแต่งตัวไปเรียนยังไง

thâa yaŋ-ŋán nák-sʉ̀k-sǎa thîi ʔa-mee-ri-kaa tɛ̀ŋ-tua pay rian yaŋ-ŋay.

- So, what kind of clothes do American students wear to class?

B ใส่อะไรก็ได้

sày ʔa-ray kɔ̂-dâay.

- (They wear) anything.

C ที่มหาวิทยาลัยพระนคร นักศึกษาไม่ต้องใส่เครื่องแบบก็ได้ใช่ไหม

thîi ma-hǎa-wít-tha-yaa-lay phrá-ná-khɔɔn nák-sʉ̀k-sǎa mây tɔ̂ŋ sày khrʉ̂aŋ-bɛ̀ɛp kɔ̂-dâay chây máy.

- At Phra Nakhon University, students don't have to wear a uniform, do they?

A ใช่ แต่ต้องใส่เสื้อผ้าสุภาพ กางเกงขายาว หรือ กระโปรงสำหรับผู้หญิง แต่ใส่กางเกงขาสั้นไม่ได้ ผู้หญิงใส่เสื้อสายเดี่ยว เสื้อเกาะอก ก็ไม่ได้

chây. tɛ̀ɛ tɔ̂ŋ sày sʉ̂a-phâa sù-phâap. kaaŋ-keeŋ khǎa-yaaw. rʉ̌ʉ kra-prooŋ sǎm-ràp phûu-yǐŋ. tɛ̀ɛ sày kaaŋ-keeŋ khǎa-sân mây dâay. phûu-yǐŋ sày sʉ̂a sǎay-dìaw sʉ̂a kɔ̀-ʔòk kɔ̂ mây dâay

- No, they don't, but they have to wear respectable clothes like long trousers, or skirts for women, and you cannot wear shorts. Women also cannot wear "Sua saai diaw" and "Sua ko ok."

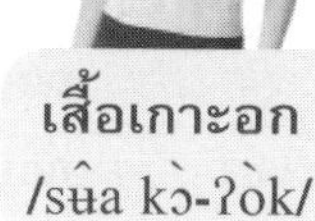

เสื้อเกาะอก
/sʉ̂a kɔ̀-ʔɔ̀k/

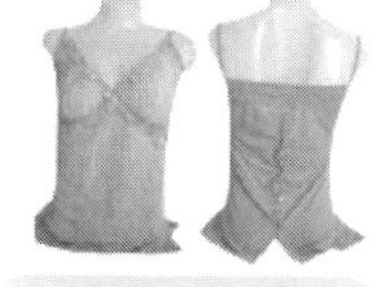

เสื้อสายเดี่ยว
/sʉ̂a sǎay-dìaw/

B เสื้อสายเดี่ยวกับเสื้อเกาะอกเป็นยังไง
sʉ̂a sǎay-dìaw kàp sʉ̂a kɔ̀-ʔɔ̀k pen yaŋ-ŋay.
- What are "sua saai diaw" and "Sua ko ok" like?

A เสื้อสายเดี่ยว คือ เสื้อไม่มีแขน แต่มีเส้นเล็ก ๆ
เสื้อเกาะอก คือเสื้อที่ไม่มีแขน คาดอก
sʉ̂a sǎay-dìaw khʉʉ sʉ̂a mây mii khɛ̌ɛn tɛ̀ɛ mii sên lék-lék.
sʉ̂a kɔ̀-ʔɔ̀k khʉʉ sʉ̂a thîi mây mii khɛ̌ɛn khâat ʔòk.
- "Sua saai diaw" is a sleeveless top with thin straps [i.e. a spaghetti strap tank top]. "Sua ko ok" is a top that is sleeveless and wraps around the chest [i.e., a tube top].

C ที่ฮาวาย นักศึกษามหาวิทยาลัยใส่อะไรก็ได้ไปเรียน กางเกงขาสั้น เสื้อสายเดี่ยว เสื้อเกาะอก
thîi haa-waay nák-sʉ̀k-sǎa ma-hǎa-wít-tha-yaa-lay sày ʔa-ray kɔ̂-dâay pay rian.
kaŋ-keeŋ khǎa-sân sʉ̂a sǎay-dìaw sʉ̂a kɔ̀-ʔɔ̀k
- In Hawaii, college students can wear anything to school; shorts, spaghetti strap tank tops, or tube tops.

B ที่วิสคอนซินเหมือนกัน หน้าร้อนเอมี่ก็จะใส่ขาสั้น เสื้อสายเดี่ยว เสื้อเกาะอกไปเรียน
thîi wís-khɔn-sîn mʉ̌an kan. nâa rɔ́ɔn ʔee-mîi kɔ̂ ca sày khǎa-sân sʉ̂a sǎay-dìaw sʉ̂a kɔ̀-ʔɔ̀k pay rian.
- In Wisconsin too. In summer, I also wear shorts, spaghetti strap tank tops, and tube tops to school.

Dialog 6.1.3

Amy (A) and Suda (B) discuss respectable clothes.

A	พรุ่งนี้ แดนกับเอมี่จะไปเที่ยววัดพระแก้วและวัง จะต้องแต่งตัวสุภาพ ใช่ไหมคะ	phrûŋ-níi dɛɛn kàp ʔee-mîi ca pay thîaw wát phrá-kɛ̂ɛw lɛ́ waŋ. ca tɔ̂ŋ tɛ̀ŋ-tua sù-phâap chây máy khá.	Tomorrow Dan and I are going to visit the Temple of the Emerald Buddha and the (Grand) Palace. We need to dress respectably, don't we?
B	ใช่	chây.	Yes.
A	แต่งตัวยังไงดีคะ	tɛ̀ŋ-tua yaŋ-ŋay dii khá.	How should I dress?
B	อย่าใส่กางเกงขาสั้น หรือ เสื้อไม่มีแขน หรือ กระโปรงสั้นมากเกินไป	yàa sày kaŋ-keeŋ khǎa-sân rʉ̌ʉ sʉ̂a mây mii khɛ̌ɛn rʉ̌ʉ kra-prooŋ sân mâak kəən pay.	Don't wear shorts or a sleeveless top or a skirt too short.
A	ถ้านักท่องเที่ยวแต่งตัวไม่สุภาพ จะเข้าวัด เข้าวังไม่ได้ใช่ไหมคะ	thâa nák thɔ̂ŋ-thîaw tɛ̀ŋ-tua mây sù-phâap ca khâw wát khâw waŋ mây dâay chây-máy khá.	If a tourist does not dress properly, s/he cannot enter a temple or a palace, right?

B ใช่ แต่ที่วัดพระแก้ว นักท่องเที่ยวผู้หญิงจะเช่าผ้านุ่งได้ ใส่ทับกางเกงขาสั้นหรือกระโปรงสั้น	châay. tɛ́ɛ thîi wát phrá-kɛ̂ɛw nák thɔ̂ŋ-thîaw phûu-yǐŋ ca châw phâa-nûŋ dâay. sày tháp kaaŋ-keeŋ khǎa sân rɨ́ɨ kra-prooŋ sân.	Yes, but at the Temple of the Emerald Buddha, female tourists can rent a tube skirt to wear over shorts or a short skirt.

นักท่องเที่ยวใส่ผ้านุ่งเช่าที่วัดพระแก้ว
/nák thɔ̂ŋ-thîaw sày phâa-nûŋ châw thîi wát phrá-kɛ̂ɛw/

Proverb ...สุภาษิต /su-phaa-sìt/

ไก่ งาม เพราะ ขน คน งาม เพราะ แต่ง kày ŋaam phrɔ́ khǒn khon ŋaam phrɔ́ tɛ̀ŋ	Rooster + to be beautiful + because + feathers People + to be beautiful +, because + to ornate	A rooster is beautiful because of its feathers; People are beautiful because they dress up.

"Fine feathers make fine birds."

Vocabulary ...ศัพท์ /sàp/

โอ้โฮ	ʔôo-hoo	excl. Gosh! Wow! Oh!
เหรอ	rɔ̌ɔ	excl. Is that so? (expressing surprise at what was said)
จริงๆ	ciŋ-ciŋ	adv. really, very
ขอบใจ	khɔ̀ɔp-cay	v. to thank (someone)
หรอก	rɔ̀ɔk, rɔ̀k	prt. particle meaning "not so"; often used with statements of negation, contradiction, or those correcting a misapprehension. Usually makes a statement milder, less abrupt, or expresses reassurance

สนใจ	sǒn-cay	v. to be interested (in)
สุภาพ	sù-phâap	v. to be polite, respectable
สถาบัน	sa-thǎa-ban	n. institute (clf. แห่ง /hɛ̀ŋ/)
โปรด	pròot	v. please (do such and such)
แต่งกาย	tɛ̀ŋ-kaay	v. to dress (= แต่งตัว /tɛ̀ŋ-tua/)
เดี่ยว	dìaw	v. to be single, sole
เกาะ	kɔ̀ʔ	v. to cling to
อก	ʔòk	n. chest, breast
อะไรก็ได้	ʔa-ray-kɔ̂-dâay	Anything will do. Anything whatever.
วัง	waŋ	n. palace
เกินไป	kəən-pay	adv. excessively, too
ทับ	tháp	v. to put on top of, overlay, superimpose
งาม	ŋaam	v. to be beautiful
ขน	khǒn	n. fur, hair (of body) (clf. เส้น /sên/); feathers (clf. ขน /khǒn/)

Language Notes

1. Talking about wearing items of clothing in Thai: *ใส่* /sày/, *สวม* /sǔam/, *นุ่ง* /nûŋ/, *คาด* /khâat/, *ผูก* /phùuk/

Thai has a number of words to talk about "wearing" clothes or ornaments. The generic verb "to wear" or "to put on" for clothing is ใส่ /sày/ or สวม /sǔam/, and both are used with garments and some accessories such as shoes, socks, hats and jewelry.

Other words with more restricted usages that refer specifically to the manner of wearing the item are:

นุ่ง /nûŋ/ : used with lower garment only, such as pants, skirts, and Thai ผ้านุ่ง /phâa-nûŋ/ (see Culture Note below).

คาด /khâat/: used with เข็มขัด /khěm-khàt/ "belt" only.

ผูก /phùuk/: used with เนคไท /nék-thay/ "necktie" only.

2. In Unit 5.4 of Book 1, we see ห้าม /hâam/ "It is prohibited to" used in a "prohibited" sign, but for a sign that requests cooperation, words like กรุณา /kà-rú-naa/ or โปรด /pròot/ "Please (do such and such)" are used, as shown in the two signs in this lesson.

3. Some expressive expressions in colloquial Thai

The dialogs in this lesson present some more expressive exclamations or words that are commonly used in casual conversations among friends.

- โอ้โฮ /ʔôo-hoo/ is an exclamation expressing surprise or excitement. The pronunciation varies according to the degree of excitement of speakers, for example, /ʔôo-hǒo/, /ʔûu-hǔu/, or shortened to /hǒo/.
- จัง /caŋ/ "very" and จริงๆ /ciŋ-ciŋ/ "really" are colloquial degree adverbs equivalent of มาก /mâak/.
- หรอก /rɔ̀k/ is a sentence final attitude particle, used in conjunction with a negator ไม่/mây/ or ไม่ได้ /mây-dây/ in correcting an assumption (see Structure Note 3c. in Unit 5.4). For example, in Dialog 6.1.1, when Suda says: ตุ๊ก**ไม่ได้**มีนัดกับใคร**หรอก** /túk mây-dây mii nát kàp khray rɔ̀k/, she is correcting Chai's assumption that she's having a date with someone.

4. Indefinite pronouns

a. The wh-question words mentioned in Unit 1.2: ใคร /khray/, อะไร /ʔa-ray/, ที่ไหน /thîi-nǎy/, เมื่อไร /mɨ̂a-rày/ also function as indefinite pronouns.

	as Question Word	as Indefinite Pronoun
ใคร /khray/	who	someone, anyone
อะไร /ʔa-ray/	what	something, anything
ที่ไหน /thîi-nǎy/	where	some where, anywhere
เมื่อไร /mɨ̂a-rày/	when	any time

An example of this indefinite pronoun usage is in Dialog 6.1.1, also discussed above:

ตุ๊กไม่ได้มีนัดกับ**ใคร**หรอก /túk mây-dây mii nát kàp khray rɔ̀k/ "I did not have a date with anyone."

b. Repetition of the above indefinite pronouns gives the meaning of unspecified "every" or "-ever":

	as Indefinite Pronoun
ใครๆ /khray-khray/	everybody, whoever
อะไรๆ /ʔa-ray-ʔa-ray/	everything, whatever
ที่ไหนๆ /thîi-nǎy-thîi-nǎy/	everywhere, wherever
เมื่อไรๆ /mɨ̂a-rày-mɨ̂a-rày/	whenever

For example:

ใคร ๆ ก็ บอกว่า อาหารไทย อร่อย	khray-khray kɔ̂ bɔ̀ɔk-wâa ʔa-haan thay ʔa-rɔ̀y	Everybody says that Thai food is delicious.
ที่ร้านนี้ ***อะไร ๆ*** ก็อร่อย	thîi ráan níi ʔa-ray-ʔa-ray kɔ̂ ʔa-rɔ̀y	At this place, everything is delicious.

c. When ***ก็ได้*** /kɔ̂-dâay/ is added to an indefinite pronoun, it makes an expression equivalent to "Any-X will do." In Dialog 6.1.2, for example, Dan uses อะไรก็ได้ /ʔa-ray kɔ̂-dâay/ when asked about what American university students wear to school.

อะไรก็ได้ /ʔa-ray kɔ̂-dâay/	Anything will do. Whatever.
ใครก็ได้ /khray kɔ̂-dâay/	Anyone will do. Whoever.
ที่ไหนก็ได้ /thîi-nǎy kɔ̂-dâay/	Anywhere will do. Wherever.
เมื่อไหร่ก็ได้ /mʉ̂a-rày kɔ̂-dâay/	Any time will do. Whenever.
ยังไงก็ได้ /yaŋ-ŋay kɔ̂-dâay/	Whatever manner. However.
เท่าไรก็ได้ /thaw-ray kɔ̂-dâay/	Whatever amount.
<u>*Clf*</u> ไหนก็ได้ /<u>*Clf*</u> nǎy kɔ̂-dâay/	Whichever item/unit.

5. Replying to a negative question with ใช่ไหม /chây-máy/

In Unit 1.3, you learn that ใช่ไหม /chây-máy/ is used to ask for confirmation, in the same way as tag questions in English. To reply in confirmation of the statement, one replies by asserting with ใช่ /chây/, and to contradict the statement, one replies with ไม่ใช่ /mây-chây/.

In this respect,ใช่ /chây/ and ไม่ใช่ /mây-chây/ are NOT used in quite the same way as English "yes" and "no." English "yes" is used ***only*** with a positive statement, and "no" is used *only* with a negative statement. But notice that ใช่ /chây/ is used to confirm or agree with a statement, whether positive or negative statement, and ไม่ใช่ /mây-chây/ is used to contradict or disagree with a statement, whether positive or negative.

In Dialog 6.1.2 and 6.1.3, you see two examples of negative questions with ใช่ไหม /chây-máy/

ที่มหาวิทยาลัยพระนคร นักศึกษา<u>*ไม่*</u>ต้องใส่ เครื่องแบบก็ได้<u>***ใช่ไหม***</u>	thîi ma-hǎa-wít-tha-yaa-lay phrá-ná-khɔɔn nák-sʉ̀k-sǎa <u>mây</u> tɔ̂ŋ sày khrʉ̂aŋ-bɛ̀ɛp kɔ̂-dâay <u>chây-máy</u>.	At Phra Nakhon University, students don't have to wear a uniform, do they?

ถ้านักท่องเที่ยวแต่งตัวไม่สุภาพ จะเข้าวัดเข้าวังไม่ได้ ใช่ไหม	thâa nák thɔ̂ŋ-thîaw tɛ̀ŋ-tua mây sù-phâap ca khâw wát khâw waŋ mây dâay chây-máy	If a tourist does not dress properly, s/he cannot enter a temple or a palace, right?

Notice that in confirming such negative questions, ใช่ /chây/ is used, whereas in English, one confirm such negative statements with "No."

So, keep in mind that ใช่ /chây/ in Thai is not equivalent to English "yes." Think of ใช่ /chây/ as "I confirm your statement," or "Your statement is correct."

Culture Notes

1. In addition to the beliefs about activities that one should or should not do on a given day of the week as mentioned in Unit 4.3, some Thais also associate an auspicious color with each day of the week. The daily colors presented in this lesson are considered to be "lucky colors" for each day.

2. Appearance and self-presentation is an important part of the social etiquette in Thai society and an indicator of one's status. This includes proper attire for the occasion and place. Respectable/proper attire is the norm for visiting or conducting business with government offices, temples and educational institutions.

3. Thais do not wear shoes in the interior of their homes or inside a chapel in a temple. So, remember to take your shoes off when you visit Thai homes and temple chapels.

4. In this lesson, a number of well known places that are tourist attractions in Bangkok are mentioned.

จตุจักร /cà-tu-cak/: is the name of a park and a weekend "swap meet" market north of Bangkok. This name has been written in various spellings in English, such as Jatujak and Chatuchak. Some foreigners also know this market as "JJ Market."

This market covers an area of 35 acres, contains more than 15,000 shops and stalls selling extensive range of products at bargain price. The products on sale include household accessories, handicrafts, religious artifacts, art works, antiques, live animals, books, music, clothes, food, plants and flowers.

วัดพระแก้ว /wát phrá-kɛ̂ɛw/ (Lit. temple of the precious stone Buddha) is the informal short name of the Temple of the Emerald Buddha, located in the compound of the Grand Palace (**พระบรมมหาราชวัง** /phrá-bɔ-rom-ma-hǎa-râat-cha-waŋ/).

A virtual tour of this palace and temple and other royal palaces of the Bureau of the Royal Household can be viewed from its official website: http://www.palaces.thai.net/

วัดพระแก้ว
/wát phrá-kɛ̂ɛw/

พระบรมมหาราชวัง
/phrá-bɔ-rom-ma-hǎa-râat-cha-waŋ/

5. Traditionally, Thais wear ผ้านุ่ง /phâa-nûŋ/ as a lower garment. This cloth can be worn as a wrap around tube skirt, or in a pant-like "dhoti" fashion called โจงกระเบน /cooŋ-kra-been/.

บทที่ ๒

Lesson 2

Skills: To talk about size and fittings; and request specific items of clothing

Size ...ขนาด /kha-nàat/

ขนาด	kha-nàat	size
เบอร์	bɔɔ	number
เล็ก	lék	small
กลาง	klaaŋ	medium
ใหญ่	yày	large
ฟรีไซส์	frii-sáy	free size (from English)

คุณใส่<u>เสื้อ</u>ขนาดอะไร คุณใส่<u>เสื้อ</u>เบอร์อะไร	khun sày <u>sɨ̂a</u> kha-nàat ʔa-ray khun sày <u>sɨ̂a</u> bɔɔ ʔa-ray	What size of *<u>blouse/shirt</u>* do you wear? What number of *<u>blouse/shirt</u>* do you wear?
ฉันใส่<u>เสื้อ</u>ขนาด<u>กลาง</u> ฉันใส่<u>เสื้อ</u>เบอร์ <u>8</u>	chán sày <u>sɨ̂a</u> kha-nàat <u>klaaŋ</u> chán sày <u>sɨ̂a</u> bɔɔ <u>pɛ̀ɛt</u>	I wear a size *<u>medium</u> <u>blouse/shirt</u>*. I wear a size *<u>8</u> <u>blouse/shirt</u>*.

Fitting

พอดี	phɔɔ-dii	v. to be just right (in size, amount, etc.)
กำลังดี	kam-laŋ-dii	v. to be just right (in size, amount, etc.)
ใส่พอดี	sày phɔɔ-dii	(It) fits just right.
ใส่ไม่ได้	sày mây dâay	(It) doesn't fit.
หลวม	lǔam	v. to be loose
คับ	kháp	v. to be tight, tight-fitting
ฟิต	fít	v. to be tight, tight-fitting (from English "fit")
ใหญ่	yày	v. to be big
เล็ก	lék	v. to be small

Talking about fit

เสื้อใส่เป็นยังไง sɨ̂a sày pen yaŋ-ŋay	*blouse/shirt* + to wear + "how is it"	How does the *blouse/shirt* fit?
เสื้อใส่ดีไหม sɨ̂a sày dii máy	*blouse/shirt* + to wear + well + q. prt.	Does the *blouse/shirt* fit well?
เสื้อใส่ได้ไหม sɨ̂a sày dâay máy	*blouse/shirt* + to wear + able + q. prt.	Does the *blouse/shirt* fit?
เสื้อใส่พอดี sɨ̂a sày phɔɔ-dii	*blouse/shirt* + to wear + to be just right	The *blouse/shirt* fits just right.
เสื้อหลวมเกินไป sɨ̂a lǔam kəən pay	*blouse/shirt* + to be loose + excessively	The *blouse/shirt* is too loose.
เสื้อหลวมไป sɨ̂a lǔam pay	*blouse/shirt* + to be loose + excessively	
กางเกงสั้นมาก kaŋ-keeŋ sân mâak	*pants* + to be short + very	The *pants* are very short.
รองเท้าคับนิดหน่อย rɔɔŋ-tháaw kháp nít-nɔ̀y	*shoes* + to be tight + a little	The *shoes* are a little tight.
ส้นสูงไปหน่อย sôn sǔuŋ pay nɔ̀y	*heels* + to be high + excessively + a little	The *heels* are a bit too high.

ขอลองเสื้อดูหน่อยนะ khɔ̌ɔ lɔɔŋ sɨ̂a duu nɔ̀y ná	Can I try on the *blouse/shirt* please?
มีเสื้อขนาดเล็กกว่านี้ไหม mii sɨ̂a kha-nàat lék kwàa níi máy	Do you have a *smaller* size of the *blouse/shirt*?

Asking about and referring to a specific piece or item

เสื้อตัวไหน sɨ̂a tua nǎy	blouse/shirt + clf. + which	Which blouse? (Lit. Which one of the blouses?)
เสื้อตัวนี้ sɨ̂a tua níi	blouse/shirt + clf. + this	This blouse.
กางเกงตัวนั้น kaŋ-keeŋ tua nán	pants + clf. + that	That (pair of) pants.

รองเท้าคู่สีน้ำเงิน rɔɔŋ-tháaw khûu sǐi nám-ŋən	shoes + clf. pair + to be blue	The blue (pair of) shoes.
หมวกใบใหญ่ mùak bay yày	hat + clf. + to be big	The big hat.
เข็มขัดเส้นสีแดง khěm-khàt sên sǐi dɛɛŋ	belt + clf. + to be red	The red belt.

Talking about shades of color

เข้ม	khêm	v. to be dark (of color)
แก่	kɛ̀ɛ	v. to be dark (of color)
อ่อน	ʔɔ̀ɔn	v. to be light (of color)
สด	sòt	v. to be bright (of hue)
สว่าง	sa-wàaŋ	v. to be bright (of hue)
มืด	mʉ̂ʉt	v. to be dark (of hue)

Talking about kinds of fabric and fabric qualities

(ผ้า) ฝ้าย	(phâa) fâay	cotton
(ผ้า) ไหม	(phâa) mǎy	silk
หนัง	nǎŋ	leather
ผ้ายืด	phâa yʉ̂ʉt	stretchable fabric

หนา	nǎa	v. to be thick
บาง	baaŋ	v. to be thin
สีตก	sǐi tòk	v. to be non colorfast (Lit. color fades)
สีไม่ตก	sǐi mây tòk	v. to be colorfast
ยืด	yʉ̂ʉt	v. to stretch
หด	hòt	v. to shrink

เสื้อตัวนี้ซักด้วยเครื่องได้ไหม sʉ̂a tua níi sák dûay khrʉ̂aŋ dây-máy เสื้อตัวนี้ซักเครื่องได้ไหม sʉ̂a tua níi sák khrʉ̂aŋ dây-máy	Is this *shirt/blouse* machine washable?
เสื้อตัวนี้ซักเครื่องไม่ได้ ต้องซักด้วยมือเท่านั้น sʉ̂a tua níi sák khrʉ̂aŋ mây dâay tɔ̂ŋ sák dûay mʉʉ thâw-nán	This *shirt/blouse* is not machine washable, only hand washable.
เสื้อตัวนี้ทำจากอะไร sʉ̂a tua níi tham-càak ʔa-ray เสื้อตัวนี้ทำด้วยอะไร sʉ̂a tua níi tham-dûay ʔa-ray	What is this *shirt/blouse* made of?
เสื้อตัวนี้ทำจากผ้าไหม sʉ̂a tua níi tham-càak phâa-mǎy เสื้อตัวนี้ทำด้วยผ้าไหม sʉ̂a tua níi tham-dûay phâa-mǎy	This *shirt/blouse* is made of *silk*.

Dialogs ...บทสนทนา /bòt sǒn-tha-naa/

Dialog 6.2.1 At a clothing shop

Suda (B) talks to the vendor (A).

A รับอะไรดีคะ

ráp ʔa-ray dii khá.

- What would you like?

B ขอดูกระโปรงตัวนี้หน่อยได้ไหมคะ

khɔ̌ɔ duu kra-prooŋ tua nán nɔ̀y dây-máy khá.

- May I take a look at this skirt?

A ตัวสีแดง ใช่ไหมคะ คุณใส่ไซส์อะไรคะ

tua sǐi dɛɛŋ chây-máy khá. khun sày sáy ʔa-ray khá.

- That red one? What size do you wear?

B ไซส์ M ค่ะ ขอลองกระโปรงดูหน่อยนะคะ มีห้องลองไหมคะ

sáy ʔem khâ. khɔ̌ɔ lɔɔŋ kra-prooŋ duu nɔ̀y ná khá. mii hɔ̂ŋ-lɔɔŋ máy khá.

- M. May I try on the skirt? Do you have a fitting room?

A ได้ค่ะ ห้องลองอยู่ทางโน้นค่ะ

dâay khâ. hɔ̂ŋ-lɔɔŋ yùu thaaŋ nóon khâ.

- Yes. The fitting room is over there.

Suda returns.

A	ใส่เป็นยังไงคะ พอดีไหมคะ	sày pen yaŋ-ŋay khá. phɔɔ-dii máy khá.	How is it? Does it fit?
B	ขนาดพอดีค่ะ แต่สั้นไปหน่อย มียาวกว่านี้ไหมคะ	kha-nàat phɔɔ-dii khâ tɛ̀ɛ sân pay nɔ̀y. mii yaaw kwàa níi máy khá.	The size fits, but the skirt is too short. Do you have a longer one?
A	ถ้ากระโปรงแบบนี้ ไม่มียาวกว่านี้ค่ะ คุณลองแบบนี้ดูไหมคะ	thâa kra-prooŋ bɛ̀ɛp níi mây mii yaaw kwàa níi khâ. khun lɔɔŋ bɛ̀ɛp níi duu máy khá.	If it is this style of skirt, I don't have a longer one. Please try on this style.

Suda returns.

A	เป็นยังไงคะ ใส่ดีไหมคะ	pen yaŋ-ŋay khá. sày dii máy khá.	How is it? Does it fit?
B	พอดีค่ะ ตัวละเท่าไหร่คะ	phɔɔ-dii khâ. tua la thâw-rày khá.	It fits well. How much is it?
A	200 บาทค่ะ ขนาดนี้มีหลายสี จะรับกี่ตัวดีคะ	sɔ̌ɔŋ-rɔ́ɔy bàat khâ. kha-nàat níi mii lǎay sǐi. ca ráp kìi tua dii khá.	200 Baht. This size comes in many colors. How many do you want?
B	เอาตัวสีเขียวนี้ตัวเดียวเท่านั้นค่ะ	ʔaw tua sǐi khǐaw níi tua diaw thâw-nán khâ.	Only this green one.
A	ได้ค่ะ	dâay khâ.	Ok.

Dialog 6.2.2

At a pants shop, Suda (A) talks to the vendor (B).

A ขอลองกางเกงแบบนี้ เบอร์ M หน่อยค่ะ

khɔ̌ɔ lɔɔŋ kaŋ-keeŋ bɛ̀ɛp níi bəə ʔem nɔ̀y khâ.

• I'd like to try on this pair of pants, size M, please.

B นี่ค่ะ

nîi khâ.

• Here you are.

Later on.

B	เป็นยังไง ใส่ได้ไหมคะ	pen yaŋ-ŋay. sày dâay máy khá.	How are they? Do they fit?
A	ใส่พอดีค่ะ แต่ขายาวไปหน่อย จะแก้ให้ได้ไหมคะ	sày phɔɔ-dii khâ. tɛ̀ɛ khǎa yaaw pay nɔ̀y. ca kɛ̂ɛ hây dây-máy khá.	They fit, but they are too long (Lit. the legs are too long). Can you alter them?
B	ได้ค่ะ เราจะตัดขาให้ แต่ใช้เวลา 1 วัน พรุ่งนี้คุณมารับได้ไหมคะ	dâay khâ. raw ca tàt khǎa hây. tɛ̀ɛ cháy wee-laa nɯ̀ŋ wan. phrûŋ-níi khun maa ráp dây-máy khá.	Yes. We can shorten them (Lit. cut the legs), but it takes a day. Can you pick them up tomorrow?

A	ได้ค่ะ อ้อ แล้วตัวนี้สีตกไหมคะ	dâay khâ. ʔɔ̂ɔ. lɛ́ɛw tua níi sǐi tòk máy khá.	Yes. By the way, will the color of these fade?
B	สีไม่ตกค่ะ ซักเครื่องได้ ไม่ยืด และ ไม่หด คุณจะรับสีอื่นด้วยไหมคะ	sǐi mây tòk khâ. sák khrɨ̂aŋ dâay. mây yɨ̂ɨt lɛ́ mây hòt. khun ca ráp sǐi ʔɨ̀ɨn dûay máy khá.	No. They're colorfast. They're machine washable, do not stretch and do not shrink. Would you like to get other colors too?
A	ไม่ค่ะ รับตัวนี้ตัวเดียวเท่านั้น	mây khâ. ráp tua níi tua diaw thâw-nán.	No. Just this one only.
B	ค่ะ	khâ.	Ok.

Proverbs ...สุภาษิต /su-phaa-sìt/

หัวล้านได้หวี hǔa-láan dâay wǐi	to be bald + to get + comb	A bald man acquires a comb.
	"To cast pearls before swine."	

ตาบอดได้แว่น taa-bɔ̀ɔt dâay wɛ̂n	to be blind + to get + spectacles	A blind man acquires a pair of spectacles.
	"To cast pearls before swine."	

Vocabulary ...ศัพท์ /sàp/

ส้น	sôn	n. heel (of the foot or shoes)
มือ	mɨɨ	n. hand
แบบ	bɛ̀ɛp	n. style, model (clf. แบบ /bɛ̀ɛp/)
ห้องลอง	hɔ̂ŋ-lɔɔŋ	n. fitting room
โน้น	nóon	d.a. over there
หลาย	lǎay	quant. many, several
แก้	kɛ̂ɛ	v. to undo (an error), correct, revise, alter
ตัด	tàt	v. to cut, sever
ให้	hây	prep. for
หัวล้าน	hǔa-láan	v. to be bald-headed
หวี	wǐi	n. comb (clf. อัน /ʔan/)
ตาบอด	taa-bɔ̀ɔt	v. to be blind
แว่น	wɛ̂n	n. glasses, spectacles (clf. อัน /ʔan/)

Language Notes

1. In Dialogs 6.1.1 and 6.1.2, we see another use of ลองดู /lɔɔŋ-duu/ (introduced in Unit 3.4) in the context of "trying on" items of clothing.

2. In talking about sizes of clothing, English abbreviation loans such as: S, M, L, XL are also used, but may be pronounced the Thai way, adjusting to the Thai sound system, for example: /ʔéet/ for "S," /ʔɛɛw/ or /ʔɛɛn/for "L," /ʔék-ʔɛɛw/ or /ʔék-ʔɛɛn/for "XL," since Thai does not have "s" or "l" as final consonant sounds.

3. Another popular English loanword used in talking about fitting is the word ฟิต /fít/ from English "fit." However, in the Thai usage, it has changed its meaning to "to be tight."

4. In this lesson, you see more examples of ***ขอ* /khɔ̌ɔ/ + *Verb***, a request for the speaker to do something and ***ขอ* /khɔ̌ɔ/ + *Noun***, a request for an item, discussed in Unit 3.3.

Structure Notes

1. The structure used for talking about the result of trying on clothes is the same as the structure for expressing an evaluative result introduced in Unit 1.3 and 1.4.

2a. Subject + Verb + Object + (ไม่ mây) + Evaluative Post-verb + (Adverb-degree)

เสื้อใส่พอดี sʉ̂a sày phɔɔ-dii	shirt/blouse + to wear + to fit	The blouse/shirt fits.
เสื้อใส่ไม่พอดี sʉ̂a sày mây phɔɔ-dii	shirt/blouse + to wear + not + to fit	The blouse/shirt does not fit.

2. The structure used to refer to a specific item, by specifying a certain property or attribute of the item is the same as the demonstrative noun phrase structure #1, *Noun+ Classifier + Demonstrative*, discussed in Unit 1.4, with a "specifier" or modifying attribute occupying the same position as a demonstrative.

1a. Noun + Classifier + Specifier

There can also be a sequence of *Classifier + Specifier* modifying the noun. The sequence can also be used with *Classifier + Demonstrative* as the last modifying element. In this case of a sequence of noun modifiers, there only needs to be one classifier at the end.

1b. Noun + (Classifier + Specifier) + (Classifier + Demonstrative)

เสื้อตัวสีแดง sʉ̂a tua sǐi-dɛɛŋ	blouse/shirt + clf. + to be red	The red blouse/shirt.
เสื้อตัวสีแดงตัวนี้ sʉ̂a tua sǐi-dɛɛŋ tua níi	blouse/shirt + clf. + to be red + clf. + this	This red blouse/shirt.
เสื้อสีแดงตัวนี้ sʉ̂a sǐi-dɛɛŋ tua níi	blouse/shirt + to be red + clf. + this	This red blouse/shirt.

The corresponding question with ไหน /nǎy/ "which" has the same structure:

1c. Noun + Classifier + ไหน /nǎy/

เสื้อตัวไหน sʉ̂a tua nǎy	blouse/shirt + clf. + which	Which blouse/shirt?
หนังสือเล่มไหน naŋ-sʉ̌ʉ lêm nǎy	book + clf. + which	Which book?

Culture Note

The sizes for clothes can be given as: S, M, L, XL etc., or as numbers, in which case, the number follows the European size number (such as Size 38, 40, 42 etc. for women's clothing). However, since there is no standard shoe and clothing size in Thailand, especially in small shops or stalls, one always asks to try on the item. Fitting rooms are typically available only in department stores or some big clothing stores. When shopping for clothes from street vendors or stalls, Thais try on the clothing by putting them on top of whatever they are wearing.

บทที่ ๓

Lesson 3

Skills: To talk about shapes and colors; describe objects; learn about Thai fruits; and review the names of months

Shapes ...รูปร่าง /rûup-râaŋ/

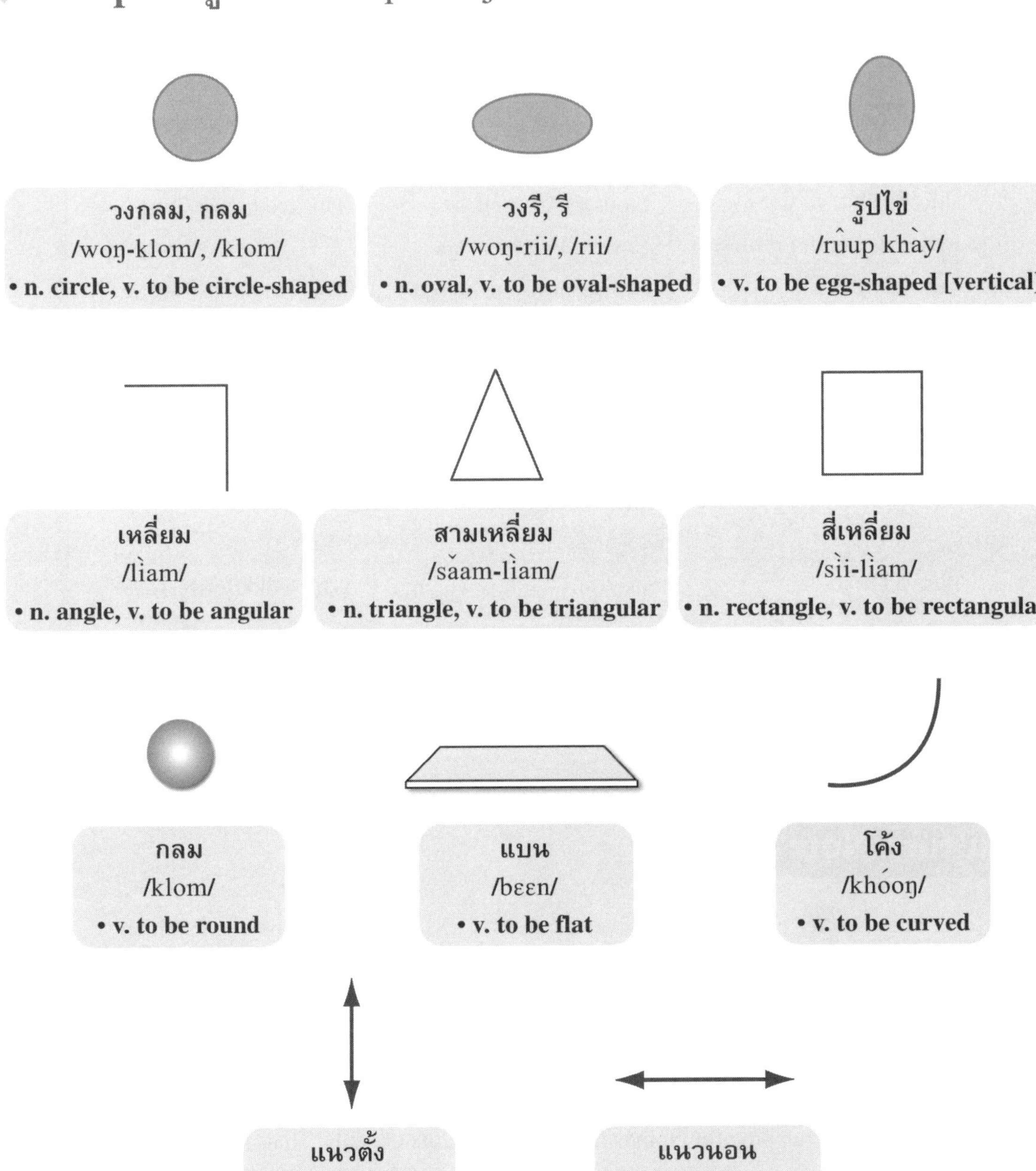

Listening Practice ...ฝึกหัด ฟัง /fɨ̀k-hàt faŋ/

Choosing a frame for eyeglasses
เลือกกรอบแว่นตา /lɨ̂ak krɔ̀ɔp wɛ̂n-taa/

คนหน้ากลม ควรจะเลือกกรอบแว่นตารูปสี่เหลี่ยม

khon nâa klom khuan-ca lɨ̂ak krɔ̀ɔp wɛ̂n-taa rûup sìi-lìam

- A person with a round-shaped face should choose rectangular/square eyeglass frames.

คนหน้าสี่เหลี่ยม ควรจะเลือกกรอบแว่นตารูปกลมหรือรูปวงรี

khon nâa sìi-lìam khuan-ca lɨ̂ak krɔ̀ɔp wɛ̂n-taa rûup klom rɨ̌ɨ rûup woŋ-rii

- A person with a square-shaped face should choose round or oval eyeglass frames.

คนหน้าสามเหลี่ยม ควรจะเลือกกรอบแว่นตารูปสี่เหลี่ยม

khon nâa sǎam-lìam khuan-ca lɨ̂ak krɔ̀ɔp wɛ̂n-taa rûup sìi-lìam

- A person with a triangle-shaped face should choose rectangular/square eyeglass frames.

คนหน้ารูปไข่ ใส่แว่นตากรอบรูปอะไรก็ได้

khon nâa rûup-khày sày wɛ̂n-taa krɔ̀ɔp rûup ʔa-ray kɔ̂-dâay

- A person with an oval-shaped face can wear eyeglass frames of any shape.

Thai Fruit Seasons
...หน้าผลไม้ไทย /nâa phǒn-la-máay thay/

	กล้วย kluây **banana**	ตลอดปี ta-lɔ̀ɔt pii all year round 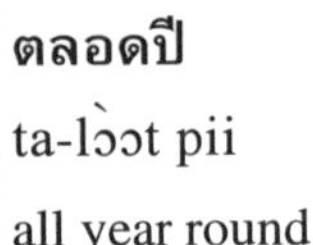		ทุเรียน thú-rian **durian**	พฤษภาคม-สิงหาคม phrʉ́t-sa-phaa-khom thʉ̌ŋ sǐŋ-hǎa-khom May-August
	องุ่น ʔa-ŋùn **grape**	กันยายน-มีนาคม kan-yaa-yon thʉ̌ŋ mii-naa-khom September-March	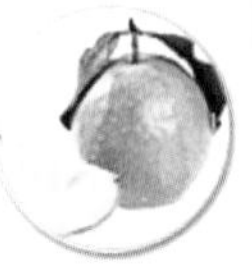	ฝรั่ง fa-ràŋ **guava**	ตลอดปี ta-lɔ̀ɔt pii all year round
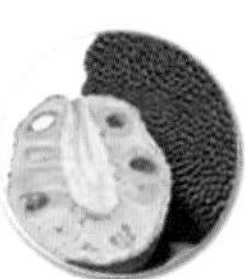	ขนุน kha-nǔn **jackfruit**	มกราคม-พฤษภาคม mók-ka-raa-khom thʉ̌ŋ phrʉ́t-sa-phaa-khom January-May		ลางสาด ลองกอง laaŋ-sàat lɔɔŋ-kɔɔŋ **lansa** **longkong**	สิงหาคม-ตุลาคม sǐŋ-hǎa-khom thʉ̌ŋ tù-laa-khom August-October
	ลิ้นจี่ lín-cìi **lychee**	เมษายน-มิถุนายน mee-sǎa-yon thʉ̌ŋ mí-thu-naa-yon April-June		ลำไย **lam-yay** **longan**	มิถุนายน-สิงหาคม mí-thu-naa-yon thʉ̌ŋ sǐŋ-hǎa-khom June-August
	มะม่วง má-mûaŋ **mango**	มกราคม-พฤษภาคม mók-ka-raa-khom thʉ̌ŋ phrʉ́t-sa-phaa-khom January-May		มังคุด maŋ-khút **mangosteen**	พฤษภาคม-ตุลาคม phrʉ́t-sa-phaa-khom thʉ̌ŋ tù-laa-khom May-October
	มะละกอ má-lá-kɔɔ **papaya**	ตลอดปี ta-lɔ̀ɔt pii all year round		ส้มโอ sôm-ʔoo pomelo	สิงหาคม-พฤศจิกายน sǐŋ-hǎa-khom thʉ̌ŋ phrʉ́t-sa-cì-kaa-yon August-November

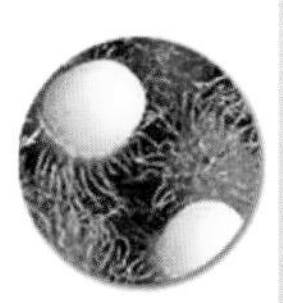

เงาะ
ŋɔ́ʔ
rambutan

พฤษภาคม-กันยายน
phrʉ́t-sa-phaa-khom
thʉ̌ŋ kan-yaa-yon
May-September

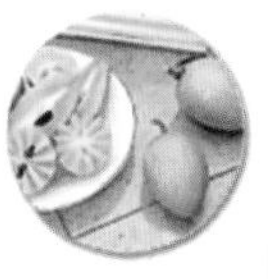

ละมุด
la-mút
sapodilla

กันยายน-ธันวาคม
kan-yaa-yon
thʉ̌ŋ than-waa-khom
September-December

น้อยหน่า
nɔ́ɔy-nàa
custard apple

มิถุนายน-กันยายน
mí-thu-naa-yon
thʉ̌ŋ kan-yaa-yon
June-September

ส้ม
sôm
tangerine

กันยายน-กุมภาพันธ์
kan-yaa-yon
thʉ̌ŋ kum-phaa-phan
September-February

มะพร้าว
má-phráaw
coconut

ตลอดปี
ta-lɔ̀ɔt pii
all year round

สับปะรด
sàp-pa-rót
pineapple

ธันวาคม-มกราคม
than-waa-khom
thʉ̌ŋ mók-ka-raa-khom
December-January

เมษายน-มิถุนายน
mee-sǎa-yon
thʉ̌ŋ mí-thu-naa-yon
April-June

ชมพู่
chom-phûu
rose apple

มิถุนายน-กันยายน
mí-thu-naa-yon
thʉ̌ŋ kan-yaa-yon
June-September

พฤศจิกายน-มีนาคม
phrʉ́t-sa-cì-kaa-yon
thʉ̌ŋ mii-naa-khom
November-March

มะเฟือง
má-fʉʉaŋ
star fruit

ตลอดปี
ta-lɔ̀ɔt pii
all year round

ทับทิม
tháp-thim
pomegranate

ตุลาคม-กุมภาพันธ์
tù-laa-khom
thʉ̌ŋ kum-phaa-phan
October-February

แตงโม
tɛɛŋ-moo
watermelon

มกราคม-มีนาคม
mók-ka-raa-khom
thʉ̌ŋ mii-naa-khom
January-March

Dialogs ...บทสนทนา /bòt sǒn-tha-naa/

Dialog 6.3.1

Suda (A) talks about Thai fruits with Amy (B) and Dan (C).

A แดนกับเอมี่ ลองกินผลไม้ไทยหรือยัง ชอบกินผลไม้อะไรบ้าง

dɛɛn kàp ʔee-mîi lɔɔŋ kin phǒn-la-máay thay rʉ̌-yaŋ. chɔ̂ɔp kin phǒn-la-máay ʔa-ray bâaŋ.

- Dan and Amy, have you tried tasting some Thai fruits? What kinds do you like?

B เอมี่ ชอบผลไม้ลูกสีแดงๆ กลมๆ มีขนสีเขียว มีเม็ดรีๆ สีขาว กับ ลูกสีแดงกลมๆ เล็กๆ แต่ไม่มีขน มีเม็ดกลมๆ สีดำ ภาษาไทยเรียกว่าอะไรนะ

ʔee-mîi chɔ̂ɔp phǒn-la-máay lûuk sǐi dɛɛŋ-dɛɛŋ klom-klom. mii khǒn sǐi khǐaw. mii mét rii-rii sǐi khǎaw. kàp lûuk sǐi dɛɛŋ klom-klom lék-lék. tɛ̀ɛ mây mii khǒn. mii mét klom-klom sǐi dam. pha-sǎa thay rîak-wâa ʔa-ray ná.

- I like a round, reddish fruit with green sprouts, and a white oval-shaped seed. I also like a small, round, red but hairless fruit with round black seeds. What are they called in Thai?

A อ๋อ ลูกสีแดง กลมๆ มีขน คือ เงาะ และลูกสีแดงกลมๆ ไม่มีขน และหวานมาก คือ ลิ้นจี่

ʔɔ̌ɔ. lûuk sǐi dɛɛŋ-dɛɛŋ klom-klom mii khǒn khʉʉ ŋɔ́ʔ.
lɛ́ lûuk sǐi dɛɛŋ klom-klom mây mii khǒn lɛ́ wǎan mâak khʉʉ lín-cìi.

- Oh! The reddish, round hairy fruit is called "ngo" [rambutan]. And the round, red, hairless, and very sweet fruit is called "linchee" [lychee].

เงาะ
/ŋɔ́ʔ/

B *(repeating the names)* เงาะ กับ ลิ้นจี่ ถูกไหม

ŋɔ́ʔ kàp lín-cìi. thùuk máy.

- "ngo" [rambutan] and "linchee" [lychee], right?

ลิ้นจี่
/lín-cìi/

A ใช่แล้ว แล้วแดนล่ะ ชอบอะไร

chây lɛ́ɛw. lɛ́ɛw dɛɛn lâ chɔ̂ɔp ʔa-ray.

- That's right. And what about you Dan, what do you like?

C ผมชอบ ผลไม้ลูกกลมๆ ขนาดใหญ่ สีเขียว มีเม็ดสีดำเยอะ หวานมาก รูปร่างเหมือน hand grenade เรียกว่า อะไรครับ

phǒm chɔ̂ɔp phǒn-la-máay lûuk klom-klom kha-nàat yày sǐi khǐaw. mii mét sǐi dam yə́ʔ. wǎan mâak. rûup-râaŋ mʉ̌an "hand grenade." rîak-wâa ʔa-ray khráp.

- I like the round, large, green fruit, with a lot of black seeds, and very sweet. Its shape is like a hand grenade. What is it called?

A น้อยหน่า รู้ไหมว่า คนไทยเรียก hand grenade ลูกระเบิดมือว่า ลูกน้อยหน่าเหล็ก เพราะรูปร่าง เหมือนลูกน้อยหน่า

nɔ́ɔy-nàa. rúu máy wâa khon thay rîak "hand grenade" [lûuk ra-bə̀ət-mʉʉ] wâa lûuk nɔ́ɔy-nàa lèk phrɔ́ʔ rûup-râaŋ mʉ̌an lûuk nɔ́ɔy-nàa.

- "Noina." Do you know that Thais call the hand grenade "iron noina" because the shape is like the noina fruit?

น้อยหน่า
/nɔ́ɔy-nàa/

C อ้อ จริงๆเหรอ แล้วผมก็ชอบ ผลไม้ลูกกลมๆ เปลือกหนาๆ สีม่วงแดง เนื้อสีขาว หวานมาก ภาษาอังกฤษเรียกว่า mangosteen

ʔɔ̂ɔ. ciŋ-ciŋ-rə̌ə. lɛ́ɛw phǒm kɔ̂ chɔ̂ɔp phǒn-la-máay lûuk klom-klom plʉ̀ak nǎa-nǎa sǐi mûaŋ-dɛɛŋ. nʉ́a sǐi khǎaw. wǎan mâak. pha-sǎa ʔaŋ-krìt rîak-wâa "mangosteen."

- Really? By the way, I also like a round fruit with thick reddish purple skin, white meat, very sweet. It's called "mangosteen" in English.

A อ๋อ ภาษาไทยเรียกว่า มังคุด

ʔɔ̌ɔ. pha-sǎa thay rîak-wâa maŋ-khút.

- Ah! It's called "mang khut" in Thai.

C *(repeating the names)* น้อยหน่า กับ มังคุด

nɔ́ɔy-nàa kàp maŋ-khút

- "Noina" and "mang khut."

B แล้วตุ๊กล่ะ ชอบกินผลไม้อะไรที่สุด

lɛ́ɛw túk lâ. chɔ̂ɔp kin phǒn-la-máay ʔa-ray thîi-sùt.

- And what about you? What fruit do you like to eat the most?

C ตุ๊กชอบ ลำไย ที่สุด แต่ลำไยมีเฉพาะหน้าร้อนของไทย เดือนมิถุนายน ถึงสิงหาคม เท่านั้น

túk chɔ̂ɔp lam-yay thîi-sùt. tɛ̀ɛ lam-yay mii cha-phɔ́ nâa-rɔ́ɔn khɔ̌ŋ thay. dʉan mí-thu-naa-yon thʉ̌ŋ dʉan sǐŋ-hǎa-khom thâw-nán.

- I like "lamyai" best. But there are "lamyai" only during the Thai summer, June to August.

B ลำไย รูปร่างเป็นยังไง

lam-yay rûup-râaŋ pen yaŋ-ŋay.

- What does "lamyai" look like?

ลำไย
/lam-yay/

A ลูกกลมๆ เล็กๆเท่าลิ้นจี่ สีน้ำตาล เนื้อสีขาว หวานมาก

lûuk klom-klom lék-lék thâw lín-cìi. sǐi nám-taan nʉ́a sǐi khǎaw. wǎan mâak.

- Small, round fruit, about the size of lychee, with brown skin, white meat, and very sweet.

C ผมคิดว่า ผมเคยเห็นที่ฮาวาย เขาเรียกว่า dragon eye หรือ longan แต่ที่ฮาวายแพงมาก

phom khít wâa phǒm khəəy hěn thîi haa-waay. kháw rîak-wâa "dragon eye" rʉ̌ʉ "longan." tɛ̀ɛ thîi haa-waay phɛɛŋ mâak.

- I think I've seen it in Hawaii. It's called "dragon eye" or "longan." But they are very expensive in Hawaii.

Idioms ...สำนวน /sǎm-nuan/

ปอกกล้วยเข้าปาก pɔ̀ɔk klûay khâw pàak	to peel + banana + to enter + the mouth	(as easy as) to peel a banana to eat
"a piece of cake, as easy as pie."		

เรื่องกล้วยๆ rʉ̂aŋ klûay-klûay	It's a cinch, a piece of cake.
เรื่องหมูๆ rʉ̂aŋ mǔu-mǔu	

Vocabulary ...ศัพท์ /sàp/

รูป	rûup	n. form, shape
วง	woŋ	n. circle, ring, group (clf. วง /woŋ/)
แนว	nɛɛw	n. line, row, strip (clf. แนว /nɛɛw/)
เลือก	lʉ̂ak	v. to choose, pick out, elect, select
กรอบ	krɔ̀ɔp	n. frame (clf. อัน /ʔan/)
ควรจะ	khuan-ca	aux. ought to, should
ตลอด	ta-lɔ̀ɔt	prep. through, all over, throughout
เม็ด	mét	n. seed, kernel, grain (clf. เม็ด /mét/)
อ๋อ	ʔɔ̌ɔ	excl. Oh! (I see; I get it)
ระเบิด	ra-bə̀ət	v. to explode, burst, blast
ลูกระเบิด	lûuk ra-bə̀ət	n. bomb (clf. ลูก /lûuk/)
เหล็ก	lèk	n. iron (the metal)
เนื้อ	nʉ́a	n. meat
เปลือก	plʉ̀ak	n. natural outer covering, such as husk (of rice), peel, skin, rind (of fruit), shell (of egg, nut), crust (of bread), bark (of tree), etc.
เฉพาะ	cha-phɔ́ʔ	v. particularly, especially, exclusively
ปอก	pɔ̀ɔk	v. to peel, pare, shell
เรื่อง	rʉ̂aŋ	n. story, subject, subject matter

Language Notes

1. Note that in conversational Thai, repetition of attributes (usually one-syllable words) is used in a description of a person or an object. The repetition functions similarly to the suffix "-ish" in English. Observe such usage in Dialog 6.3.1.

2. Dialog 6.3.1 also introduces two more colloquial expressions.

อ๋อ /ʔɔ̌ɔ/ is an exclamation of realization, giving the meaning of "I see" or "I get it." This is a more intensified exclamation of realization than อ้อ /ʔɔ̂ɔ/.

จริง ๆ เหรอ /ciŋ-ciŋ rɘ̌ɘ/, /ciŋ-ciŋ lɘ̌ɘ/ is an expression of surprise or excitement, similar to English "Really?" The literal meaning of this expression is: Is it true?

Unit 7

หน่วยที่ ๗

lesson 1

Provide and obtain preferences about leisure activities

lesson 2

Make telephone calls; learn Thai telephone phrases and etiquette; and learn about emotion compounds with ใจ /cay/

Lesson 1

Skills: To provide and obtain preferences about leisure activities

Hobbies ...งานอดิเรก /ŋaan-ʔa-di-rèek/

เวลาว่างคุณชอบทำอะไร	wee-laa wâaŋ khun chɔ̂ɔp tham ʔa-ray.	What do you like to do in your free time?

อ่านหนังสือ
/ʔàan nǎŋ-sʉ̌ʉ/
• **read (Lit. read books)**

อ่านหนังสือพิมพ์
/ʔàan nǎŋ-sʉ̌ʉ phim/
• **read the newspaper**

ฟังเพลง, ฟังวิทยุ
/faŋ phlɛɛŋ, faŋ wít-tha-yú/
• **listen to music, listen to the radio**

ดูทีวี, ดูโทรทัศน์
/duu thii-wii/, /duu thoo-ra-thát/
• **watch TV**

ดูหนัง
/duu nǎŋ/
• **watch movies**

เล่นคอมพิวเตอร์
/lên khɔm-phiw-tə̂ə/
• **play games on the computer**

เล่นอินเทอร์เน็ต
/lên ʔin-thəə-nèt/
• **surf the net**

เล่นดนตรี
/lên don-trii/
• **play musical instruments**

เล่นกีฬา
/lên kii-laa/
• **play sports**

เล่นไพ่
/lên phây/
• **play cards**

เต้นรำ
/tên-ram/
• **dance**

ออกกำลัง
/ʔɔ̀ɔk kam-laŋ/
• **exercise**

พูดโทรศัพท์กับเพื่อน
/phûut thoo-ra-sàp kàp phɨ̂an/
• **chat on the phone with friends**

ว่ายน้ำ
/wâay-náam/
• **swim**

เดินเล่น
/dəən lên/
• **go for a walk**

ซื้อของ, ไปช็อปปิ้ง
/sɨ́ɨ khɔ̌ɔŋ/, /pay chɔ́p-pîŋ/
• **go shopping**

ไปเที่ยว
/pay thîaw/
• **go out (for fun)**

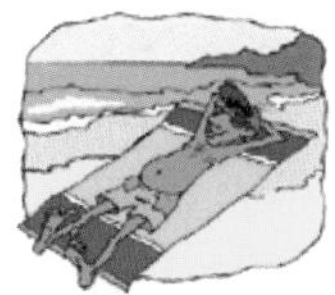

ไปชายหาด
/pay chaay-hàat/
• **go to the beach**

Geographical Locations

คุณชอบไปเที่ยวที่ไหน	khun chɔ̂ɔp pay thîaw thîi-nǎy	Where do you like to go for fun?
ฉันชอบไปเที่ยว _____	chán chɔ̂ɔp pay thîaw _____	I like to go (for fun) to _____.

แม่น้ำ
/mɛ̂ɛ-náam/
• **river**

น้ำตก
/nám-tòk/
• **waterfall**

ชายหาด, ชายทะเล
/chaay-hàat/, /chaay-tha-lee/
• **beach, seaside**

ภูเขา
/phuu-khǎw/
• **mountain**

ทะเล
/tha-lee/
• **sea**

Sports ...กีฬา /kii-laa/

คุณชอบเล่นกีฬาอะไร	khun chɔ̂ɔp lên kii-laa ʔa-ray.	What sports do you like to play?
ฉันชอบเล่น _______	chán chɔ̂ɔp lên _______	I like to play _______.

อเมริกันฟุตบอล
/ʔa-mee-ri-kan fút-bɔn/
• n. American football

ฟุตบอล
/fút-bɔn/, /fút-bɔl/
• n. soccer

แบดมินตัน
/bὲt-min-tân/
• n. badminton

เทนนิส
/then-nít/, /then-nís/
• n. tennis

บาสเก็ตบอล
/báas-kêt-bɔn/
• n. basketball

วอลเล่ย์บอล
/wɔn-lê-bɔn/
• n. volleyball

โต้คลื่น
/tôo-khlʉ̂ʉn/
• n. surfing, v. to surf, ride the waves

เรือใบ
/rʉa-bay/
• n. sailing, sailboat

สกี
/sa-kii/
• n. skiing, ski

ตะกร้อ
/ta-krɔ̂ɔ/
• n. sepak-takraw, foot volleyball

ลูกตะกร้อ
/lûuk ta-krɔ̂ɔ/

T.V. Programs ...รายการทีวี /raay-kaan thii-wii/

คุณชอบดูรายการทีวีอะไร	khun chɔ̂ɔp duu raay-kaan thii-wii ʔa-ray	What TV programs do you like to watch?
คุณชอบดูรายการโทรทัศน์อะไร	khun chɔ̂ɔp duu raay-kaan thoo-ra-thát ʔa-ray	
ฉันชอบดูรายการ _____	chán chɔ̂ɔp duu raay-kaan _____	I like to watch _____.

ข่าว	khàaw	news
บันเทิง	ban-thəəŋ	entertainment
สารคดี	sǎa-rá-kha-dii	documentary
กีฬา	kii-laa	sports
ละคร	la-khɔɔn	soap opera, play
หนัง	nǎŋ	movie
เกมโชว์	keem-choo	game show
สัมภาษณ์	sǎm-phâat	n. interview, v. to interview
วาไรตี้	waa-ray-tîi	variety show (from English)

Movies ...หนัง /nǎŋ/

คุณชอบดูหนังแบบไหน	khun chɔ̂ɔp duu nǎŋ bɛ̀ɛp nǎy	What kinds of movies do you like to watch?
ฉันชอบดู _______	chán chɔ̂ɔp duu _______	I like to watch _______.

หนังรัก	nǎŋ rák	love story
หนังชีวิต	nǎŋ chii-wít	drama
หนังตลก	nǎŋ ta-lòk	comedy
หนังบู๊	nǎŋ búu	action movie
หนังผี	nǎŋ phǐi	ghost movie
หนังสยองขวัญ	nǎŋ sa-yɔ̌ɔŋ-khwǎn	horror movie
หนังนักสืบ	nǎŋ nák-sɨ̀ɨp	detective movie
หนังสืบสวน	nǎŋ sɨ̀ɨp-sǔan	detective movie
หนังลึกลับ	nǎŋ lɨ́k-láp	mystery
หนังผจญภัย	nǎŋ pha-con-phay	adventure movie
หนังวิทยาศาสตร์	nǎŋ wít-tha-yaa-sàat	sci fi movie
หนังการ์ตูน	nǎŋ kaa-tuun	animation, cartoon

คุณชอบอ่านหนังสืออะไร	khun chɔ̂ɔp ʔàan nǎŋ-sʉ̌ʉ ʔa-ray	What do you like to read?
ฉันชอบอ่าน _______	chán chɔ̂ɔp ʔàan _______	I like to read _______.

นิยาย	ní-yaay	novel, fiction (clf. เรื่อง /rʉ̂aŋ/)
เรื่องสั้น	rʉ̂aŋ-sân	short story (clf. เรื่อง /rʉ̂aŋ/)
สารคดี	sǎa-rá-kha-dii	documentary (clf. เรื่อง /rʉ̂aŋ/)
นิตยสาร	nít-ta-yá-sǎan	magazine (clf. เล่ม /lêm/, ฉบับ /cha-bàp/)
แมกกาซีน	mέk-kaa-siin	magazine (clf. เล่ม /lêm/, ฉบับ /cha-bàp/)
วารสาร	waa-ra-sǎan	magazine (clf. เล่ม /lêm/, ฉบับ /cha-bàp/)
การ์ตูน	kaa-tuun	comic book, manga

Vocabulary ...ศัพท์ /sàp/

งานอดิเรก	ŋaan ʔà-di-rèek	n. hobby
อินเทอร์เน็ต	ʔin-thəə-nèt	n. Internet
ดนตรี	don-trii	n. music (clf. แบบ /bὲεp/, อย่าง /yàaŋ/)
ไพ่	phây	n. playing cards (clf. สำรับ /sǎm-ráp/)
ช็อปปิ้ง	chɔ́p-pîŋ	n. shopping (from English)
คลื่น	khlʉ̂ʉn	n. wave
โต้	tôo	v. to counter, resist, withstand
รายการ	raay-kaan	n. list, list of items (clf. รายการ /raay-kaan/)
แบบ	bὲεp	clf. classifier for models, types, styles, patterns, forms
รัก	rák	v. to love
ชีวิต	chii-wít	n. life
ตลก	ta-lòk	v. to be funny, comical, farcical
บู๊	búu	v. to fight
ผี	phǐi	n. ghost, spirit (clf. ตน /ton/)
ขวัญ	khwǎn	n. spirits, morale (clf. ขวัญ /khwǎn/)
สยอง	sà-yɔ̌ɔŋ, sa-yɔ̌ɔŋ	v. to terrify, frighten, scare
สยองขวัญ	sa-yɔ̌ɔŋ khwǎn	v. be terrified, be horrified, be frightened

สืบ	sɨ̀ɨp	v. to search for the facts, seek clues
สืบสวน	sɨ̀ɨp-sǔan	v. to investigate
ลึกลับ	lɨ́k-láp	v. to be mysterious
ภัย	phay	n. danger, peril (clf. อย่าง /yàaŋ/)
ผจญ	pha-con	v. to encounter, meet, face, fight
ผจญภัย	pha-con phay	v. to encounter danger, face danger
วิทยาศาสตร์	wít-tha-yaa-sàat	n. science, the sciences
การ์ตูน	kaa-tuun	n. cartoon (clf. เรื่อง /rɨ̂aŋ/)
เรื่อง	rɨ̂aŋ	1. n. story, subject, subject matter, 2. clf. classifier for stories, plays, anecdotes

Dialogs ...บทสนทนา /bòt sǒn-tha-naa/

Dialog 7.1.1

After Friday afternoon's class, Chai (A), Dan (B) and Amy (C) discuss what to do.

A	เราไปไหนกันดี	raw pay nǎy kan dii.	Where should we go?
B	ไม่รู้ซิ เอมี่อยากทำอะไรกันล่ะ	mây rúu sì. ʔee-mîi yàak tham ʔa-ray kan lâ.	I don't know. Amy, what do you want to do?
C	อะไรก็ได้ ไปกินข้าว ไปดูหนัง ไปเต้นรำ ได้ทั้งนั้น	ʔa-ray kɔ̂-dâay. pay kin khâaw. pay duu nǎŋ. pay tên-ram. dâay tháŋ-nán.	Anything will do. Eating out, going to a movie, dancing. They're all fine with me.
A	แล้วปกติ วันศุกร์เย็น คุณทำอะไรล่ะ	lɛ́ɛw pa-ka-tì wan sùk yen khun tham ʔa-ray lâ.	Normally, Friday evenings, what do you do?
B	ผมไปออกกำลัง แล้วก็ไป ดูหนัง หรือ กินข้าว และ ฟังเพลงที่ผับแถว ๆ ถนนพระอาทิตย์	phǒm pay ʔɔ̀ɔk-kam-laŋ lɛ́ɛw-kɔ̂ɔ pay duu nǎŋ rɨ̌ɨ kin khâaw lɛ́ faŋ phleeŋ thîi phàp thɛ̌w-thɛ̌ɛw tha-nǒn phrá-ʔaa-thít.	I go exercise, and then go see a movie or have dinner, and listen to music at a pub around Phra Athit Road.
C	ถ้ายังงั้น เราไปดูหนัง แล้วก็กินข้าวเย็นกันไหม	thâa-yaŋ-ŋán raw pay duu nǎŋ lɛ́ɛw-kɔ̂ɔ kin khâaw yen kan máy.	In that case, should we go see a movie, and then have dinner?
A	ดี เราไปดูหนังกันเถอะ	dii. raw pay duu nǎŋ kan thə̀.	(Sounds) good. Let's go see a movie.

Dialog 7.1.2

Amy (A) and Suda (B) talk about their leisure activities.

A	เวลาว่าง วันเสาร์วันอาทิตย์ ตุ๊กทำอะไร	wee-laa wâaŋ wan sǎw wan ʔaa-thît túk tham ʔa-ray.	What do you do during your free time on weekends?
B	ชอบไปเดินดูของที่จตุจักร ที่นั่นมีของกระจุกกระจิก เยอะแยะ	chɔ̂ɔp pay dəən duu khɔ̌ɔŋ thîi cà-tu-càk. thîi nân mii khɔ̌ɔŋ ka-cùk ka-cìk yə́ʔ-yɛ́ʔ.	I like to go window shopping at Chatuchak. There are a lot of knick-knacks there.
A	เหรอ ปกติไปกับใครล่ะ	rə̌ə. pà-ka-tì pay kàp khray lâ.	Really? Who do you normally go with?
B	ปกติ ไปคนเดียว แต่บางที ก็ไปกับน้องชาย	pà-ka-tì pay khon diaw. tɛ̀ɛ baaŋ thii kɔ̂ɔ pay kàp nɔ́ɔŋ-chaay.	I usually go by myself, but sometimes I go with my brother.
A	เหรอ เอมี่ก็อยากไปเดิน จตุจักรเหมือนกัน ถ้าอาทิตย์นี้ตุ๊กไป เอมี่ขอ ไปกับตุ๊กด้วยคนได้ไหม	rə̌ə. ʔee-mîi kɔ̂ɔ yàak pay dəən cà-tu-càk mʉ̌an-kan. thâa ʔaa-thít níi túk pay ʔee-mîi khɔ̌ɔ pay kàp túk dûay khon dâay máy.	Is that so? I'd like to look around Chatuchak as well. If you go this Sunday, can I go with you?
B	ได้สิ ตุ๊กชอบมีเพื่อนเดินด้วย ไปกันวันอาทิตย์นี้ไหม	dâay sì. túk chɔ̂ɔp mii phʉ̂an dəən dûay. pay kan wan ʔaa-thít níi máy.	Of course! I like having company. Should we go this Sunday?

Dialog 7.1.3

Chai (A) and Dan (B) discuss sports.

A	แดน ที่ฮาวาย เวลาว่าง แดนชอบทำอะไร	dɛɛn. thîi haa-waay wee-laa wâaŋ dɛɛn chɔ̂ɔp tham ʔa-ray.	Dan, in Hawaii what do you like to do in your free time?
B	ผมชอบไปชายหาด ไปเล่น surfing ภาษาไทยเรียก surfing ว่าอะไรนะ	phǒm chɔ̂ɔp pay chaay-hàat. pay lên "surfing." phaa-sǎa thay rîak "surfing" wâa ʔa-ray ná.	I like to go to the beach and go surfing. What is "surfing" called in Thai?
A	เรียกว่า เล่นโต้คลื่น แดนเล่นโต้คลื่นเก่งไหม	rîak wâa lên tôo-khlʉ̂ʉn. dɛɛn lên tôo-khlʉ̂ʉn kèŋ máy.	It's called "lên tôo-khlʉ̂ʉn." Are you good at surfing?
B	ผมเล่นโต้คลื่นได้ แต่ยังไม่เก่ง แล้วชัยล่ะ เล่นโต้คลื่นเป็นไหม	phǒm lên tôo-khlʉ̂ʉn dâay tɛ̀ɛ yaŋ mây kèŋ. lɛ́ɛw chay lâ lên tôo-khlʉ̂ʉn pen máy.	I can surf, but not very well. What about you, Chai, can you surf?
A	ไม่เป็นครับ ที่เมืองไทย คนยังไม่ค่อยรู้จักเล่นโต้คลื่น	mây pen khráp. thîi mʉaŋ-thay khon yaŋ mây khɔ̂y rúu-càk lên tôo-khlʉ̂ʉn.	No. In Thailand, people still are not familiar with surfing.

B	ครับ แล้วก็ชายหาดที่เมืองไทยก็ไม่มีคลื่นใหญ่ๆ สำหรับโต้คลื่นด้วย	khráp. lɛ́ɛw-kɔ̂ɔ chaay-hàat thîi mʉaŋ-thay kɔ̂ɔ mây mii khlʉ̂ʉn yày-yày sǎm-ràp tôo-khlʉ̂ʉn dûay.	Right. And besides, beaches in Thailand don't have big waves for surfing.

Dialog 7.1.4

Chai (A) and Amy (B) discuss Thai TV programs.

A	เอมี่ ดูทีวีบ้างหรือเปล่า	ʔee-mîi duu thii-wii bâaŋ rʉ́-plàaw.	Amy, do you ever watch TV?
B	ดูบ้างเหมือนกัน	duu bâaŋ mʉ̌an-kan.	I watch some.
A	ปกติ ดูช่องไหน รายการอะไร	pà-ka-tì duu chɔ̂ɔŋ nǎy. raay-kaan ʔa-ray.	What channels and what programs do you usually watch?
B	ดูเคเบิลทีวี ดูหนังกับรายการทีวีจากอเมริกา	duu khee-bôl thii-wii. duu nǎŋ kàp raay-kaan thii-wii càak ʔa-mee-ri-kaa.	I watch cable TV. I watch movies and TV programs from America.
A	ดูรายการทีวีไทยบ้างหรือเปล่า	duu raay-kaan thii-wii thay bâaŋ rʉ́-plàaw.	Do you watch any Thai TV programs?
B	ไม่ค่อยดู ทีวีไทยไม่น่าสนใจ มีแต่ละครกับเกมส์โชว์ เอมี่ฟังไม่ค่อยรู้เรื่องด้วย	mây khɔ̂y duu. thii-wii thay mây nâa sǒn-cay. mii tɛɛ la-khɔɔn kàp keem-choo. ʔee-mîi faŋ mây-khɔ̂y rúu-rʉ̂aŋ dûay.	Not a lot. Thai TV (programs) are not interesting. There are only soaps and game shows. And besides I can't understand them very well.
A	จริงด้วย แต่รายการข่าว รายการสารคดี กับ รายการวาไรตี้ของไทย อย่าง "ที่นี่ประเทศไทย" น่าสนใจนะ	ciŋ dûay. tɛ̀ɛ raay-kaan khàaw raay-kaan sǎa-rá-kha-dii kàp raay-kaan waa-ray-tîi khɔ̌ɔŋ thay yàaŋ "thîi-nîi prà-thêt-thay" nâa sǒn-cay ná.	That's true. But news programs, documentary programs, and Thai variety shows such as "This is Thailand" are interesting.
B	เหรอ รายการนี้ มีช่องไหน วันไหน กี่โมง	rɔ̌ɔ. raay-kaan níi mii chɔ̂ŋ nǎy. wan nǎy. kìi mooŋ.	Are they? That show, what channel is it on, what day, what time?
A	ช่อง 5 ทุกวันจันทร์ถึงวันศุกร์ เวลาสามทุ่มยี่สิบนาที หลังรายการข่าวภาคค่ำ เอมี่ กับแดน น่าจะดูรายการนี้ จะได้ฟังภาษาไทยเก่ง แล้วพูดภาษาไทยคล่อง	chɔ̂ŋ hâa. thúk wan can thʉ̌ŋ wan sùk wee-laa sǎam thûm yîi sìp naa-thii lǎŋ raay-kaan khàaw. ʔee-mîi kàp dɛɛn nâa-ca duu raay-kaan níi ca-dâay faŋ phaa-sǎa thay kèŋ lɛ́ɛw phûut phaa-sǎa thay khlɔ̂ŋ.	Channel 5, every Monday to Friday at 9.20 pm after the evening news. You and Dan should watch this program so that you can improve your Thai listening skill and your speaking fluency.
B	ตกลง เอมี่จะลองดู	tòk-loŋ. ʔee-mîi ca lɔɔŋ-duu.	Okay. I'll take a look.

Idiom ...สำนวน /sǎm-nuan/

เส้นผมบังภูเขา sên-phǒm baŋ phuu-khǎw	strand of hair + to hide + mountain	a strand of hair hiding a mountain

"Cannot see the forest for the trees."

Vocabulary ...ศัพท์ /sàp/

ทั้งนั้น	tháŋ-nán	all of them, any of them, all or any of them, every last one; everything, anything, everything and anything
ได้ทั้งนั้น	dâay tháŋ-nán	Anything will do. Anything is acceptable.
ล่ะ	lâ	prt. particle which is mildly entreating in force
ผับ	phàp	n. pub; bar; tavern (from British English)
แถวๆ	thɛ̌ɛw-thɛ̌ɛw	n. = บริเวณ /bɔɔ-ri-ween/, area, neighborhood; region; zone; vicinity
กระจุกกระจิก	kra-cùk-kra-cìk	v. to be trifling, insignificant, petty (also pronounced ka-cùk-ka-cìk)
ของกระจุกกระจิก	khɔ̌ɔŋ kra-cùk-kra-cìk	n. odds and ends, knick-knacks
ด้วยคน	dûay khon	adv. along, together with
ขอไปด้วยคน	khɔ̌ɔ pay dûay khon	May I join in (going)?
เป็น	pen	v. to be able to, know how to
ช่อง	chɔ̂ŋ	n. channel
น่า-	nâa-	v. prefix. leading (to), arousing, inducing, interesting (to), worth (doing), -able, -ing, -ingly, placed before verbs to make new verb derivatives
น่าสนใจ	nâa-sǒn-cay	v. to be interesting
รู้เรื่อง	rúu-rʉ̂aŋ	v. to understand
อย่าง	yàaŋ	conj. for instance, such as, like
น่าจะ	nâa-ca	aux. ought to, might like to
คล่อง	khlɔ̂ŋ	v. to be active, nimble, fluent

จะได้	ca-dâay	conj. shortened from เพื่อจะได้ /phʉ̂a ca-dâay/ 1. in order to, in order that, in order to get to (do something). 2. in order to get, obtain.
ผม	phǒm	n. hair
เส้นผม	sên-phǒm	n. strand of hair (clf. เส้น /sên/)
บัง	baŋ	v. to obstruct one's view

Language Notes

1. Mood particles

In the dialogs in this lesson, observe more examples of the usage of the following conversational mood particles: ละ /lâ/, /là/, /la/ (emphasis), นะ /ná/, ซิ, สิ /si/, /sí/, /sì/ and เถอะ /thə̀/ (request, urging). Also, note that among friends and peers, polite particles can be dropped. If used at all, women usually use informal polite particles จ้ะ /câ/ or จ๊ะ /cá/ instead of the formal ค่ะ /khâ/ or คะ /khá/.

Of special note are the following conversational particles:

• **เหรอ /rɔ̌ɔ/** also pronounced /lɔ̌ɔ/, used as a conversational signal of acknowkledgement and a signal that the listener is listening, similar to English- "yes," "right," "uh-huh," "really?"

• **ละ /lâ/, /là/, /la/** is used for emphasis after a statement or a question. Other variant colloquial pronunciations of ละ that are now commonly used in conversational Thai are /ʔâ/, /ʔà/, /ʔa/, which sometimes are seen written informally such as in chat room language as อ้ะ, อ่ะ, อะ.

Structure Notes

1. Two usages of เหมือนกัน /mʉ̌an-kan/

This lesson demonstrates two usages of เหมือนกัน /mʉ̌an-kan/:

a. as an adverb meaning "likewise," "as well," placed at the end of the sentence (Dialog 7.1.2, see also Unit 1.2), and usually used in conjunction with a pre-verb ก็ /kɔ̂ɔ/.

เอมี่ ก็อยากไปเดิน จตุจักรเหมือนกัน	ʔee-mîi kɔ̂ɔ yàak pay dɛɛn cà-tu-càk mʉ̌an-kan.	I'd like to go look around Chatuchak as well.

b. as a degree adverb meaning "somewhat" or "rather" (Dialog 7.1.4) in the pattern 2d. ***Subject + (NEG) + Verb (+ Object) (+ Adverb)***. The following is a revised degree-scale chart from Unit 4.4 with ***เหมือนกัน*** /mʉ̌an-kan/ added.

(Negative) Degree	Verb (Attributive)	Degree	Strength
	ชอบ /chɔ̂ɔp/	ที่สุด /thîi-sùt/	+++
	ชอบ /chɔ̂ɔp/	มาก /mâak/	++
	ชอบ /chɔ̂ɔp/		+
	ชอบ /chɔ̂ɔp/	เหมือนกัน /mʉ̌an-kan/	0
ไม่ /mây/	ชอบ /chɔ̂ɔp/	มาก /mâak/	-
ไม่ /mây/	ชอบ /chɔ̂ɔp/	นัก /nák/	-
ไม่ /mây/	ชอบ /chɔ̂ɔp/	เท่าไร /thâw-rày/	-
ไม่ค่อย /mây-khɔ̂y/	ชอบ /chɔ̂ɔp/		-
ไม่ /mây/	ชอบ /chɔ̂ɔp/		- -
ไม่ /mây/	ชอบ /chɔ̂ɔp/	เลย /ləəy/	- - -

2. Ability/capability/evaluative post-verbs: ได้ /dâay/, เป็น /pen/, เก่ง /kèŋ/, คล่อง /khlɔ̂ŋ/, รู้เรื่อง /rúu-rʉ̂aŋ/

This set of evaluative post-verbs expressing capability/ability appears in pattern 2a. ***Subject + Verb+ Object + (ไม่** mây**)+ Evaluative Post-verb + (Adverb-degree)*** discussed in Unit 1.3 and 1.4. In this lesson, in addition to ได้ /dâay/ "to be able to," "to be allowed," "permitted" introduced in Unit 1.3, we see the following post-verbs:

เป็น /pen/: to know how
เก่ง /kèŋ/: to be good at, to be proficient
คล่อง /khlɔ̂ŋ/: to be fluent, skillful
รู้เรื่อง /rúu-rʉ̂aŋ/: to understand the subject matter

and also in this set of post-verbs:

ไหว /wǎy/: to be physically able
ออก /ʔɔ̀ɔk/: to come out, to figure out

Verb	Negative (degree)	Capability, Evaluative	Adverb	
พูดภาษาไทย phûut pha-sǎa thay		เก่ง kèŋ		to speak Thai well
		ได้ dâay		to be able to speak Thai
		เป็น pen		to know how to speak Thai
		คล่อง khlɔ̂ŋ		to be fluent in speaking Thai
ฟังภาษาไทย faŋ pha-sǎa thay	ไม่ค่อย mây-khɔ̂y	รู้เรื่อง rúu-rʉ̂aŋ		to not quite understand spoken Thai (by listening)
ว่ายน้ำ wâay-naam	ไม่ค่อย mây-khɔ̂y	เก่ง kèŋ	มาก mâak	to be not very good at swimming
วิ่ง wîŋ	ไม่ mây	ไหว wǎy		to not be physically able to run, to not have the strength to run
อ่านภาษาไทย ʔàan pha-sǎa thay	ไม่ mây	ออก ʔɔ̀ɔk		to not be able to read Thai

For the post-verb ออก /ʔɔ̀ɔk/, there are two expressions about the capability of literacy, as follows:

อ่านออกเขียนได้ /ʔàan ʔɔ̀ɔk khǐan dâay/ "to be literate" (Lit. able to read and write), and อ่านไม่ออกเขียนไม่ได้ /ʔàan mây ʔɔ̀ɔk khǐan mây dâay/ "to be illiterate" (Lit. not able to read and write).

3. Word formation

น่า /nâa/ + Verb

น่า /nâa/ is one of the very few active prefix-like elements in Thai word formation. It is attached to verbs to form a new attributive verb derivative with the meaning of "inviting," "inducing," "arousing one to do (verb)," "to be worth doing (verb)."

In Dialog 7.1.4, we see น่าสนใจ /nâa sǒn-cay/ "to be interesting," from adding น่า to the verb สนใจ /sǒn-cay/ "to be interested in."

The following are more examples of attributive verbs with น่า-

น่า /nâa/ + กิน /kin/: to eat
น่า /nâa/ + เที่ยว /thîaw/: to go for fun, to sightsee
น่า /nâa/ + ดู /duu/: to watch, look
น่า /nâa/ + อ่าน /ʔàan/: to read

อาหารที่ร้านนี้น่ากิน ʔa-hǎan thîi ráan níi nâa-kin	food + at + shop + this + to be inviting to eat	The food at this shop looks delicious.
กรุงเทพฯ เป็นเมืองที่น่าเที่ยว kruŋ-thêep pen mʉaŋ thîi nâa-thîaw	Bangkok + to be + city + that + to be inviting to visit	Bangkok is a city worth visiting.
หนังเรื่องนี้น่าดู nǎŋ rʉ̂aŋ níi nâa-duu หนังสือเล่มนี้น่าอ่าน nǎŋ-sʉ̌ʉ rʉ̂aŋ níi nâa-ʔàan	movie + clf. + this + to be inviting to watch book + clf. + this + to be inviting to read	This movie is worth watching. This book is worth reading.

4. Purpose conjunction: เพื่อ...จะได้ /phʉ̂a...ca-dâay/, จะได้ /ca-dâay/

จะได้ /ca-dâay/, a conjunction of purpose that you see in Dialog 7.1.4, is a conversational shortened form of เพื่อ...จะได้ /phʉ̂a...ca-dâay/ with เพื่อ /phʉ̂a/ "for the purpose of" omitted. The following sentence pattern is used.

7a. Clause 1	Purpose Conjunction	Clause 2
	เพื่อ /phʉ̂a/	*(Subject)* จะได้ /cà-dâay/ + Verb

The element **จะได้** /cà-dâay/ appears before the verb of the second clause. However, as the subject of Clause 2 is the same as the subject of Clause 1, it is typically omitted in Thai. **เพื่อจะได้** /phʉ̂a cà-dâay/ is mostly seen together as one unit.

เอมี่ น่าจะดูรายการนี้ ʔee-mîi nâa-cà duu raay-kaan níi	เพื่อ (เอมี่) จะได้ฟังภาษาไทยเก่ง phʉ̂a ʔee-mîi cà-dâay faŋ phaa-sǎa thay kèŋ
Amy + should + to watch + program + this	***เพื่อ*** phʉ̂a Amy **จะได้** cà-dâay + to listen + Thai language + proficiently
You (Amy) should watch this program, so that (you) will be good at listening to Thai.	

Culture Notes

1. ตะกร้อ /ta-krɔ̂ɔ/ is a popular ball game played in Thailand and also Malaysia and the Philippines, where it is known as "sepak" or "sipak." The oldest form of kicking the "takraw" balls (woven from rattan or bamboo) was for players to stand in a circle and try to keep the ball in the air as long as possible without using their hands or arms. The modern form of competitive "takraw" adds a net and a set of rules similar to volleyball. Therefore, it is now also known as "foot volleyball."

2. In Thai movie theaters, the Royal Anthem (see Appendix 2) is played before the feature film or performance begins, along with a display of pictures or video clips honoring the King. The audience is expected to stand up to pay respect to the King while the Anthem is playing.

3. ขวัญ /khwǎn/ is part of the traditional Thai belief system. It refers to the spirit, soul, morale or psyche of a person. The belief is that a person's ขวัญ has to reside peacefully within one's body for the person to be healthy in body and in spirit. ขวัญ can leave the body in fright if a person encounters a disturbing experience, and this will result in ill health for the person. There are various ceremonies and rituals for inviting the ขวัญ back, or consoling the ขวัญ. There are also many compounds in the language involving ขวัญ. In addition to the term สยองขวัญ /sa-yɔ̌ɔŋ khwǎn/ (Lit. to scare ขวัญ) that we see in this lesson, there is also ของขวัญ /khɔ̌ɔŋ-khwǎn/ "gift" (Lit. things for ขวัญ).

4. ถนนพระอาทิตย์ /tha-nǒn phra-ʔa-thít/ Phra Athit Road is a road that lines the Chao Phraya river bank on the city's old outer wall between the Banglamphu area and Thammasat University in Bangkok. There are old buildings lining the street, including Phra Sumen Fort, one of the two remaining forts of the original 14 built under King Rama I. Since the year 2000, the street has become a trendy spot populated with cafés, bars and restaurants with live music, catering for university students in the area.

บทที่ ๒

Lesson **2**

Skills: To make telephone calls; to learn Thai telephone phrases and etiquette; and learn about emotion compounds with ใจ /cay/

Commonly used phrases in telephone calls

ฮัลโหล	han-lǒo	Hello.
ฮัลโหล ที่นี่ *number or place*	han-lǒo thîi-nîi *number or place*	Hello. This is *number or place*.
นี่ *name* พูด	nîi *name* phûut.	This is *name* speaking.
ขอพูดกับ *person*	khɔ̌ɔ phûut kàp *person*	May I speak to *person*?
ขอเรียนสายกับ *person*	khɔ̌ɔ rian-sǎay kàp *person* (formal to a superior)	
กรุณา รอสักครู่	ka-ru-naa rɔɔ sák khrûu	Please wait just a moment.
รอประเดี๋ยว	rɔɔ pra-dǐaw	Wait a minute.
รอเดี๋ยว	rɔɔ dǐaw	Wait a second.
จะฝากข้อความไว้ไหม	ca fàak khɔ̂ɔ-khwaam wáy máy	Would you like to leave a message?
จะสั่งอะไรไว้ไหม	ca sàŋ ʔa-ray wáy máy	
ช่วยบอก *person* ว่า *message*	chûay bɔ̀ɔk *person* wâa *message*	Please tell *person* that *message*.
ช่วยเรียน *person* ว่า *message*	chûay rian *person* wâa *message* (to a superior)	

โทร	thoo	v. to telephone (shortened from โทรศัพท์)
ต่อโทรศัพท์	tɔ̀ɔ thoo-ra-sàp	v. to dial a number
หมุนโทรศัพท์	mǔn thoo-ra-sàp	v. to dial a number
สายไม่ว่าง	sǎay mây wâaŋ	The line is busy.
รับโทรศัพท์	ráp thoo-ra-sàp	v. to answer the phone, pick up the phone
รับสาย	ráp sǎay	v. to answer the phone, pick up the phone
พูดสาย	phûut sǎay	v. to telephone, to speak (with)
ติดสาย	tìt sǎay	v. to be on the phone, to be on another line

วางสาย	waaŋ-sǎay	v. to hang up (the phone)
วางหู	waaŋ-hǔu	v. to hang up (the phone)
ถือสาย	thʉ̌ʉ sǎay	v. to hold the line
กดเครื่องหมาย # (สี่เหลี่ยม)	kòt khrʉ̂aŋ-mǎay sìi-lìam	Press the # key.
กดเครื่องหมาย * (ดอกจัน)	kòt khrʉ̂aŋ-mǎay dɔ̀ɔk-can	Press the * key.
กดรหัส	kòt ra-hàt	Enter the code.
เลขหมายโทรศัพท์	lêek-mǎay thoo-ra-sàp	n. telephone number (formal)
ฝากข้อความ	fàak khɔ̂ɔ-khwaam	v. to leave a message
มือถือ	mʉʉ-thʉ̌ʉ	n. mobile phone (informal)
โทรศัพท์ทางไกล	thoo-ra-sàp thaaŋ klay	n. long distance call.

โทรทั่วไทยราคาประหยัด
Y-Tel 1234

กด 1234 + {รหัสทางไกล / รหัสมือถือ} + เลขหมายโทรศัพท์ กด 1234 + {02,044,038 / 01} + xxxxxx / xxxxxx

thoo thûa thay raa-khaa pra-yàt
kòt **1234** + ra-hàt thaaŋ klay + lêek-mǎay thoo-ra-sàp
+ ra-hàt mʉʉ-thʉ̌ʉ

Dialogs ...บทสนทนา /bòt sǒn-tha-naa/

Dialog 7.2.1 Asking to speak to someone on the phone

Dan (B) calls Chai (C) at the dorm. Another person (A) answers the phone.

Telephone rings.

A	ฮัลโหล ที่นี่ 213-4567 ค่ะ	han-lǒo thîi-nîi sɔ̌ɔŋ nʉ̀ŋ sǎam sìi hâa hòk cèt khâ.	Hello. This is 213-4567.
B	ขอพูดกับชัยหน่อยครับ	khɔ̌ɔ phûut kàp chay nɔ̀y khráp.	May I speak to Chai?
A	กรุณารอสักครู่นะคะ	ka-rú-naa rɔɔ sák khrûu ná khá.	Please wait a minute.
	ไม่ทราบว่าใครจะพูดด้วยคะ	mây sâap wâa khray ca phûut dûay khá.	May I ask who would like to speak to him?
B	ผมชื่อ แดนครับ	phǒm chʉ̂ʉ dɛɛn khráp.	My name is Dan.
A	ค่ะ รอเดี๋ยวนะคะ	khâ. rɔɔ dǐaw ná khá.	Yes. Wait a minute please.
C	ฮัลโหล แดนเหรอ นี่ชัยพูด	han-lǒo. dɛɛn rɔ̌ɔ. nîi chay phûut.	Hello. Is this Dan? This is Chai.

Dialog 7.2.2

Suda (B) calls Chai at the dorm but he is not in. A person (A) answers the phone.

Telephone rings.

A	ฮัลโหล ที่นี่ 213-4567 ค่ะ	han-lǒo thîi-nîi sɔ̌ɔŋ nʉ̀ŋ sǎam sìi hâa hòk cèt khâ.	Hello. This is 213-4567.
B	ขอพูดกับชัยหน่อยค่ะ	khɔ̌ɔ phûut kàp chay nɔ̀y khâ.	May I speak to Chai?
A	ตอนนี้ ชัยไม่อยู่ค่ะ ออกไปข้างนอก จะฝากข้อความไว้ไหมคะ	tɔɔn-níi chay mây yùu khâ. ʔɔ̀ɔk pay khâŋ-nɔ̂ɔk. ca fàak khɔ̂ɔ-khwaam wáy máy khá.	He is not in at the moment. He went out. Would you like to leave a message?
B	ค่ะ ช่วยบอกชัยว่า ตุ๊กสุดาโทร.มานะคะ ตุ๊กจะโทร.มาใหม่ค่ะ สวัสดีค่ะ	khâ. chûay bɔ̀ɔk chay wâa túk sù-daa thoo maa ná khá. túk ca thoo maa mày khâ. khɔ̀ɔp-khun khâ. sa-wàt-dii khâ.	Yes. Please tell him that Tuk-Suda called. I will call again later. Thank you. Goodbye.
A	สวัสดีค่ะ	sa-wàt-dii khâ.	Goodbye.

Dialog 7.2.3 Dialing the wrong number

Amy (B) calls Chai, but dials the wrong number.

Telephone rings.

A	ฮัลโหล	han-lǒo	Hello.
B	ฮัลโหล ชัยอยู่ไหมคะ	han-lǒo. chay yùu máy khá.	Hello. Is Chai in?
A	ที่นี่ไม่มีใครชื่อชัยค่ะ คุณคงต่อเบอร์ผิด	thîi-nîi mây mii khray chʉ̂ʉ chay khâ. khun khoŋ tɔ̀ɔ bəə phìt.	There's no one by the name Chai here. You must have dialed the wrong number.
B	ขอโทษค่ะ	khɔ̌ɔ-thôot khâ.	I'm sorry.
A	ไม่เป็นไรค่ะ	mây-pen-ray khâ.	That's alright.

Dialog 7.2.4 Asking to speak to a professor

Chai (B) calls his professor's office. A secretary answers the phone.

Telephone rings.

A	ฮัลโหล ที่นี่คณะเศรษฐศาสตร์ค่ะ	han-lǒo. thîi-nîi kha-ná sèt-tha-sàat khâ.	Hello. This is the Faculty of Economics.
B	ขอเรียนสาย อาจารย์นริศครับ	khɔ̌ɔ rian sǎay ʔaa-caan na-rít khráp.	May I speak to Professor Naris?
A	อาจารย์ไม่อยู่ค่ะ จะฝากข้อความไว้ไหมคะ	ʔaa-caan mây yùu khâ. ca fàak khɔ̂ɔ-khwaam wáy máy khá.	He is not in. Would you like to leave a message?
B	ครับ กรุณาเรียนอาจารย์ว่า ชัย นักศึกษาในวิชาของอาจารย์โทร.มา และจะโทร.มาใหม่ครับ	khráp. ka-ru-naa rian ʔaa-caan wâa chay nák-sʉ̀k-sǎa nay wí-chaa khɔ̌ɔŋ ʔaa-caan thoo maa lɛ́ cà thoo maa mày khráp.	Yes. Please tell him that Chai, a student in his class, called and will call again later.

A	ค่ะ ดิฉันจะเรียนอาจารย์ให้	khâ. di-chán ca rian ʔaa-caan hây.	Yes. I will tell him.
B	ขอบคุณครับ สวัสดีครับ	khɔ̀ɔp-khun khráp. sa-wàt-dii khráp.	Thank you. Goodbye.
A	สวัสดีค่ะ	sa-wàt-dii khâ.	Goodbye.

Dialog 7.2.5 Requesting information from directory assistance (1133)

Suda (A) calls directory assistance (B).

A	ขอทราบเบอร์โรงแรม ดุสิตธานี ถนนชิดลม ค่ะ	khɔ̌ɔ sâap bəə rooŋ-rɛɛm dù-sìt thaa-nii tha-nǒn chít-lom khâ.	I'd like to know the number of Dusit Thani Hotel, Chidlom Road?
B	สักครู่นะคะ	sák khrûu ná khá.	Just a moment.
	เบอร์ที่หนึ่ง 02-238-0032	bəə thîi nɯ̀ŋ. sǔun sɔ̌ɔŋ sɔ̌ɔŋ sǎam pɛ̀ɛt sǔun sǔun sǎam sɔ̌ɔŋ	The first number (is): 02-238-0032.
	เบอร์ที่สอง 02-200-9000	bəə thîi sɔ̌ɔŋ. sǔun sɔ̌ɔŋ sɔ̌ɔŋ sǔun sǔun kâaw sǔun sǔun sǔun.	The second number (is): 02-200-9000.

Idiom ...สำนวน /sǎm-nuan/

ฝนตกไม่ทั่วฟ้า fǒn tòk mây thûa fáa	rain + to fall + not + throughout + sky	It's raining here and there.

"an event that does not include everyone or everything; uneven benefits."

Vocabulary ...ศัพท์ /sàp/

เรียน	rian	v. to inform, tell (particularly when speaking to a superior)
รอ	rɔɔ	v. to wait, wait for, await
ครู่	khrûu	n. moment
ประเดี๋ยว	pra-dǐaw	adv. for a moment, in a moment
ฝาก	fàak	v. to entrust, leave (something) (with someone)
ไว้	wáy	v. to keep, leave, place, put (something somewhere) for future use
ข้อความ	khɔ̂ɔ-khwaam	n. statement, message (clf. ข้อความ /khɔ̂ɔ-khwaam/)
ต่อ	tɔ̀ɔ	v. to connect
หมุน	mǔn	v. to turn, rotate, spin
วาง	waaŋ	v. to place, lay
ถือ	thɯ̌ɯ	v. to hold, carry (in the hands)
กด	kòt	v. to press, press on (something), push

◂ เครื่องหมาย	khrɨ̂aŋ-mǎay	n. sign, mark, symbol, signal (clf. อัน /an/)
◂ ดอกจัน	dɔ̀ɔk-can	n. asterisk (clf. ดอก /dɔ̀ɔk/)
◂ รหัส	ra-hàt	n. code (clf. รหัส /ra-hàt/)
◂ ทั่ว	thûa	v. to be all over, to be general
◂ ประหยัด	pra-yàt	v. to economize, to save, to be thrifty
◂ คณะ	kha-náʔ	n. faculty, college, group, team (clf. คณะ /kha-náʔ/)
◂ เศรษฐศาสตร์	sèet-tha-sàat	n. economics (as a science)
◂ วิชา	wí-chaa	n. subject (of study) (clf. วิชา /wí-chaa/)
◂ ทราบ	sâap	v. to know; to learn of (formal)
◂ ฟ้า	fáa	n. sky

Song ...เพลง /phleeŋ/

สบาย สบาย /sa-baay sa-baay/

สบาย สบาย ถูกใจก็คบกันไป	sa-baay sa-baay thùuk-cay kɔ̂ khóp kan pay	Take it easy. If we like each other, then we can continue seeing each other,
เพราะฉันเป็นคนไม่สนอะไร	phrɔ́ chán pen khon mây sǒn ʔa-ray	because I am easy going,
ไม่เคยคิดกวนใจใคร	mây khəəy khít kuan-cay khray	and have never thought about bothering anyone.
สบาย สบาย	sa-baay sa-baay	Take it easy.
หากเราจะคบกันไป	hàak raw ca khóp kan pay	If we are to continue seeing
ฉันขอเพียงความรักและจริงใจ	chán khɔ̌ɔ phiaŋ khwaam rák lɛ́ ciŋ-cay	each other, I only ask for love and sincerity.
ไม่เคยต้องการอะไร	mây khəəy tɔ̂ŋ-kaan ʔa-ray	I have never wanted anything else.
*สบาย สบาย แล้วเธอก็คงเข้าใจ	sa-baay sa-baay lɛ́ɛw thəə kɔ̂ khoŋ khâw-cay	Take it easy, and you will understand.
เรานั้นจะอยู่เรียนรู้กันไป จะทุกข์จะสุขเพียงไหน	raw nán ca yùu rian-rúu kan pay ca thúk ca sùk phiaŋ-nǎy	We will stay on to learn about each other, no matter how happy or sad.
สบาย สบาย แม้วันใดที่ใจเธอเปลี่ยน	sa-baay sa-baay mɛ́ɛ-wan-day-thîi-cay-thəə-plìan	I take it easy, even on the day that your heart changes.
ไม่เห็นจะแปลก เมื่อรู้จากปาก ว่าคิดจะจากฉันไป	mây hěn ca plɛ̀ɛk mɨ̂a rúu càak pàak wâa khít ca càak chán pay	I won't be surprised, if I learn from you that you are thinking about leaving me.

ก็คงเข้าใจว่าเธอต้องไป	kɔ̂ khoŋ khâw-cay wâa thəə tɔ̂ŋ pay	I'll understand that you have to go.
ก็คงเสียใจและคงเสียดาย	kɔ̂ khoŋ sǐa-cay lɛ́ khoŋ sǐa-daay	I'll be sorry and I'll regret it.
แต่ก็ยังสบาย หากเธอจะทิ้งกันไป	tɛ̀ɛ kɔ̂ yaŋ sa-baay hàak thəə ca thíŋ kan pay	But I'll still take it easy if you are going to leave me.
เพราะฉันเป็นคนไม่ฝืนใจใคร	phrɔ́ chán pen khon mây fʉ̌ʉn-cay khray	Because I am not the guy who makes you do anything against your will.
ก็คงเลิกรากันไปแบบสบาย	kɔ̂ khoŋ lə̂ək-raa kan pay bɛ̀ɛp sa-baay	So we will break up in an easy going way.

Vocabulary ...ศัพท์ /sàp/

ถูกใจ	thùuk-cay	v. to please; to be satisfactory, pleasing; appealing
คบ	khóp	v. to associate with, be friends with; also, คบหา /khóp-hǎa/
สน	sǒn	v. to be interested (in); (colloquial) shortened from สนใจ /sǒn-cay/
กวน	kuan	v. to trouble, bother, disturb
กวนใจ	kuan-cay	v. to disturb, bother, agitate
หาก	hàak	conj. if, in case, provided that
จริงใจ	ciŋ-cay	v. to be sincere, heartfelt
เรียนรู้	rian-rúu	v. to learn
ทุกข์	thúk	v. to suffer, to be unhappy, to be in trouble
สุข	sùk	v. to be happy; to be content; to be satisfied
แม้	mɛ́ɛ	conj. even though, even if
เห็น	hěn	1. v. to see; 2. v. to think
แปลก	plɛ̀ɛk	v. to be strange, unusual, queer
จาก	càak	v. to leave, depart, go away
เสียใจ	sǐa-cay	v. to be sorry, to feel sorry, to feel badly, to regret
เสียดาย	sǐa-daay	v. to feel sorry (about something lost, about a lost opportunity), to regret
ทิ้ง	thíŋ	v. to abandon, discard
ฝืนใจ	fʉ̌ʉn-cay	v. to force oneself (to do something) against one's will
เลิก	lə̂ək	v. to quit, finish, be through, be over; to end, discontinue; to give up; to break up
เลิกรา	lə̂ək-raa	v. to break up, to separate, to end.

Language Notes

1. ทราบ /sâap/ "to know" is a formal word used in a formal situation or to express politeness. Its neutral counterpart is รู้ /rúu/.

ทราบ /sâap/ is normally used in an expression to request for information or an expression of inquiry. Commonly used expressions with ทราบ /sâap/ are:

ขอทราบ ______	khɔ̌ɔ sâap ______	I'd like to know ______.
อยากทราบว่า ______	yàak sâap wâa ______	I'd like to know if ______?
ไม่ทราบว่า ______	mây sâap wâa ______	May I ask if ______?

Note that as an expression, ไม่ทราบว่า /mây sâap wâa/ has lost its negative meaning, and is understood as a formulaic expression to request information.

2. Another formal word in this lesson is เรียน /rian/, equivalent to English "to inform." Its neutral counterpart is บอก /bɔ̀ɔk/ "to tell."

เรียน /rian/ is also used in a formal/official letter as a formulaic expression to address the recipient of the letter, similar to English "Dear," for example, เรียน คุณสุดา /rian khun su-daa/ "Dear Ms. Suda," and also in addressing the recipient on the envelope.

In a phone call situation, a related expression เรียนสาย /rian-sǎay/ "to speak on the line" is also popularly used in a formal situation such as in Dialog 7.2.4, when Chai asks to speak to his professor. However, this particular expression is not yet approved as "proper" usage of Thai by the Thai language authority. Nonetheless, it is commonly used.

3. It is mentioned in Unit 3.1 that some occupation terms can be used as pronouns. Observe the use of อาจารย์ /ʔaa-caan/ in Dialog 7.2.4 of this lesson as a third person pronoun, and also as a title before the name.

4. Some nicknames are popular. In one's circle, one might come across many people with the same nicknames. Therefore when leaving a message, it is common practice to give one's full first name along with one's nickname as Suda does in Dialog 7.2.2.

5. In giving a telephone number in telephone conversation, โท /thoo/, an Indic number for "two" is also used instead of สอง /sɔ̌ɔŋ/ for the number 2. This is to avoid a possible confusion between the number 2 สอง /sɔ̌ɔŋ/ and 3 สาม /sǎam/ which can sound alike on the telephone line.

Culture Notes

1. Thai local "land line" telephone numbers have nine digits, starting with 0. For example, the telephone numbers in Bangkok and its suburbs start with 02. Starting in November 2006, local mobile phone numbers have ten digits, beginning with 08. Special numbers for public services and some commercial services can be three digits or four digits. Some useful Thai public service phone numbers are:

Emergency: 191 **Directory Assistance: 1133**

2. Thai etiquette dictates that the ผู้น้อย "junior" should not inconvenience the ผู้ใหญ่ "senior". Therefore, in leaving a message for a senior, one does not ask the senior to return one's call, the ผู้น้อย "junior" should be the one who attempts to contact the "senior."

3. The actual Dusit Thani Hotel is located on Silom Road (ถนน สีลม /tha-non sǐi-lom/) in Bangkok.

Structure Notes

1. Word formation: compounds with ใจ /cay/ "heart"

There are more than 700 compounds with the word ใจ /cay/ "heart" in Thai that express feelings, emotions, state of mind and also the temperament and personality of a person. There are two types of word formations with ใจ /cay/.

1. Verb + ใจ /cay/

This forms a verb compound to express emotions and feelings and a person's state of mind. We see some examples of such compounds in the song.

- ถูกใจ /thùuk-cay/: from ถูก /thùuk/ "to touch" + ใจ /cay/
- กวนใจ /kuan-cay/: from กวน /kuan/ "to stir," "disturb," "annoy" + ใจ /cay/
- จริงใจ /ciŋ-cay/: from จริง /ciŋ/ "to be true" + ใจ /cay/
- เข้าใจ /khâw-cay/: from เข้า /khâw/ "to enter" + ใจ /cay/
- เสียใจ /sǐa-cay/: from เสีย /sǐa/ "to lose" + ใจ /cay/
- ฝืนใจ /fɯ̌ɯn-cay/: from ฝืน /fɯ̌ɯn/ "to do something against (the law, one's will)" + ใจ /cay/

Other common ใจ /cay/ compounds that you should know are: ดีใจ /dii-cay/ "to be glad" and แปลกใจ "to be surprised, amazed" /plɛ̀ɛk-cay/, from แปลก /plɛ̀ɛk/ "to be strange, unusual."

Another common ใจ /cay/ compound introduced in Unit 6.1 is สนใจ /sǒn-cay/ "to be interested in."

For ถูกใจ /thùuk-cay/, recently there is a new ใจ compound replacing it in colloquial use: โดนใจ /doon-cay/, from โดน /doon/ "to touch" + ใจ /cay/.

2. ใจ /cay/ + Verb

This forms a verb compound which describes the personality or temperament of a person. The following are some commonly used ใจ /cay/ compounds of this type:

ใจดี /cay-dii/ "to be kind," "good-hearted"	ใจ /cay/ + ดี /dii/ "to be good"
ใจร้าย /cay-ráay/ "to be cruel," "mean," "vicious"	ใจ /cay/ + ร้าย /ráay/ "to be bad"
ใจดำ /cay-dam/ "to be mean," "unkind"	ใจ /cay/ + ดำ /dam/ "to be black"
ใจเย็น /cay-yen/ "to be patient"	ใจ /cay/ + เย็น /yen/ "to be cool"
ใจร้อน /cay-rɔ́ɔn/ "to be impatient"	ใจ /cay/ + ร้อน /rɔ́ɔn/ "to be hot"
ใจกว้าง /cay-kwâaŋ/ "to be generous," "open-minded"	ใจ /cay/ + กว้าง /kwâaŋ/ "to be wide"
ใจแคบ /cay-khɛ̂ɛp/ "to be narrow-minded," "ungenerous"	ใจ /cay/ + แคบ /khɛ̂ɛp/ "to be narrow"
ใจลอย /cay-lɔɔy/ "to be absent-minded"	ใจ /cay/ +ลอย /lɔɔy/ "to float"

The compounds with ใจ /cay/ are usually listed as sub-entries under ใจ /cay/ in Thai dictionaries. You can also see more examples of ใจ /cay/ compounds at the website: http://www.thaihearttalk.info which is based on a book about Thai ใจ /cay/ compounds.

2. Condition conjunctions: หาก /hàak/, แม้ /mɛ́ɛ/, เมื่อ /mʉ̂a/

These are all condition conjunctions, meaning "if" or "even if," following the pattern of ถ้า /tha(a/ discussed in Unit 3.1.

6. Condition Conjunction	+ Clause 1	ก็ Clause 2
ถ้า /thâa/ เมื่อ /mʉ̂a/ หาก /hàak/ แม้ /mɛ́ɛ/		____ (ก็ /kɔ̂/) + Verb ____

The conjunctions หาก /hàak/ and แม้ /mɛ́ɛ/ are usually seen in formal and poetic use, including in lyrics. As for เมื่อ /mʉ̂a/, it is generally used as a time conjunction (see Unit 4.1), but in certain contexts, it can be interpreted as a condition conjunction.

8 Unit

หน่วยที่ ๘

lesson 1

Learn about body parts; talk about daily personal hygiene and grooming; and talk about common illnesses and ailments

lesson 2

Provide and obtain information about health, physical condition and ailments

บทที่ ๑ Lesson 1

Skills: To learn about body parts; to talk about daily personal hygiene and grooming; to talk about common illnesses and ailments

Our body ...ร่างกายของเรา /râaŋ-kaay khɔ̌ɔŋ raw/

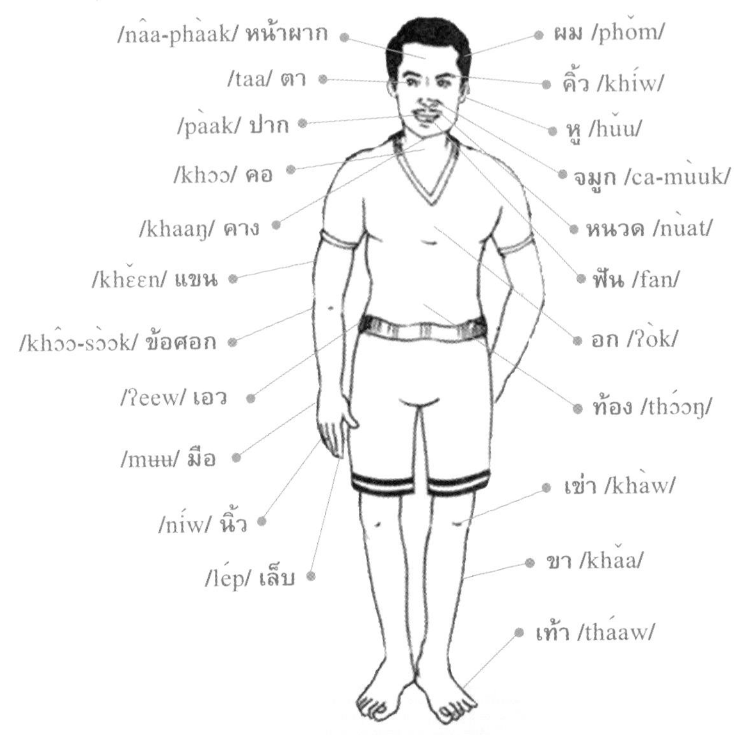

หน้าผาก	nâa-phàak	forehead
ตา	taa	eye
ปาก	pàak	mouth
คอ	khɔɔ	neck
คาง	khaaŋ	chin
แขน	khɛ̌ɛn	arm
ข้อศอก	khɔ̂ɔ-sɔ̀ɔk	elbow
เอว	ʔeew	waist
มือ	mʉʉ	hand
นิ้ว	níw	finger
ขา	khǎa	leg

ผม	phǒm	hair
คิ้ว	khíw	eye-brow
หู	hǔu	ear
จมูก	ca-mùuk	nose
หนวด	nùat	moustache
ฟัน	fan	teeth
อก	ʔòk	chest
ท้อง	thɔ́ɔŋ	abdomen, stomach
เข่า	khàw	knee
เล็บ	lép	nail
เท้า	tháaw	foot

Daily Personal Routine
...กิจวัตรส่วนตัว /kìt-ca-wát sùan-tua/

เขากำลังทำอะไร	kháw kam-laŋ tham ʔa-ray	What is s/he doing?
เขากำลัง *verb*	kháw kam-laŋ *verb*	S/he is *verb*.

ล้างหน้า
/láaŋ-nâa/
• **v. to wash one's face**

แปรงฟัน
/prɛɛŋ-fan/
• **v. to brush one's teeth**

บ้วนปาก
/bûan-pàak/
• **v. to rinse one's mouth**

อาบน้ำ
/ʔàap-náam/
v. to take a bath/shower

ล้างมือ
/láaŋ-mʉʉ/
v. to wash one's hands

สระผม
/sà-phǒm/
• **v. to wash one's hair**

หวีผม
/wǐi-phǒm/
• **v. to comb one's hair**

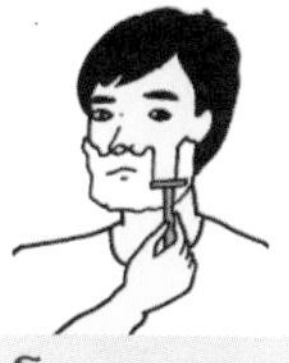

โกนหนวด
/koon-nùat/
• **v. to shave**

แต่งหน้า
/tɛ̀ŋ-nâa/
• **v. to put makeup on**

แต่งตัว
/tɛ̀ŋ-tua/
• **v. to get dressed**

ทาปาก
/thaa-pàak/
• **v. to put on lipstick**

ตัดผม
/tàt-phǒm/
• **v. to have one's hair cut**

Toiletries

แปรงสีฟัน	prɛɛŋ-sǐi-fan	n. toothbrush (clf. อัน /an/)
ยาสีฟัน	yaa-sǐi-fan	n. toothpaste
ไหมขัดฟัน	mǎy-khàt-fan	n. dental floss
สบู่	sa-bùu	n. soap (clf. ก้อน /kɔ̂ɔn/)
ยาสระผม	yaa-sà-phǒm	n. shampoo
แชมพู	chɛm-phuu	n. shampoo
น้ำยาบ้วนปาก	nám-yaa bûan-pàak	n. mouthwash
ครีมโกนหนวด	khriim koon-nùat	n. shaving cream
แป้ง	pɛ̂ɛŋ	n. talcum powder

Aches and Pains ...อาการเจ็บปวด /ʔaa-kaan cèp-pùat/

ปวด	pùat	v. to ache, to be in (aching) pain (including muscle pain and cramps)
เจ็บ	cèp	v. to hurt, to feel piercing pain, to feel sore (from wound, infection etc.)
ชา	chaa	v. to feel numb
เมื่อย	mɯ̂ay	v. to feel stiff, tired (in the muscles)

คุณเป็นอะไรไป	khun pen ʔa-ray pay	What's the matter?
ฉัน ___*verb*___	chán ___*verb*___	I ___*verb*___.

ปวดฟัน	pùat fan	(I) have a toothache.
ปวดท้อง	pùat thɔ́ɔŋ	(I) have a stomach ache.
ปวดคอ	pùat khɔɔ	(I) have neck pain.
ปวดหลัง	pùat lǎŋ	(I) have back pain.
ปวดขา	pùat khǎa	(My) legs ache.
เจ็บคอ	cèp khɔɔ	(I) have a sore throat.

◂ เจ็บเท้า	cèp tháaw	(My) legs hurt.
◂ เมื่อยขา	mɨ̂ay khǎa	(my) legs are tired, stiff, sore.
◂ เมื่อยคอ	mɨ̂ay khɔɔ	(My) neck is stiff.
◂ ชาเท้า	chaa tháaw	(My) feet are numb.
◂ ชานิ้ว	chaa níw	(My) fingers are numb.

Physical Expressions

เขากำลังทำอะไร	kháw kam-laŋ tham ʔa-ray	What is s/he doing?
เขากำลัง ___*verb*___	kháw kam-laŋ ___*verb*___	S/he is ___*verb*___.

ยิ้ม
/yím/
• v. to smile

หัวเราะ
/hǔa-rɔ́ʔ/
• v. to laugh

ร้องไห้
/rɔ́ɔŋ-hâay/
• v. to weep, cry

Vocabulary ...ศัพท์ /sàp/

◂ กิจวัตร	kìt-ca-wát	n. routine; routine matter
◂ ส่วนตัว	sùan-tua	n. private, personal, individual
◂ แปรง	prɛɛŋ	v. to brush
◂ โกน	koon	v. to shave
◂ ทา	thaa	v. to coat, apply, spread (on)
◂ ยา	yaa	n. medicine, drug (clf. ชนิด /cha-nít/, อย่าง /yàaŋ/, ขนาน /kha-nǎan/)
◂ สีฟัน	sǐi-fan	v. to brush the teeth; = แปรงฟัน /prɛɛŋ fan/
◂ ไหม	mǎy	n. silk
◂ น้ำยา	nám-yaa	n. chemical solution (non-technical term)
◂ แป้ง	pɛ̂ɛŋ	n. powder, flour
◂ อาการ	ʔaa-kaan	n. symptom, condition (as of one's health)

Dialogs ...บทสนทนา /bòt sǒn-tha-naa/

Dialog 8.1.1

Dan (A) and Suda (B) discuss their morning routines.

A	แย่แล้ว ผมมาเรียนสาย อีกแล้ว	yɛ̂ɛ lɛ́ɛw. phǒm maa rian sǎay ʔìik lɛ́ɛw.	Oh gosh, I'm late for class again.
B	ทำไมล่ะจ๊ะ	tham-may lâ cá.	Why?
A	ผมตื่นสาย	phǒm tɯ̀ɯn sǎay.	I got up late.
B	ปกติ แดนตื่นกี่โมง	pòk-ka-tì dɛɛn tɯ̀ɯn kìi mooŋ.	What time do you usually get up?
A	เจ็ดโมงครึ่ง	cèt mooŋ khrɯ̂ŋ.	7:30.
B	โอ้โฮ แดนตื่นเจ็ดโมงครึ่ง แต่มาเรียนทันแปดโมงเช้า แดนทำได้ยังไง	ʔôo-hoo. dɛɛn tɯ̀ɯn cèt mooŋ khrɯ̂ŋ tɛ̀ɛ maa rian than pɛ̀ɛt mooŋ cháaw. dɛɛn tham dây yaŋ-ŋay.	Wow! You get up at 7:30 but you make it to an 8 a.m. class. How do you do that?
A	ผมก็เข้าห้องน้ำ แปรงฟัน ล้างหน้า หวีผม แต่งตัว แล้วก็มามหา'ลัยเลย แล้วตุ๊กล่ะครับ	phǒm kɔ̂ khâw hɔ̂ŋ-náam prɛɛŋ-fan láaŋ-nâa wǐi-phǒm tɛ̀ŋ-tua lɛ́ɛw kɔ̂ maa ma-hǎa-lay ləəy. lɛ́ɛw túk la khráp.	I go into the bathroom, brush my teeth, wash my face, comb my hair, get dressed and then come to school. How about you?
B	ตายแล้ว ตอนเช้าเธอไม่ได้ อาบน้ำเหรอ ฉันน่ะ ต้องอาบน้ำตอนเช้าด้วยจ้ะ แล้วก็ฉันก็ต้องใช้เวลา แต่งหน้าทำผมด้วย	taay-lɛ́ɛw. tɔɔn cháaw thəə mây-dây ʔàap-náam rə̌ə. chán nâ tɔ̂ŋ ʔàap-náam tɔɔn cháaw dûay cà. lɛ́ɛw kɔ̂ chán kɔ̂ tɔ̂ŋ cháy wee-laa tɛ̀ŋ-nâa tham phǒm dûay.	What? You don't bathe in the morning? For me, I have to take a bath in the morning, and I have to spend some time putting makeup on and doing my hair too.

Dialog 8.1.2

Suda (A) asks about Amy's (B) condition.

A	เอมี่เป็นอะไร หน้าตา ไม่สบาย	ʔee-mîi pen ʔa-ray. nâa-taa mây sa-baay.	Amy, what's wrong? You don't look well.
B	ปวดหัว	pùat-hǔa.	I have a headache.
A	กินยาแล้วหรือยัง	kin yaa lɛ́ɛw-rɯ̌-yaŋ.	Have you taken medicine?
B	กินแล้ว กำลังจะไป นอนพักที่บ้าน	kin lɛ́ɛw. kam-laŋ-ca pay nɔɔn-phák thîi bâan.	Yes. I'm going to rest in bed at home.

Dialog 8.1.3

Chai (A) asks about Dan's (B) condition.

A	เป็นอะไรไป	pen ʔa-ray pay.	What's wrong?
B	ปวดฟัน	pùat fan.	I have a toothache.
A	ไปหาหมอแล้วหรือยัง	pay hǎa mɔ̌ɔ lɛ́ɛw-rɯ̌-yaŋ.	have you seen a doctor?
B	กำลังจะไปหาหมอฟันของมหา'ลัย	kam-laŋ-ca pay hǎa mɔ̌ɔ-fan khɔ̌ŋ ma-hǎa-lay.	I'm going to see the university dentist.

Dialog 8.1.4

At Chai's dorm, a neighbor (A) talks to Chai (B).

A	ชัย มีพลาสเตอร์ปิดแผลไหม	chay. mii phláas-tɤ̂ɤ pìt phlɛ̌ɛ máy.	Chai, do you have a bandage?
B	มี ใครเป็นอะไรเหรอ	mii. khray pen ʔa-ray rɤ̌ɤ.	Yes. Did something happen to someone?
A	ผมเอง โดนมีดบาดนิ้วนิดหน่อย ใส่ยาแล้ว แต่ยังไม่มีพลาสเตอร์	phǒm ʔeeŋ. doon mîit bàat níw nít-nɔ̀y. sày yaa lɛ́ɛw. tɛ̀ɛ yaŋ mây mii phláas-tɤ̂ɤ.	It's me. I cut my finger a little with a knife. I put on some ointment but I don't have a bandage.
B	นี่ครับ	nîi khráp.	Here it is.
A	ขอบคุณครับ	khɔ̀ɔp-khun khráp.	Thank you.

Idioms ...สำนวน /sǎm-nuan/

ลูบหน้าปะจมูก lûup nâa pàʔ ca-mùuk	to rub + face + to encounter + nose	to rub a face and encounter a nose

"To come upon something one wasn't looking for."
(as in an investigation where evidence implicating the investigator turns up);
"To hold back doing something for fear of affecting one's own clique."

ตบหัวแล้วลูบหลัง tòp hǔa lɛ́ɛw lûup lǎŋ	to slap + head + then + to stroke + back	to slap someone on the head and then rub his back

"To offend and then mollify."

Vocabulary ...ศัพท์ /sàp/

แย่	yɛ̂ɛ	v. to be in trouble, in a bad way
แย่แล้ว	yɛ̂ɛ-lɛ́ɛw	excl. I'm in trouble. There's trouble.
ทัน	than	v. to be on time, in time
ตาย	taay	v. to die
ตายแล้ว	taay-lɛ́ɛw	excl. exclamation expressing dismay or alarm; "My goodness."
ทำผม	tham-phǒm	v. to style a hairdo
หน้าตา	nâa-taa	n. look, appearance
พลาสเตอร์	phláas-tə̂ə	n. adhesive bandage
ปิด	pìt	v. to cover, to cover up
แผล	phlɛ̌ɛ	n. wound, cut
โดน	doon	aux. element used in making passive construction
บาด	bàat	v. to cut (as of a sharp object), wound, scar
ลูบ	lûup	v. to stroke, pat, pet, rub
ปะ	pàʔ	v. to meet, encounter
ตบ	tòp	v. to slap, clap, pat

Language Notes

1. Washing in Thai: ล้าง /láaŋ/, สระ /sà/, ซัก /sák/

ล้าง /láaŋ/ is a general word for washing objects and most body parts.

ซัก /sák/ is used only with washing clothing items, as seen in Unit 4.2.

สระ /sà/ is used with washing hair only.

2. Verb compounds expressing aches and pains

Notice that the verb compounds expressing feelings or symptoms of aches and pains in Thai are composed of the following pattern:

Types of pain + Body parts affected

For example:

ปวด /pùat/ + หัว /hǔa/ "head"
เจ็บ /cèp/ + คอ /khɔɔ/ "neck"
เมื่อย /mûay/ + ขา /khǎa/ "leg"
ชา /chaa/ + นิ้ว /níw/ "finger"

3. มหา'ลัย /ma-hǎa-lay/, shortened from มหาวิทยาลัย /ma-hǎa-wít-tha-yaa-lay/, is commonly used in casual conversation.

4. In the dialogs in this lesson, observe the use of the particles จ้ะ /câ/ จ๊ะ /cá/ by women among friends, instead of the more formal ค่ะ /khâ/, คะ /khá/ (see also Unit 1.1). Also notice that the set of pronouns that one uses can express one's attitudes and emotions. In Dialog 8.1.1, Suda switches to use the ฉัน /chán/ - เธอ /thəə/ set in jest of Dan's morning routine.

Culture Note

Thai Etiquette about the head and feet

The concept of hierarchy in Thai society and social interaction also applies to body parts. The head is considered the highest (i.e. the most important) and the feet the lowest (i.e. the most insignificant) in the hierarchy. This is also related to the belief about ขวัญ /khwǎn/ "soul" or "psyche" mentioned in Unit 7.1 Culture Note, as the head is believed to be where the ขวัญ resides. Thais therefore also show respect to those higher in status through gestures, such as lowering one's head and bowing slightly to make one's head lower than a superior's head, especially when that person is sitting or standing in a lower place.

The feet are considered the lowliest part of the body. Therefore Thais are offended when a person uses his/her foot to point at something. Likewise, since the head is the most important part, Thais do not like people to touch their heads, even playfully.

The pronoun ผม /phǒm/ for men originated from the meaning "hair" and is used as a means to show respect to others. ผม /phǒm/ is believed to be a shortened form of กระผม /kra-phǒm/ "hair" which is derived from a deferential first person pronoun เกล้ากระผม /klâaw kra-phǒm/ "hair of the head" used by a male commoner in speaking to high ranking non-royalty noblemen. This follows a court tradition of verbal expression of respect in the "royal vocabulary" (terms used when speaking to the royalty) in which euphemisms are used to avoid direct reference to the King and to royalty. In the royal vocabulary, one equates the reference to oneself with the highest part (and hence the most important part) of one's body, and never directly addresses royalty but merely to the "dust under the sole of the feet" of the royalty. Thus, when one places one's highest part in relation to another person's low(li)-est part, this is considered by Thais to be the utmost form of respect.

This concept of knowing one's place in the hierarchy is expressed in Thai as "knowing one's high and low places" รู้จักที่ต่ำที่สูง /rúu-càk thîi tàm thîi sǔuŋ/.

Skills: To provide and obtain information about health, physical condition and ailment

Asking about one's health and physical condition

เป็นอะไรไป	pen ʔa-ray pay	What's the matter? What's wrong?
คุณเป็นยังไงบ้าง	khun pen yaŋ-ŋay bâaŋ	How are you?
คุณเป็นอะไรหรือเปล่า	khun pen ʔa-ray rɨ́-plàaw	Are you alright?
ฉัน(รู้สึก) ___verb___	chán (rúu-sɨ̀k) ___verb___	I (feel) ___verb___.

ง่วงนอน	ŋûaŋ-nɔɔn	v. to be sleepy
เหนื่อย	nɨ̀ay	v. to be tired, exhausted
ไม่สบาย	mây sa-baay	v. to be not well, to be ill
ไม่ค่อยสบาย	mây-khɔ̂y sa-baay	v. to be not very well
ป่วย	pùay	v. to be sick, ill, unwell
ค่อยยังชั่ว	khɔ̂y-yaŋ-chûa	v. to feel better, to get better
หายดีแล้ว	hǎay dii lɛ́ɛw	I am cured. I have recovered.

คุณมีอาการยังไงบ้าง	khun mii ʔaa-kaan yaŋ-ŋay bâaŋ	What symptoms do you have?
ฉัน ___verb___	chán ___verb___	I ___verb___.

คลื่นไส้	khlɨ̂ɨn-sây	v. to be sick (in the stomach), to feel nauseated
อาเจียน	ʔaa-cian	v. to vomit (formal)
อ้วก	ʔûak	v. to vomit (informal)
ไอ	ʔay	v. to cough
จาม	caam	v. to sneeze
ตัวร้อน	tua-rɔ́ɔn	v. to have a high body temperature, to be feverish

◂ ครั่นเนื้อครั่นตัว	khrân-nʉ́a khrân-tua	v. to feel feverish, to have a chill
◂ แพ้อากาศ	phɛ́ɛ ʔaa-kàat	v. to have hay fever (Lit. to be allergic to the weather)
◂ คัน	khan	v. to itch, to be itchy
◂ เป็นไข้	pen khây	v. to have a fever
◂ เป็นหวัด	pen wàt	v. to have a cold
◂ เป็นไข้หวัด	pen khây-wàt	v. to have a cold with fever
◂ เป็นเหน็บ	pen nèp	v. to lose sensation in a given part of the body, usually limbs, to go to sleep (as of a limb).
◂ เป็นตะคริว	pen ta-khriw	v. to have cramps
◂ เป็นผด	pen phòt	v. to have prickly heat, a heat rash
◂ เป็นผื่น	pen phʉ̀ʉn	v. to have hives, a rash
◂ เป็นแผล	pen phlɛ̌ɛ	v. to have a wound, an injury
◂ เป็นลม	pen-lom	v. to swoon, faint
◂ ท้องอืด	thɔ́ɔŋ-ʔʉ̀ʉt	v. to have indigestion, to feel bloated
◂ ท้องเฟ้อ	thɔ́ɔŋ-fɔ́ɔ	v. to have heartburn
◂ ท้องเสีย	thɔ́ɔŋ-sǐa	v. to have an upset stomach
◂ ท้องเดิน	thɔ́ɔŋ-dəən	v. to have diarrhea
◂ ท้องผูก	thɔ́ɔŋ-phùuk	v. to have constipation
◂ เสียดท้อง	sìat-thɔ́ɔŋ	v. to feel a sharp pain in the stomach, to have heartburn
◂ น้ำมูกไหล	nám-mûuk lǎy	v. to have a runny nose
◂ มีน้ำมูก	mii nám-mûuk	v. to have nasal discharge
◂ มีเสมหะ	mii sěem-hàʔ	v. to have phlegm

Other commonly heard expressions

หายดีหรือยัง	hǎay dii rʉ́-yaŋ	Are you feeling well yet?
หายเร็ว ๆ	hǎay rew-rew	Get well soon.
รักษาเนื้อรักษาตัวดี ๆ	rák-sǎa nʉ́a rák-sǎa tua dii dii	Take good care of your health.

ยากิน
/yaa-kin/
• **oral medicine**

ยาเม็ด
/yaa-mét/
• **pill, tablet**

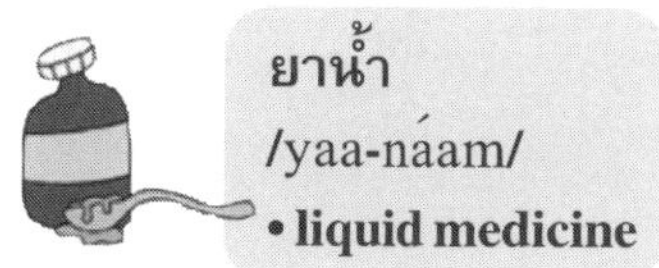

ยาน้ำ
/yaa-náam/
• **liquid medicine**

ยาทา
/yaa-thaa/
• **ointment**

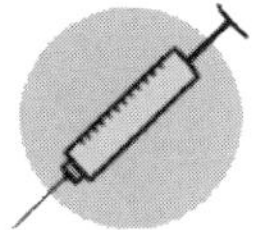

ยาฉีด
/yaa-chìit/
• **injection**

Types of Medecine ...ยาชนิดต่าง ๆ /yaa cha-nít tàaŋ-tàaŋ/

ยาแก้ไข้	yaa kɛ̂ɛ khây	fever medicine
ยาแก้ไอ	yaa kɛ̂ɛ ʔay	cough medicine
ยาแก้ปวด	yaa kɛ̂ɛ pùat	pain killer
ยาฆ่าเชื้อ	yaa khâa chúa	antibiotics (informal)
ยาปฏิชีวนะ	yaa pa-tì-chii-wa-ná	antibiotics (formal)
ยาแก้แพ้	yaa kɛ̂ɛ phɛ́ɛ	allergy medicine
ยาหม่อง	yaa mɔ̀ɔŋ	mentholated ointment, balm

Vocabulary ...ศัพท์ /sàp/

หาย	hǎay	v. to recover, to get well, to be cured, healed
หายป่วย	hǎay-pùay	v. to recover, get well
แพ้	phɛ́ɛ	v. to be allergic to
ไข้	khây	v. fever, illness
หวัด	wàt	n. common cold
ไข้หวัด	khây-wàt	n. fever due to a common cold
เหน็บ	nèp	n. numbness
ตะคริว	ta-khriw	n. cramp, painful spasmodic muscular contraction
ผด	phòt	n. prickly heat, heat rash

ผื่น	phʉ̀ʉn	n. rash
อืด	ʔʉ̀ʉt	n. to be swollen, distended
เฟ้อ	fə́ə	v. to be in excess
ผูก	phùuk	v. tie, bind, fasten
น้ำมูก	nám-mûuk	n. nasal mucus, nasal discharge
ไหล	lǎy	v. to flow, run
เสมหะ	sěem-hàʔ	n. phlegm, sputum
รักษา	rák-sǎa	v. to treat (illness), cure; remedy; heal; have a treatment
ชนิด	cha-nít	clf. kind, type, variety, description, sort, species
ต่าง ๆ	tàaŋ-tàaŋ	d.a. different, various
ฉีด	chìit	v. to inject, inoculate
แก้	kɛ̂ɛ	v. to remedy, relieve (an illness)
ฆ่า	khâa	v. to kill, execute, destroy
เชื้อ	chʉ́a	n. germ, bacteria
ปฏิชีวนะ	pà-tì-chii-wa-ná	n. antibiotic

วันที่...
ชื่อ...
รับประทานครั้งละ..............................**เม็ด**
วันละ..**เวลา**
ก่อนอาหาร
หลังอาหาร **เช้า กลางวัน เย็น ก่อนนอน**
หรือ ทุก..................................**ชั่วโมง**
เวลา...
คำแนะนำ...

wan thîi..........................
chʉ̂ʉ..
ráp-pra-thaan khráŋ la............mét
wan-la..............................wee-laa
kɔ̀ɔn ʔaa-hǎan
lǎŋ-ʔaa-hǎan cháaw klaaŋ-wan yen kɔ̀ɔn-nɔɔn
rʉ̌ʉ thúk...............chûa-mooŋ
wee-laa..
kham-nɛ́-nam..............................

Dialogs ...บทสนทนา /bòt sǒn-tha-naa/

Dialog 8.2.1 Asking about someone's condition

Suda (A) asks about Chai's (B) condition.

A	หวัดดีจ้ะ ชัย เป็นอะไร	wàt-dii câ chay. pen ʔa-ray	Hello Chai. What's wrong
	หรือเปล่า หน้าตาไม่สบาย	rʉ́ plàaw. nâa-taa mây sa-baay.	with you? You don't look well.
B	เป็นหวัดนิดหน่อยครับ	pen wàt nít nɔ̀y khráp.	I have a little cold.
A	ไปหาหมอ หรือ กินยาแล้ว	pay hǎa mɔ̌ɔ rʉ̌ʉ kin yaa	Have you seen the doctor or
	หรือยัง	lɛ́ɛw-rʉ́-yaŋ.	taken any medicine yet?
B	ผมไปหาหมอมา แล้วหมอ	phǒm pay hǎa mɔ̌ɔ maa.	I saw the doctor, and he gave
	ก็ให้ยาแก้ไข้มากินแล้วครับ	lɛ́ɛw mɔ̌ɔ kɔ̂ɔ hây yaa kɛ̂ɛ	me some fever medicine.
		khây maa kin lɛ́ɛw khráp.	

Dialog 8.2.2

Dan sneezes a couple of times. Suda (A) asks him (B) about his condition.

A	แดน เป็นอะไรหรือเปล่า	dɛɛn pen ʔa-ray rʉ́-plàaw.	Dan, are you alright? Today,
	วันนี้ จามหลายครั้งแล้วนะ	wan-níi caam lǎay khráŋ	you've been sneezing many
	เป็นหวัดหรือเปล่า	lɛ́ɛw ná. pen wàt rʉ́-plàaw.	times. Do you have a cold?
B	เปล่าครับ วันนี้ผมมี	plàaw khráp. wan-níi phǒm	No. I have "hay fever."
	hay fever ภาษาไทยเรียก	mii "hay fever". pha-sǎa-thay	What is that called in Thai?
	อะไรนะครับ	rîak ʔa-ray ná khráp.	
A	เรียกว่า แพ้อากาศ	rîak-wâa phɛ́ɛ ʔaa-kàat.	It's called "phae aakaat."
	แล้วแดนกินยาแก้แพ้	lɛ́ɛw dɛɛn kin yaa kɛ̂ɛ phɛ́ɛ	Have you taken allergy
	แล้วหรือยังคะ	lɛ́ɛw-rʉ́-yaŋ khá.	medicine yet?
B	กินยาแล้วครับ	kin yaa lɛ́ɛw khráp.	Yes. The sneezing should
	เดี๋ยวคงจะหยุดจาม	dǐaw khoŋ-ca yùt caam.	stop soon.

Dialog 8.2.3

Chai (A) calls Suda (B) about their plan.

A	ฮัลโหล ตุ๊ก ผมชัยนะ	han-lǒo túk. phǒm chay ná.	Hello, Tuk, it's Chai.
	วันนี้ผมไม่สบาย	wan-níi phǒm mây sa-baay.	I'm sick today. I have a cold
	เป็นไข้หวัด คงจะไป	pen khây wàt. khoŋ ca pay duu	and won't be able to go see
	ดูหนังกับพวกคุณไม่ได้	nǎŋ kàp phûak khun mây-dâay.	a movie with you guys.

B	ไม่เป็นไรหรอกจ้ะ	mây-pen-ray rɔ̀k câ. khɔ̀ɔp-cay	That's alright. Thanks for
	ขอบใจที่โทร.มาบอกนะ	thîi thoo maa bɔ̀ɔk ná. rák-sǎa	calling to let us know.
	รักษาเนื้อรักษาตัวดีๆ	nʉ́a rák-sǎa tua dii dii lɛ́ɛw-kan.	Take good care of yourself
	แล้วกัน แล้วหายเร็วๆล่ะ	lɛ́ɛw hǎay rew-rew ná.	and get well soon.
A	ขอบใจ ดูหนังให้สนุก	khɔ̀ɔp-cay. duu nǎŋ hây sa-nùk	Thanks. Have fun at the movie.
	ก็แล้วกัน หวัดดีนะ	kɔ̂-lɛ́ɛw-kan. wàt-dii ná.	Bye.
B	หวัดดีจ้ะ	wàt-dii câ.	Bye.

Dialog 8.2.4

Suda (A) asks about Dan's (B) condition.

A	แดน ไปไหนมา	dɛɛn pay nǎy maa.	Dan, where have you been?
B	ไปหาหมอมา	pay hǎa mɔ̌ɔ maa.	I went to see a doctor.
A	เป็นอะไรเหรอ	pen ʔa-ray rə̌ə.	Is something the matter?
B	เมื่อคืนนี้ ผมปวดท้องและ	mʉ̂a-khʉʉn-níi phǒm pùat-	Last night I had a stomach
	ท้องเสีย คิดว่าผมคงจะ	thɔ́ɔŋ lɛ́ thɔ́ɔŋ-sǐa. khít wâa	ache and diarrhea. I think
	กินอาหารเผ็ดมากไป	phǒm khoŋ ca kin ʔaa-hǎan	I might have eaten food that
	หน่อย	phèt mâak pay nɔ̀y.	was too spicy.
A	แล้วตอนนี้หายดีหรือยังจ๊ะ	lɛ́ɛw tɔɔn-níi hǎay dii rʉ̌-yaŋ cá.	Are you feeling better yet?
B	ค่อยยังชั่วแล้วครับ	khɔ̂y-yaŋ-chûa lɛ́ɛw khráp.	I'm better now.

Dialog 8.2.5

At the drug store, Chai (B) talks to the vendor (A).

A	รับอะไรดีครับ	ráp ʔa-ray dii khráp.	What would you like?
B	มียาแก้ไอ และแก้เจ็บคอ	mii yaa kɛ̂ɛ ʔay lɛ́ kɛ̂ɛ cèp	Do you have cough and sore
	ไหมครับ	khɔɔ máy khráp.	throat medicine?
A	จะรับยาน้ำหรือยาเม็ด	ca ráp yaa-náam rʉ̌ yaa-mét	Would you like them as liquid
	ครับ	khráp.	or pills?

B ยาน้ำดีกว่าครับ

yaa-náam dii-kwàa khráp.

• I prefer liquid.

A นี่ครับ จะรับอย่างอื่นอีกไหมครับ

nîi khráp. ca ráp yàaŋ ʔʉ̀ʉn ʔìik máy khráp.

• Here they are. Would you like anything else?

B ไม่ละครับ

mây la khráp.

• No.

Dialog 8.2.6

Chai (B) at the doctor's (A) clinic.

A คุณมีอาการยังไงบ้างครับ

khun mii ʔaa-kaan yaŋ-ŋay bâaŋ khráp.

• What symptoms do you have?

B ผมเจ็บคอ มีไข้ครับ

phǒm cèp khɔɔ mii khây khráp.

• I have a sore throat and a fever.

A ไอ และ มีน้ำมูกด้วยหรือเปล่า

ʔay lɛ́ mii náam-mûuk dûay rʉ̌-plàaw.

• Do you cough and have nasal discharge also?

B ครับ

khráp.

• Yes.

A ขอหมอตรวจดูหน่อยนะครับ อ้าปากกว้างๆครับ

khɔ̌ɔ mɔ̌ɔ trùat duu nɔ̀y ná khráp. ʔâa pàak kwâaŋ-kwâaŋ khráp.

• Let me take a look. Open your mouth wide.

A คุณเป็นไข้หวัด คออักเสบนิดหน่อย หมอจะให้ยาแก้ไข้ ยาแก้ไอ และยาฆ่าเชื้อนะ
ยาฆ่าเชื้อกินวันละ 4 ครั้ง ครั้งละ 2 เม็ด หลังอาหาร และ ก่อนนอน
ยาแก้ไข้ กินวันละ 4 ครั้ง ครั้งละ 1 เม็ด หลังอาหาร และ ก่อนนอนเหมือนกัน
สำหรับยาแก้ไอ ให้กินเวลาไอ ยาฆ่าเชื้อต้องกินให้หมดด้วยนะ
ดื่มน้ำมากๆ และนอนพักให้มากๆ ด้วยนะ

khun pen khây-wàt. khɔɔ ʔàk-sèep nít-nɔ̀y. mɔ̌ɔ ca hây yaa kɛ̂ɛ khây yaa kɛ̂ɛ ʔay lɛ́ yaa khâa chʉ́a ná.

yaa khâa chʉ́a kin wan lá sìi khráŋ. khráŋ lá sɔ̌ɔŋ mét lǎŋ ʔaa-hǎan lɛ́ kɔ̀ɔn nɔɔn.

yaa kɛ̂ɛ khây kin wan lá sìi khráŋ. khráŋ lá mét lǎŋ ʔaa-haan lɛ́ kɔ̀ɔn nɔɔn mʉ̌an kan.

sǎm-ràp yaa kɛ̂ɛ ʔay hây kin wee-laa ʔay. yaa khâa chʉ́a tɔ̂ŋ kin hây mòt dûay ná.

dʉ̀ʉm náam mâak-mâak lɛ́ nɔɔn-phák hây mâak-mâak dûay ná.

• You have a cold. A little throat inflammation. I will prescribe fever medicine, cough medicine, and antibiotics. For the antibiotics, take 2 pills, 4 times a day after meals and before going to bed. For the fever medicine, take one pill 4 times a day, after meals and before bedtime too. As for the cough medicine, take it when you cough. Take the antibiotics until they are gone. Drink a lot of water and rest in bed a lot.

Idioms ...สำนวน /sǎm-nuan/

ตีตนไปก่อนไข้ tii ton pay kɔ̀ɔn khây	to beat + self + v. dir + before + fever	to beat oneself up before a fever

"To cross one's bridges before coming to them; to be a pessimist a defeatist."

ยืมจมูกคนอื่นหายใจ yʉʉm ca-mùuk kon-ʔʉ̀ʉn hǎay-cay	to borrow + nose + other people + to breathe	to borrow another's nose to breathe

"To be dependent on others."

Vocabulary ...ศัพท์ /sàp/

พวก	phûak	n. group, party
สนุก	sa-nùk	v. to have fun, to be fun
ตรวจ	trùat	v. to inspect, examine, check
อ้า	ʔâa	v. to open (e.g. the mouth)
กว้าง	kwâaŋ	v. to be broad, wide
อักเสบ	ʔàk-sèep	v. to be infected, inflamed
หมด	mòt	v. to be used up, exhausted (in supply)
ตี	tii	v. to hit, beat, strike
ยืม	yʉʉm	v. to borrow
อื่น	ʔʉ̀ʉn	n. other; others
หายใจ	hǎay-cay	v. to breathe

Structure Notes

1. Word formation: ailment verb compounds

In Thai, expressions for symptoms of ailments are verb compounds. In Unit 8.1, we see a set of verb compounds expressing aches and pains with the pattern: ***type of pain + body part affected.***

For symptoms other than aches and pains affecting body parts, the verb compounds typically follow the pattern:

Body Part Affected + Symptom

For example:

ท้องเสีย /thɔ́ɔŋ-sǐa/ from ท้อง + เสีย /sǐa/ "to be bad"

คออักเสบ /khɔɔ ʔàk-sèep/ from คอ + อักเสบ /ʔàk-sèep/ "to be inflamed"

For symptoms that do not affect a particular body part, the pattern ***เป็น /pen/*** + **ailment/disease** is commonly used.

2. ปฏิชีวนะ /pa-tì-chii-wa-ná/ is a formal coined word from Indic loans for "antibiotic." In conversational Thai, ยาฆ่าเชื้อ /yaa khâa chʉ́a/ is more commonly used.

3. Three functions of ให้ /hây/

ให้ /hây/ is another commonly used multi-function word. So far, we have seen three usages of ให้ /hây/:

a. ให้ /hây/ as a verb, "to give"

It follows basic pattern #2. ***Subject + Verb (+ Object) (+ Adverb)***, with the addition that it can have two objects: ***direct object + indirect object***.

In formal use, the indirect object can be preceded by a preposition แก่ /kὲε/ "to"

2h. Subject + Verb (+ Direct Object) (+ Indirect Object) (+ Adverb)

หมอให้ยาแก่ชัย mɔ̌ɔ hây yaa kὲε chay	doctor + ***ให้*** /hây/ + medicine + to + Chai	The doctor gave (= prescribed) the medicine to Chai.
แม่ให้เงินลูก mɛ̂ɛ hây ŋən lûuk	mother + ***ให้*** /hây/ + money + child	The mother gave money to her child.

b. ให้ /hây/ as a preposition/conjunction indicating a desired result or purpose. The pattern of this usage is similar to the Evaluative Post Verb pattern 2a.

2i. Subject + Verb + Object + (ไม่ mây) *ให้* /hây/ + Evaluative Post-verb + (Adverb-degree)

But typically, it is used as an instruction or command.

กินยาให้หมด kin yaa hây mòt	to eat + medicine + **ให้** /hây/ + to be used up	Use up all the medicine.
นอนให้มาก nɔɔn hây mâak	to sleep + **ให้** /hây/ + a lot	Get a lot of sleep.
ดูหนังให้สนุก duu nǎŋ hây sa-nùk	to watch movie + **ให้** /hây/ + to have fun	Have fun at the movie.

c. ให้ /hây/ as a preposition/conjunction indicating "for the benefit of someone," or "on behalf of someone."

We see an example of this usage in Unit 6.2. If the person receiving the beneift is omitted, it usually refers to the hearer.

เราจะตัดขากางเกงให้ raw ca tàt khǎa kaaŋ-keeŋ hây	we + to cut + leg + pants + **ให้** /hây/	We will shorten (the leg of) the pants (for you).
จะบอกชัยให้ ca bɔ̀ɔk chay hây	will + to tell + Chai + **ให้** /hây/	(I) will tell Chai (for you).

Culture Note

Drug stores in Thailand sell most drugs over the counter. Even "prescription" drugs can be purchased without any prescription. So, for minor illnesses, Thais usually just get the drugs, as well as suggestions for which drugs to take, directly from the drug stores.

9 Unit

หน่วยที่ ๙

lesson 1

Understand and express words and phrases related to mishaps, emergencies and accidents; be able to ask for help, give warnings and report emergencies

lesson 2

Understand and express words and phrases related to banking transactions, posting and shipping

บทที่ ๑ Lesson 1

Skills: To understand and express words and phrases related to mishaps, emergencies and accidents; to be able to ask for help, give warnings and report emergencies

Talking about mishaps, emergencies and accidents

ช่วยด้วย	chûay-dûay	Help!
ไฟไหม้	fay-mây	Fire!
ระวัง	ra-waŋ	Watch out! Be careful!
ฉันถูกล้วงกระเป๋า	chán thùuk lúaŋ kra-pǎw	I was pick-pocketed.
ฉันถูกปล้น	chán thùuk plôn	I was robbed.
ฉันถูกขโมยเงิน	chán thùuk kha-mooy ŋən	My money was stolen.
เงินฉันถูกขโมย	ŋən chán thùuk kha-mooy	My money was stolen.
เกิดอุบัติเหตุ	kə̀ət ʔu-bàt-ti-hèet	There's an accident.
เกิดไฟไหม้	kə̀ət fay-mây	There's a fire.
เกิดน้ำท่วม	kə̀ət náam thûam	There's a flood.
มีคนบาดเจ็บ	mii khon bàat-cèp	There's someone injured. There's an injured person.
มีรถชนกัน	mii rót chon kan	There's a car collision.
เรื่องด่วน	rʉ̂aŋ dùan	n. urgent matter
เรื่องฉุกเฉิน	rʉ̂aŋ chùk-chə̌ən	n. emergency

/thaaŋ-ʔɔ̀ɔk chùk-chə̌ən/
• **Emergency Exit**

/thaaŋ nǐi fay/
• **Fire Exit**

/ra-waŋ khon khâam/
• **Caution: Pedestrian Crossing**

ระวังคนข้าม

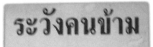

Vocabulary ...ศัพท์ /sàp/

ไหม้	mây	v. to be burned, charred
ถูก	thùuk	aux. element used in making passive constructions
ขโมย	kha-mooy	v. to steal, pilfer; n. thief
ปล้น	plôn	v. to commit a robbery
ล้วง	lúaŋ	v. to reach into (e.g. a pocket, deep drawer, hole)
กระเป๋า	kra-pǎw	n. pocket, bag (clf. ใบ /bay/)
ล้วงกระเป๋า	lúaŋ kra-pǎw	v. to pick a pocket, to put one's hand in a pocket or bag
เกิด	kə̀ət	v. to arise, occur, happen, take place
อุบัติเหตุ	ʔù-bàt-tì-hèet, ʔù-bàt-ti-hèet	n. accident (clf. ครั้ง /khráŋ/)
น้ำท่วม	náam thûam	n. flood; floodwaters
บาดเจ็บ	bàat-cèp	v. to get hurt; to be injured, wounded
ชน	chon	v. to collide, bump into, run into, butt, hit
ด่วน	dùan	v. to be urgent, hasty
ฉุกเฉิน	chùk-chə̌ən	v. to be of an emergency nature, in a state of critical disorder
หนี	nǐi	v. to flee, escape

Dialogs ...บทสนทนา /bòt sǒn-tha-naa/

Dialog 9.1.1

Amy (A) asks for Suda's (B) help concerning her stolen purse.

A	ตุ๊ก ช่วยด้วย เอมี่ถูกล้วงกระเป๋า	túk. chûay-dûay. ʔee-mîi thùuk lúaŋ kra-pǎw.	Tuk, help! My purse was stolen. (Lit. I was pick-pocketed)
B	เมื่อไหร่ ที่ไหน	mʉ̂a-rày. thîi-nǎy.	When? Where?
A	ไม่รู้ เอมี่เพิ่งรู้เดี๋ยวนี้เองว่ากระเป๋าสตางค์หาย เอมี่ต้องทำยังไงบ้าง	mây-rúu. ʔee-mîi phə̂ŋ rúu dǐaw-níi ʔeeŋ wâa kra-pǎw sa-taŋ hǎay. ʔee-mîi tɔ̂ŋ tham yaŋ-ŋay bâaŋ.	I don't know. I realized just now that my purse is missing. What do I need to do?
B	ต้องไปแจ้งความกับตำรวจ ตุ๊กจะพาไป	tɔ̂ŋ pay cɛ̂ɛŋ-khwaam kàp tam-rùat. túk ca phaa pay.	You need to report it to the police. I'll take you there.

แจ้งเอกสารหาย
DOCUMENT REPORT

/cɛ̂ɛŋ ʔèek-ka-sǎan hǎay/

แจ้งความที่สถานีตำรวจ
/cɛ̂ɛŋ-khwaam thîi sa-thǎa-nii tam-rùat/

Dialog 9.1.2

At the police station, Suda (A) helps Amy (C) report to the police (B).

A	พาเพื่อนฝรั่งมาขอ แจ้งความกระเป๋าหายค่ะ ต้องทำยังไงบ้างคะ	phaa phɨ̂an fa-ràŋ maa khɔ̌ɔ cɛ̂ɛŋ-khwaam kra-pǎw hǎay khâ. tɔ̂ŋ tham yaŋ-ŋay bâaŋ khá.	I'm bringing my farang friend to report a stolen purse. What does she need to do?
B	ขอหนังสือเดินทางของเขา ด้วยครับ	khɔ̌ɔ naŋ-sɨ̌ɨ dəən-thaaŋ khɔ̌ŋ kháw dûay khráp.	Can I have her passport?
C	นี่ค่ะ	nîi khâ.	Here it is.
B	กระเป๋าหายที่ไหนครับ	kra-pǎw hǎay thîi-nǎy khráp.	Where did you lose the purse?
C	ที่บางลำพูค่ะ คิดว่าถูก ขโมยไป	thîi baaŋ-lam-phuu khâ. khít wâa thùuk kha-mooy pay.	At Banglamphuu. I think it was stolen.
B	กระเป๋าที่ถูกขโมยไป เป็นยังไงครับ มีอะไรอยู่ใน กระเป๋าบ้างครับ	kra-pǎw thîi thùuk kha-mooy pay pen yaŋ-ŋay. mii ʔa-ray yùu nay kra-pǎw bâaŋ khráp.	The stolen purse, what does it look like? What's in it?
C	เป็นกระเป๋าสตางค์หนัง สีแดงยาวราวๆ 6 นิ้ว กว้างราวๆ 3 นิ้ว ข้างในมีเงินบาทอยู่ราวๆ 3,000 บาท เงินดอลลาร์ ราวๆ 100 ดอลลาร์ แล้วก็ บัตรต่างๆ เช่น บัตร นักศึกษา บัตรเอทีเอ็ม ธนาคารไทยพาณิชย์ และ บัตรเครดิตวีซ่า	pen kra-pǎw sa-taŋ nǎŋ sǐi-dɛɛŋ yaaw raw-raaw hòk níw kwâaŋ raw-raaw sǎam níw. khâŋ-nay mii ŋən bàat yùu raw-raaw sǎam-phan bàat ŋən dɔn-lâa raw-raaw rɔ́ɔy dɔn-lâa lɛ́ɛw kɔ̂ bàt tàaŋ-tàaŋ chên bàt nák-sɨ̀k-sǎa bàt ʔee-thii-ʔem bàt tha-naa-kaan thay-phaa-nít lɛ́ bàt khree-dit wii-sâa.	It's a red leather purse, about 6 inches long and 3 inches wide. In the purse, there is about 3,000 Baht, around 100 dollars and some cards, such as a student ID card, a Siam Commercial bank ATM card and a Visa credit card.
B	บัตรวีซ่าของไทยหรือ ต่างประเทศครับ	bàt wii-sâa khɔ̌ŋ thay rɨ̌ɨ tàaŋ-pra-thêet khráp.	Is it a Thai or foreign Visa card?
C	บัตรวีซ่าของอเมริกาค่ะ	bàt wii-sâa khɔ̌ɔŋ ʔa-mee-ri-kaa khâ.	An American Visa card.

B	ผมแนะนำว่าคุณควรจะอายัดบัตรเครดิต และบัตรเอทีเอ็มนะครับ	phǒm nɛ́-nam wâa khun khuan-ca ʔaa-yát bàt khree-dit lɛ́ bàt ʔee-thii-ʔem ná khráp.	I suggest that you should /aayat/ the credit card and the ATM card.
C	อายัด แปลว่า cancel ใช่ไหมคะ	ʔaa-yát plɛɛ-wâa "cancel" chây-máy khá.	/aayat/ means cancel, right?
B	ใช่ครับ	chây khráp.	Yes.

(The officer fills in the form)

/tam-rùat thɔ̂ŋ-thîaw/

B นี่ครับ ใบรับแจ้งเอกสารหายเป็นภาษาไทย คุณเอาไปใช้เป็นเอกสารสำหรับขอบัตรใหม่ได้ แต่สำหรับบัตรในเมืองไทยเท่านั้น ถ้าเป็นบัตรจากต่างประเทศ คุณต้องติดต่อตำรวจท่องเที่ยว เขาจะออกเอกสารเป็นภาษาอังกฤษให้ได้ครับ

nîi khráp. bay ráp cɛ̂ɛŋ ʔèek-ka-sǎan hǎay pen pha-sǎa-thay. khun ʔaw pay cháy pen ʔèek-ka-sǎan sǎm-ràp khɔ̌ɔ bàt mày dâay. tɛ̀ɛ sǎm-ràp nay mʉaŋ-thay thâw-nán. thâa pen bàt càak tàaŋ-pra-thêet khun tɔ̂ŋ tìt-tɔ̀ɔ tam-rùat thɔ̂ŋ-thîaw. kháw ca ʔɔ̀ɔk ʔèek-ka-sǎan pen pha-sǎa-ʔaŋ-krìt hây dâay khráp.

- Here. This is an acknowledgement of the missing document report in Thai. You can use this as a document for getting new ID cards, but only for cards in Thailand. If it is a foreign card, you need to contact the Tourist Police. They will issue you a document in English.

A,C	ขอบคุณค่ะ	khɔ̀p-khun khâ.	Thank you.

Dialog 9.1.3

Suda (A) talks to Chai (B).

A	ชัย ทำไมวันนี้มาสาย	chay tham-may wan-níi maa sǎay.	Chai, why are you late today?
B	โอ้โห วันนี้รถติดมากเลย มีอุบัติเหตุ รถเมล์ชนกับรถยนต์ ตำรวจปิดถนนตั้ง 1 เลน	ʔôo-hǒo. wan-níi rót-tìt mâak ləəy. mii ʔu-bàt-ti-hèet. rót mee chon kàp rót yon. tam-rùat pìt tha-nǒn tâŋ nʉ̀ŋ leen.	Man!! The traffic today was really jammed up. There was an accident. A bus collided with a car. The police closed off one lane.
A	มีคนบาดเจ็บหรือเปล่า	mii khon bàat-cèp rʉ̌-plàaw.	Was there anyone injured?
B	คิดว่าอาจจะมี มีรถพยาบาลมาด้วย	khít-wâa ʔàat-ca mii. mii rót pha-yaa-baan maa dûay.	I think there might be. An ambulance came also.
A	เหรอ	rɔ̌ɔ	Is that so?

Vocabulary ...ศัพท์ /sàp/

เพิ่ง	phə̌ŋ	adv. just, just now
แจ้ง	cɛ̂ɛŋ	v. to tell, inform, report, make known
แจ้งความ	cɛ̂ɛŋ-khwaam	v. to report, inform, notify
กระเป๋าสตางค์	kra-pǎw sa-taaŋ	v. purse, wallet (clf. ใบ /bay/)
บัตรเอทีเอ็ม	bàt ʔee-thii-ʔem	n. ATM card
อายัด	ʔaa-yát	v. to seize, attach; freeze; detain
เอกสาร	ʔèek-ka-sǎan	n. document (clf. ใบ /bay/, ฉบับ cha-bàp)
ติดต่อ	tìt-tɔ̀ɔ	v. to get in touch (with)
เลน	leen	v. lane (from English)
รถพยาบาล	rót pha-yaa-baan	n. ambulance

Listening Practice ...ฝึกหัด ฟัง /fɨ̀k-hàt faŋ/

วันนี้ ไมค์นั่งรถแท็กซี่ไปทำธุระข้างนอกที่ทำงาน เขาลืมกระเป๋าเอกสารไว้ในรถแท็กซี่ เขาจึงไปแจ้งความที่สถานีตำรวจ ตำรวจแนะนำให้เขาโทรศัพท์ไปแจ้งที่รายการวิทยุ จส.100 ด้วย เพื่อให้รายการวิทยุประกาศข่าว ราว ๆ 2 ชั่วโมงต่อมา คนขับรถแท็กซี่ก็นำกระเป๋าเอกสารที่ไมค์ลืมไว้ในรถมาคืนที่สถานีตำรวจ ไมค์ดีใจมาก เขาขอบคุณคนขับรถแท็กซี่ และให้เงิน 1000 บาทเป็นรางวัล

wan-nii Mike nâŋ rót thɛ́k-sîi pay tham thú-rá khâŋ-nɔ̂ɔk thîi tham-ŋaan. kháw lɨɨm ʔèek-ka-sǎan wáy nay rót thɛ́k-sîi. kháw cɨŋ pay cɛ̂ɛŋ-khwaam thîi sa-thǎa-nii tam-rùat. tam-rùat nɛ́ʔ-nam hây kháw thoo-ra-sàp pay cɛ̂ɛŋ thîi raay-kaan wít-tha-yúʔ cɔɔ-sɔ̌ɔ-rɔ́ɔy dûay phɨ̂a-hây raay-kaan wít-tha-yúʔ pra-kàat khàaw. raw-raaw sɔ̌ɔŋ chûa-mooŋ tɔ̀ɔ-maa khon khàp-rót thɛ́k-sîi kɔ̂ɔ nam kra-pǎw ʔèek-ka-sǎan thîi Mike lɨɨm wáy nay rót maa khɨɨn thîi sa-thǎa-nii tam-rùat. Mike dii-cay mâak. kháw khɔ̀ɔp-khun khon khàp-rót thɛ́k-sîi lɛ́ hây ŋən nɨ̀ŋ-phan bàat pen raaŋ-wan.

- Today, Mike took a taxi to conduct business outside his office. He forgot his briefcase in the taxi. He therefore went to report this to the police. The police suggested that he call and report this to Jor Sor 100 radio program as well, for the program to make an announcement. About two hours later, the taxi driver brought the briefcase that Mike left in the car to the police station. Mike was very happy. He thanked the taxi driver and gave him 1000 Baht as a reward.

Proverb ...สุภาษิต /su-phaa-sìt/

หนีเสือปะจระเข้ nǐi sʉ̌a pàʔ cɔɔ-ra-khêe	to escape + tiger +to meet + crocodile	Escape from the tiger; meet the crocodile.
	"Out of the frying pan into the fire."	

Idiom ...สำนวน /sǎm-nuan/

ฟังหู ไว้หู faŋ hǔu wáy hǔu	to listen + ear + keep + ear	To listen with one ear and keep it in another ear.
	"To take something with a grain of salt."	

Vocabulary ...ศัพท์ /sàp/

ทำธุระ	tham thú-rá	v. to have business to do
ลืม	lʉʉm	v. to forget
กระเป๋าเอกสาร	kra-pǎw ʔèek-ka-sǎan	n. briefcase, portfolio (clf. ใบ /bay/)
จึง	cʉŋ	conj. so, therefore, as a consequence
ประกาศ	pra-kàat	v. to announce, proclaim, declare
ต่อมา	tɔ̀ɔ-maa	conj. later on (in time), afterwards; subsequently; after that
รางวัล	raaŋ-wan	n. prize, reward, award (clf. รางวัล /raaŋ-wan/)
เสือ	sʉ̌a	n. tiger (clf. ตัว /tua/)
จระเข้	cɔɔ-ra-khêe	n. crocodile (clf. ตัว /tua/)

Structure Notes

1. Passive sentence with ถูก /thùuk/

Passive sentences are the sentences in which the affected entity of the action is highlighted. In English, the passive sentence is marked by the reversal of the positions of the noun phrases acting as subject and object in the counterpart basic "active" sentences. In Thai, a passive sentence is marked by a special auxiliary verb such as ถูก /thùuk/, with the highlighted "object" of the active sentence appearing as a subject of the sentence in front of ถูก /thùuk/, as follows:

8. Affected Subject + ถูก /thùuk/ (+Agent) + Verb Phrase (+ Adverb)

The following shows how the above passive structure corresponds with the "active" basic structure (pattern # 2):

Active	2. Subject X + Verb + Object Y (+ Adverb)
Passive	8. Affected Subject **Y + ถูก** /thùuk/ (+Agent X) + Verb Phrase (+ Adverb)

As in English passive sentences, the Agent noun phrase is usually omitted.

In Unit 8.2, another passive auxiliary โดน /doon/ was already mentioned. However, it has a more restricted use than ถูก /thùuk/.

Examples.

Active	หมากัดเด็ก mǎa kàt dèk	dog + to bite + child	A dog bites a child.
Passive	เด็กถูกหมากัด dèk thùuk mǎa kàt	child + ***ถูก*** /thùuk/ + dog + to bite	A child is bitten by the dog.

Active	คนขโมยนาฬิกาเขา khon kha-mooy naa-li-kaa kháw	person + to steal + watch + s/he	Someone stole his/her watch.
Passive 1	นาฬิกาเขาถูกขโมย naa-li-kaa kháw thùuk kha-mooy	watch + s/he + ***ถูก*** /thùuk/ + to steal	His/her watch was stolen.
Passive 2	เขาถูกขโมยนาฬิกา kháw thùuk kha-mooy naa-li-kaa	s/he + ***ถูก*** /thùuk/ + to steal + watch	His/her watch was stolen. (Lit. S/he was watch-stolen.)

2. Presentation sentence with เกิด /kə̀ət/ and มี /mii/

In Unit 5.4, the presentational มี /mii/ is discussed in Structure Note 1a. (มี /mii/ + Clause). เกิด/kə̀ət/ is another such presentational verb, used in presenting an event or happening. The pattern of usage is the same as the presentational มี /mii/, i.e. เกิด /kə̀ət/ + clause.

3. Phrasal verb: ไว้ /wáy/

ไว้ /wáy/ as a main verb means "to keep or put for future use," but it is normally seen as a secondary verb in a phrasal verb compound of placing, storing, keeping and gives the meaning of "to be left in a certain position" or "to have on hand for future use or for safe keeping." The closest English equivalent is perhaps "away" in a phrasal verb such as "to put (something) away."

We see examples of such usage of ไว้ /wáy/ in Unit 7.2, and here in this unit.

คุณจะฝากข้อความไว้ไหมคะ khun ca fàak khɔ̂ɔ-khwaam wáy máy khá.	you + to leave + message + ไว้ /wáy/ + question prt. + prt.	Would you like to leave a message?
เขาลืมเอกสารไว้ในรถแท็กซี่ kháw lɯɯm ʔèek-ka-sǎan wáy nay rót thɛ́k-sîi.	he + to forget + document + ไว้ /wáy/ + in + taxi	He forgot a document in a taxi.

4. Consequence conjunction: จึง /cɯŋ/

As a marker of a consequence clause, จึง /cɯŋ/ "therefore," "consequently" always appears before the main verb of the second clause of the sentence. The first clause, which is the "cause" clause may also have an explicit cause conjunction such as เพราะ /phrɔ́ʔ/ "because," but it can be omitted and inferred from the presence of จึง /cɯŋ/ in the second clause.

9. Cause Conjunction + Clause 1	Clause 2
(**เพราะ** /phrɔ́ʔ/) because	(subject) **จึง** /cɯŋ/ + Verb ____ consequently

เขาลืมของไว้ในรถแท็กซี่ kháw lɯɯm khɔ̌ɔŋ wáy nay rót thɛ́k-sîi. He forgot a document in a taxi,	เขา**จึง**ไปแจ้งความที่สถานีตำรวจ kháw cɯŋ pay cɛ̂ɛŋ-khwaam thîi sa-thǎa-nii tam-rùat. he therefore went to report it at a police station.
เพราะเขาสนใจเรื่องเมืองไทย phrɔ́ʔ kháw sǒn-cay rɯ̂aŋ mɯaŋ-thay Because he is interested in Thailand,	เขา**จึง**เรียนภาษาไทย kháw cɯŋ rian pha-sǎa thay he is therefore studying Thai.

Culture Notes

1. The emergency telephone number in Thailand is a special 3 digit number: 191.

2. The "Tourist Police" is a special unit of the police that is specifically responsible for matters relating to the safety and welfare of foreign visitors to Thailand. The call center's number is 1155.

3. จส. 100 /cɔɔ-sɔ̌ɔ rɔ́ɔy/ is a broadcast radio station focusing on live interactive reports of traffic conditions, news and community service announcements for Bangkok and nearby provinces. The channel emerged in response to the increase of severe traffic jams in Bangkok since 1990. It is one of two traffic report radio stations popular among Bangkok taxi drivers (the other being ร่วมด้วยช่วยกัน /rûam dûay chûay kan/. จส. 100's call center number is 1137.

Skills: To understand and express words and phrases related to banking transactions, posting and shipping

At the Bank ...ที่ธนาคาร /thîi tha-naa-khaan/

สมุดฝาก, สมุดบัญชี
/sa-mùt fàak/, /sa-mùt ban-chii/

สมุดฝาก	sa-mùt fàak	n. passbook (clf. เล่ม /lêm/)
สมุดบัญชี	sa-mùt ban-chii	n. passbook (clf. เล่ม /lêm/)
บัญชี	ban-chii	n. account (clf. บัญชี)
เปิดบัญชี	pə̀ət ban-chii	v. to open an account
ปิดบัญชี	pìt ban-chii	v. to close an account
ออมทรัพย์	ʔɔɔm-sáp	v. to save upsavings account
บัญชีออมทรัพย์	ban-chii ʔɔɔm-sáp	n. savings account
กระแสรายวัน	kra-sɛ̌ɛ-raay-wan	n. current account
บัญชีกระแสรายวัน	ban-chii kra-sɛ̌ɛ-raay-wan	n. current account
ประจำ	pra-cam	v. to be fixed, steady, regular
บัญชีฝากประจำ	ban-chii fàak pra-cam	n. fixed account
ฝากเงิน	fàak ŋən	v. deposit money
ถอนเงิน	thɔ̌ɔn ŋən	v. withdraw money
โอนเงิน	ʔoon ŋən	v. transfer money
ตัดเงิน	tàt ŋən	v. debit (from an account)
แลกเงิน	lɛ̂ɛk ŋən	v. exchange money
ค่าบริการ	khâa bɔɔ-ri-kaan	n. service fee
สกุล (เงิน)	sa-kun (ŋən)	n. currency (clf. สกุล)
อัตรา	ʔàt-traa	n. rate (clf. อัตรา)
อัตราแลกเปลี่ยน	ʔàt-traa lɛ̂ɛk-plìan	n. exchange rate

Dialogs ...บทสนทนา /bòt sǒn-tha-naa/

Dialog 9.2.1

At a currency exchange counter, Amy (A) talks to a teller (B).

A	ขอแลกเงินบาทหน่อยค่ะ	khɔ̌ɔ lɛ̂ɛk ŋən bàat nɔ̀y khâ	I'd like to exchange this money into Baht, please.
B	ขอดูหนังสือเดินทางหน่อยนะคะ	khɔ̌ɔ duu naŋ-sʉ̌ʉ dəən-thaaŋ nɔ̀y ná khá.	May I see your passport?
	ขอบคุณค่ะ จะแลกเงินสกุลอะไร เท่าไหร่คะ	khɔ̀ɔp-khun khâ. ca lɛ̂ɛk ŋən sa-kun ʔa-ray thâw-rày khá.	Thank you. What currency would you like to exchange? How much?
A	แลก 300 ดอลลาร์สหรัฐค่ะ ตอนนี้อัตราแลกเปลี่ยนเท่าไหร่คะ	lɛ́ɛk sǎam-rɔ́ɔy dɔn-lâa sa-hà-rát khâ. tɔɔn-níi ʔàt-traa lɛ̂ɛk-plìan thâw-rày khá.	300 US dollars. What is the exchange rate now?
B	แบงก์ 100 ดอลลาร์ อัตรา 1 ดอลลาร์สหรัฐต่อ 40 บาทค่ะ 300 ดอลลาร์ จะได้ 12,000 บาทนะคะ	bɛ́ŋ rɔ́ɔy dɔn-lâa ʔàt-traa nʉ̀ŋ dɔn-lâa sa-hà-rat tɔ̀ɔ sìi-sìp bàat khâ. sǎam-rɔ́ɔy dɔn-lâa ca dâay nʉ̀ŋ mʉ̀ʉn sɔ̌ɔŋ-phan bàat ná khá.	For a 100 dollar bill, the rate is 40 Baht for 1 US dollar. For 300 dollars, you will get 12,000 Baht.
	(the teller fills out the form)		
B	รอสักครู่นะคะ	rɔɔ sák khrûu ná khá.	Please wait a minute.
	(the teller brings the money)		
B	กรุณาเซ็นชื่อรับเงินตรงนี้นะคะ	ka-ru-naa sen chʉ̂ʉ ráp ŋən troŋ-níi ná khá.	Please sign the receipt for the cash here.
A	ขอบคุณค่ะ	khɔ̀ɔp-khun khâ.	Thank you.

Dialog 9.2.2

Amy (A) and Suda (B) talk about ATM machines.

A	ตุ๊ก เอมี่ไม่มีเงินไทยแล้ว เอมี่ต้องไปถอนเงินเพิ่ม บริเวณนี้มีตู้เอทีเอ็มตรงไหนบ้าง	túk ʔee-mîi mây mii ŋən thay lɛ́ɛw. ʔee-mîi tɔ̂ŋ pay thɔ̌ɔn ŋən phə̂əm. bɔɔ-ri-ween níi mii tûu ʔee-thii-ʔem troŋ-nǎy bâaŋ.	I don't have any Thai currency left. I need to withdraw some more cash. Where is there an ATM machine around here?
B	เอมี่มีบัญชีธนาคารไทยหรือเปล่า	ʔee-mîi mii ban-chii tha-naa-khaan thay rʉ̌-plàaw.	Do you have a Thai bank account?

A	ไม่มี แต่เอมี่มีบัตรเอทีเอ็ม ของ ธนาคารที่อเมริกา ถอนเงินจากตู้เอทีเอ็ม ที่มีตรา "cirrus"ได้	mây mii. tὲε ʔee-mîi mii bàt ʔee-thii-ʔem khɔ̌ŋ tha-naa-khaan thîi ʔa-mee-ri-kaa. thɔ̌ɔn ŋən càak tûu ʔee-thii-ʔem thîi mii traa "cirrus" dâay.	No, but I have an ATM card from a bank in America. I can withdraw cash from an ATM machine with the "cirrus" logo.
B	มีค่าบริการหรือเปล่า แพงไหม	mii khâa bɔɔ-ri-kaan rʉ̌-plàaw. phεεŋ máy.	Is there a service charge? Is it expensive?
A	มีค่าบริการซิ เอมี่คิดว่า ครั้งละราวๆ 4 ดอลลาร์	mii khâa bɔɔ-ri-kaan si. ʔee-mîi khít wâa khráŋ-la raaw-raaw sìi dɔn-lâa.	Yes, there is a service charge. I think it's about 4 dollars each time.

B นั่นไง ที่ธนาคารตรงนั้นมีตู้เอทีเอ็ม
nân-ŋay. thîi tha-naa-khaan troŋ-nán mii tûu ʔee-thii-ʔem.
- There! At the bank over there, there's an ATM machine.

ตู้เอทีเอ็ม
/tûu ʔee-thii-ʔem/

Dialog 9.2.3

Dan (A) opens a bank account. He talks to a bank clerk (B).

A	สวัสดีครับ ผมเป็น นักศึกษาแลกเปลี่ยน ที่มหาวิทยาลัยพระนคร อยากจะเปิดบัญชีที่นี่ครับ อยากได้บัตรเอทีเอ็ม ด้วยครับ	sa-wàt-dii khráp. phǒm pen nák-sʉ̀k-sǎa lɛ̂ɛk-plìan thîi ma-hǎa-wít-tha-yaa-lay phrá-ná-khɔɔn. yàak-ca pə̀ət ban-chii thîi nîi khráp. yàak dâay bàt ʔee-thii-ʔem dûay khráp.	Hello. I am an exchange student at Phra Nakhon University. I'd like to open an account here. I'd like to get an ATM card too.
B	ขอแนะนำให้เปิดบัญชี ออมทรัพย์นะคะ ขอหนังสือเดินทาง และ จดหมายรับรองจาก มหาวิทยาลัยด้วยค่ะ	khɔ̌ɔ né-nam hây pə̀ət ban-chii ʔɔɔm-sáp ná khá. khɔ̌ɔ naŋ-sʉ̌ʉ dəən-thaaŋ lɛ́ còt-mǎay ráp-rɔɔŋ càak ma-hǎa-wít-tha-yaa-lay dûay khâ.	I suggest that you open a savings account. Can I have your passport and a reference letter from the university?
A	นี่ครับ	nîi khráp.	Here they are.
B	กรุณา กรอกแบบฟอร์ม ขอเปิดบัญชีนะคะ จะฝากเงินเท่าไหร่คะ	ka-ru-naa krɔ̀ɔk bὲεp-fɔɔm khɔ̌ɔ pə̀ət ban-chii ná khá. ca fàak ŋən thâw-rày khá.	Please fill out the account application form. How much are you going to deposit?

A 50,000 บาทครับ นี่ครับ	hâa-mɯɯn bàat. nîi khráp.	50,000 Baht. Here it is.
B รอสักครู่นะคะ	rɔɔ sák khrûu ná khá.	Please wait a minute.
(returns with a passbook)		
B กรุณาเซ็นชื่อในสมุดบัญชีนะคะ คุณจะมารับบัตรเอทีเอ็มได้ราวๆ อาทิตย์หน้า ค่าทำบัตรเอทีเอ็ม 50 บาทค่ะ ค่าบริการบัตรเอทีเอ็ม ปีละ 100 บาท เราจะตัดจากบัญชีนี้ค่ะ	ka-ru-naa sen chɯ̂ɯ nay sa-mùt ban-chii ná khá. khun ca maa rap bàt ʔee-thii-ʔem dâay raaw-raaw ʔaa-thít nâa. khâa tham bàt ʔee-thii-ʔem hâa-sip bàat khâ. khâa bɔɔ-ri-kaan bàt ʔee-thii-ʔem pii la nɯ̀ŋ-rɔ́ɔy bàat. raw ca tàt càak ban-chii níi khâ.	Please sign in the passbook. You can pick up the ATM card around next week. The ATM card issuance fee is 50 Baht. The ATM service fee is 100 Baht per year. We debit it from this account.
A ผมจะใช้บัตรเอทีเอ็มถอนเงินได้วันละเท่าไหร่ครับ	phǒm ca cháy bàt ʔee-thii-ʔem thɔ̌ɔn ŋən dâay wan-la thâw-rày khráp.	How much cash per day can I withdraw with the ATM card?
B ถอนเงินจากตู้เอทีเอ็มครั้งละไม่เกิน 25,000 บาท ถอนกี่ครั้งก็ได้ แต่วันละไม่เกิน 50,000 บาทค่ะ	thɔ̌ɔn ŋən càak tûu ʔee-thii-ʔem khráŋ-la mây kəən sɔ̌ɔŋ-mɯ̀ɯn-hâa-phan bàat. thɔ̌ɔn kìi khráŋ kɔ̂ dâay tɛɛ wan-la mây kəən hâa-mɯ̀n-bàat khâ.	You can withdraw from an ATM machine no more than 25,000 Baht each time. You can withdraw as many times as you want, but no more than 50,000 Baht per day.

Vocabulary ...ศัพท์ /sàp/

เซ็น	sen	v. to sign
เพิ่ม	phə̂əm	v. to add, increase, augment
ตรงไหน	troŋ-nay	q. where, somewhere, anywhere = ที่ไหน /thii-nay/
ตู้	tûu	n. kiosk, closet (clf. ตู้ /tûu/)
ตรา	traa	n. trademark, seal, logo (clf. ตรา /traa/)
ไง	ŋay	prt. used to show that the speaker thinks that the statement is self-evident

นั่นไง	nâan-ŋay	There it is.
รับรอง	ráp-rɔɔŋ	v. to certify, guarantee, vouch; to confirm, sanction, recognize, approve
จดหมายรับรอง	còt-mǎay ráp-rɔɔŋ	n. reference letter, recommendation letter
กรอก	krɔ̀ɔk	v. to fill, fill out, fill in
แบบฟอร์ม	bɛ̀ɛp-fɔɔm	n. form (from English "form")
เกิน	kəən	v. to exceed, be in excess of

ตู้ไปรษณีย์
/tûu pray-sa-nii/

At the Post Office
...ที่ไปรษณีย์ /thîi pray-sa-nii/

ไปรษณีย์	pray-sa-nii	n. post, post office
ตู้ไปรษณีย์	tûu pray-sa-nii	n. postbox (clf. ตู้ /tûu/)
แสตมป์	sa-tɛm	n. stamp (clf. ดวง /duaŋ/) from English "stamp"
ซอง	sɔɔŋ	n. envelope (clf. ซอง /sɔɔŋ/ ใบ /bay/)
จดหมาย	còt-mǎay	n. letter (clf. ฉบับ /cha-bàp/)
ส่งจดหมาย	sòŋ còt-mǎay	v. to send a letter
พัสดุ	phát-sa-dùʔ	n. package, parcel (clf. กล่อง /klɔ̀ŋ/ ชิ้น /chín/)
(ไปรษณีย์) ลงทะเบียน	(pray-sa-nii) loŋ tha-bian	registered mail
(ไปรษณีย์) รับประกัน	(pray-sa-nii) ráp pra-kan	certified mail
(ไปรษณีย์) ด่วน	(pray-sa-nii) dùan	express mail
(ไปรษณีย์) ด่วนพิเศษ	(pray-sa-nii) dùan phí-sèet	EMS (Express Mail Service)
กล่อง	klɔ̀ŋ	n. box (clf. กล่อง /klɔ̀ŋ/ ใบ /bay/)
ทางอากาศ	thaaŋ ʔaa-kàat	by air
ทางเรือ	thaaŋ rʉa	by sea
ราคาเหมา	raa-khaa mǎw	n. flat rate, all inclusive price

Dialog 9.2.4

Dan (A) talks to a postal clerk (B) at the post office.

A ขอซื้อแสตมป์สำหรับส่งโปสการ์ดไปอเมริกาครับ
khɔ̌ɔ sɨ́ɨ sa-tɛm sǎm-ràp sòŋ póos-káat pay ʔa-mee-ri-kaa khráp.
- I'd like to get stamps for sending postcards to America.

B กี่ดวงครับ
kìi duaŋ khráp.
- How many?

A 20 ดวงครับ ดวงละ เท่าไหร่ครับ
yîi-sìp duaŋ khráp. duaŋ la thâw- rày khráp.
- 20 stamps. How much for each?

B ดวงละ 15 บาทครับ นี่ครับ 300 บาทครับ รับอย่างอื่นอีกไหมครับ

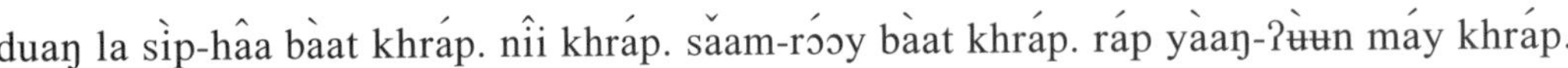

duaŋ la sìp-hâa bàat khráp. nîi khráp. sǎam-rɔ́ɔy bàat khráp. ráp yàaŋ-ʔɨ̀ɨn máy khráp.
- 15 Baht each. Here they are. 300 Baht please. Would you like to get anything else?

A	ไม่ครับ แต่ผมอยากทราบว่า ถ้าจะส่งโปสการ์ดไปประเทศอื่น ใช้แสตมป์ราคานี้เหมือนกันใช่ไหมครับ	mây khráp. tɛ̀ɛ phǒm yàak sâap wâa thâa ca sòŋ póos-káat pay pra-thêet ʔɨ̀ɨn cháy sa-tɛm raa-khaa níi mɨ̌an-kan chây-máy khráp.	No. But I'd like to know if the same stamps can also be used for sending postcards to other countries.
B	ครับ แสตมป์ 15 บาทส่งโปสการ์ดได้ทุกประเทศ	khráp. sa-tɛm sìp-hâa bàat sòŋ póos-káat dâay thúk pra-thêet.	Yes. 15 Baht stamps can be used for sending postcards to every country.
A	ขอบคุณครับ	khɔ̀ɔp-khun khráp.	Thank you.

Dialog 9.2.5

Amy (A) talks to an postal clerk (B) at the post office.

A	ส่งจดหมายด่วนอีเอ็มเอสไปอเมริกาค่ะ	sòŋ còt-mǎay dùan ʔii-ʔem-ʔées pay ʔa-mee-ri-kaa khâ.	I'd like to send a letter via EMS to America.

(the clerk gives her an EMS label)

B	คุณเขียนชื่อ ที่อยู่ บนใบนี้นะครับ	khun khǐan chɨ̂ɨ thîi-yùu bon bay níi ná khráp.	Please write the names and addresses on this label.

(the clerk weighs the envelope)

B	หนัก 500 กรัม 600 บาทครับ	nàk hâa-rɔ́ɔy kram hòk-rɔ́ɔy bàat khráp.	It weighs 500 grams. 600 Baht please.
A	จดหมายจะไปถึงเมื่อไหร่คะ	còt-mǎay ca pay thʉ̌ŋ mʉ̂a-rày khá.	When will the letter get there?
B	ราวๆ 3-4 วันครับ	raaw-raaw sǎam sìi wan khráp.	In about 3-4 days.

บริการต่าง ๆที่ไปรษณีย์
bɔɔ-ri-kaan tàaŋ tàaŋ thîi pray-sa-nii

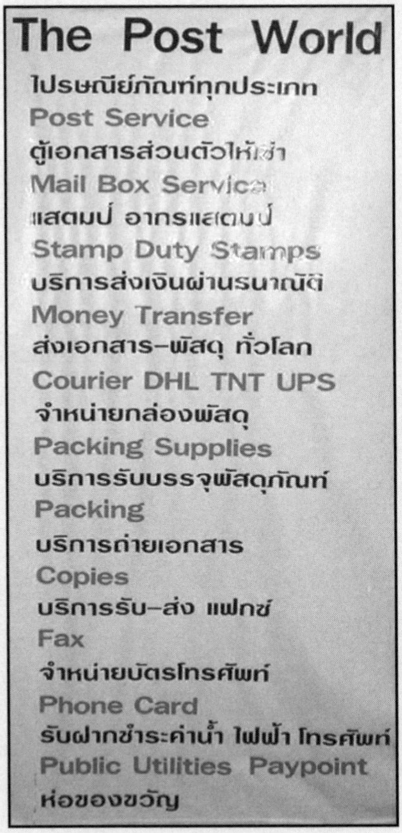

The Post World
ไปรษณียภัณฑ์ทุกประเภท
Post Service
ตู้เอกสารส่วนตัวให้เช่า
Mail Box Service
แสตมป์ อากรแสตมป์
Stamp Duty Stamps
บริการส่งเงินผ่านธนาณัติ
Money Transfer
ส่งเอกสาร-พัสดุ ทั่วโลก
Courier DHL TNT UPS
จำหน่ายกล่องพัสดุ
Packing Supplies
บริการรับบรรจุพัสดุภัณฑ์
Packing
บริการถ่ายเอกสาร
Copies
บริการรับ-ส่ง แฟกซ์
Fax
จำหน่ายบัตรโทรศัพท์
Phone Card
รับฝากชำระค่าน้ำ ไฟฟ้า โทรศัพท์
Public Utilities Paypoint
ห่อของขวัญ

ไปรษณียภัณฑ์ ทุกประเภท
pray-sa-nii-ya-phan thúk pra-phêet
ตู้เอกสารส่วนตัวให้เช่า
tûu ʔèek-ka-sǎan sùan-tua hây châw
แสตมป์ อากรแสตมป์
sa-tɛm ʔaa-kɔɔn sa-tɛm
บริการส่งเงินผ่านธนาณัติ
bɔɔ-ri-kaan sòŋ ŋən phàan tha-naa-nát
ส่งเอกสาร-พัสดุ ทั่วโลก
sòŋ ʔèek-ka-sǎan phát-sa-dù thûa lôok
จำหน่ายกล่องพัสดุ
cam-nàay klɔ̀ŋ phát-sa-dù
บริการรับบรรจุพัสดุภัณฑ์
bɔɔ-ri-kaan ráp ban-cù phát-sa-dù-phan
บริการถ่ายเอกสาร
bɔɔ-ri-kaan thàay ʔèek-ka-sǎan
บริการรับ-ส่งแฟกซ์
bɔɔ-ri-kaan ráp sòŋ fɛ̀k
จำหน่ายบัตรโทรศัพท์
cam-nàay bàt thoo-ra-sàp
รับฝากชำระค่าน้ำ ไฟฟ้า โทรศัพท์
ráp fàak cham-rá khâa náam fay-fáa thoo-ra-sàp
ห่อของขวัญ
hɔ̀ɔ khɔ̌ɔŋ-khwǎn

Dialog 9.2.6

Dan (A) discusses arrangements for sending items to Hawaii with Chai (B).

A	ชัย ผมอยากจะส่งหนังสือกับของกลับบ้านที่ฮาวาย จะส่งยังไงดี	chay phǒm yàak-ca sòŋ naŋ-sʉ̌ʉ kàp khɔ̌ɔŋ klàp bâan thîi haa-waay. ca sòŋ yaŋ-ŋay dii.	Chai, I'd like to send books and stuff back home to Hawaii. How should I send them?
B	ส่งเป็นพัสดุ ส่งที่ไปรษณีย์ก็ได้ หรือ ส่งที่บริษัทยูพีเอสก็ได้	sòŋ pen phát-sa-dù. sòŋ thîi pray-sa-nii kɔ̂ dâay rʉ̌ʉ sòŋ thîi bɔɔ-ri-sàt yuu-phii-ʔées kɔ̂ dâay.	As parcels. You can send them at the post office or at UPS.
A	ถ้าจะส่งทางอากาศล่ะ ราคาสักเท่าไหร่ แล้วกี่วันถึง	thâa ca sòŋ thaaŋ ʔaa-kàat lâ. raa-khaa sák thâw-rày. lɛ́ɛw kìi wan thʉ̌ŋ.	If I send it by air, how much will it be? And how many days will it take?
B	ค่าส่ง ขึ้นอยู่กับน้ำหนัก ผมคิดว่าพัสดุส่งทางอากาศหนัก 5 กิโล ราวๆ 3,000 บาท ใช้เวลาราวๆ อาทิตย์หนึ่งถึง 10 วัน	khâa sòŋ khʉ̂n-yùu-kàp nám-nàk. phǒm khít wâa phát-sa-dù sòŋ thaaŋ ʔaa-kàat nàk hâa ki-loo raaw-raaw sǎam-phan bàat. cháy wee-laa raaw-raaw ʔaa-thít nʉŋ thʉ̌ŋ sìp wan.	The postage depends on the weight. I think that sending a 5 kilogram package by air costs about 3,000 Baht and takes about a week or 10 days.
A	ถ้าส่งทางเรือล่ะ	thâa sòŋ thaaŋ rʉa lâ.	What about by sea?
B	แดน ผมว่า คุณส่งทางอากาศดีกว่า ถ้าคุณส่งทางเรือ ใช้เวลาอย่างน้อยตั้ง 3 เดือน	dɛɛn phǒm wâa khun sòŋ thaaŋ ʔaa-kàat dii kwàa. thâa khun sòŋ thaaŋ rʉa cháy wee-laa yàaŋ-nɔ́ɔy tâŋ sǎam dʉan.	Dan, I think you'd better send by air. If you send by sea, it takes at least 3 months.
A	แล้วส่งของทางบริษัทยูพีเอสล่ะ แพงกว่าส่งทางไปรษณีย์ไหม	lɛ́ɛw sòŋ khɔ̌ɔŋ thaaŋ bɔɔ-ri-sàt yuu-phii-ʔées lâ. phɛɛŋ kwàa sòŋ thaaŋ pray-sa-nii máy.	And what about sending by UPS, is it more expensive than sending by post?
B	ไม่รู้เหมือนกัน ผมจะโทรศัพท์ไปถามให้	mây rúu mʉ̌an kan. phǒm ca thoo-ra-sàp pay thǎam hây.	I don't know. I'll call to ask for you.

Dialog 9.2.7

Chai (B) calls UPS and talks to a clerk (A).

A สวัสดีค่ะ ยูพีเอสค่ะ

sa-wàt-dii khâ. yuu-phii-ʔées khâ.

- Hello. UPS.

B ผมขอถามอัตราค่าส่งพัสดุทางอากาศไปอเมริกาครับ

phǒm khɔ̌ɔ thǎam ʔàt-traa khâa sòŋ phát-sa-dù thaaŋ ʔaa-kàat pay ʔa-mee-ri-kaa khráp.

- I'd like to ask about the rate for sending a package to America.

A ขึ้นอยู่กับน้ำหนักนะคะ

khʉ̂n-yùu-kàp nám-nàk ná khá.

- It depends on the weight.

B คิดว่าราว ๆ 10 ถึง 20 กิโลครับ

khít wâa raaw-raaw sìp thʉ̌ŋ yîi-sìp ki-loo-kram khráp.

- I think it's about 10-20 kilograms.

A ตอนนี้ เรามีอัตราพิเศษค่ะ สำหรับกล่อง 10 กิโล ราคาเหมารวม 3,500 บาท ถ้าน้ำหนักเกินจาก 10 กิโล คิดกิโลละ 160 บาท และสำหรับกล่อง 25 กิโล ราคาเหมารวม 4,500 บาท ถ้าน้ำหนักเกิน 25 กิโล แต่ไม่เกิน 30 กิโล คิดกิโลละ 160 บาทเหมือนกัน คุณมารับกล่องพัสดุฟรีได้จากบริษัทค่ะ เรามีบริการไปรับกล่องพัสดุฟรีถึงบ้านด้วยนะคะ

tɔn níi raw mii ʔàt-traa phí-sèet khâ. sǎm-ràp klɔ̀ŋ sìp ki-loo ra-khaa mǎw ruam sǎam-phan-hâa-rɔ́ɔy bàat. thâa nám-nàk kəən càak sìp ki-loo khít ki-loo la nʉ̀ŋ-rɔ́ɔy-hòk-sìp bàat. lɛ́ sǎm-ràp klɔ̀ŋ yîi-sìp-hâa ki-loo ra-khaa mǎw ruam sìi-phan-hâa-rɔ́ɔy bàat. thâa nám-nàk kəən yîi-sìp-hâa ki-loo tɛ̀ɛ mây kəən sǎam-sìp ki-loo khít ki-loo la nʉ̀ŋ-rɔ́ɔy-hòk-sìp bàat mʉ̌an-kan. khun maa ráp klɔ̀ŋ phát-sa-dù frii dây càak bɔɔ-ri-sàt khâ. raw mii bɔɔ-ri-kaan pay ráp klɔ̀ŋ phát-sa-dù frii thʉ̌ŋ bâan dûay ná khá.

- At the moment, we have a special rate for a 10 kilogram box, the flat rate is 3,500 Baht. For any weight above 10 kilograms, the cost is 160 Baht per kilogram. And for a 25 kilogram box, the flat rate is 4,500 Baht. For any weight above 25 kilos but not exceeding 30 kilos, it's 160 Baht per kilogram as well. You can pick up free boxes from us. We also have a free package pickup service from home too.

B ส่งพัสดุกี่วันจึงจะถึงอเมริกาครับ

sòŋ phát-sa-dù kìi wan cʉŋ-ca thʉ̌ŋ ʔa-mee-ri-kaa khráp.

- How many days does it take for the package to arrive in America?

A ราว ๆ 7-10 วันค่ะ

raw-raaw cèt thʉ̌ŋ sìp wan khâ.

- About 7-10 days.

B บริษัทคุณอยู่ที่ไหนครับ

bɔɔ-ri-sàt khun yùu thîi-nǎy khráp.

- Where is your company located?

A อยู่ที่ถนนพระราม 4 ค่ะ และเรามีสำนักงานที่บางลำพูด้วย อยู่ที่ถนนตะนาว

yùu thîi tha-nǒn phra-raam-sìi khâ. lɛ́ raw mii sǎm-nák-ŋaan thîi baaŋ-lam-phuu dûay. yùu thîi tha-nǒn ta-naaw.

- On Rama IV Road. And we also have an office at Banglamphuu too, on Tanao Road.

B ขอบคุณครับ

khɔ̀ɔp-khun khráp.

- Thank you.

Listening Practice ...ฝึกหัด ฟัง /fʉ̀k-hàt faŋ/

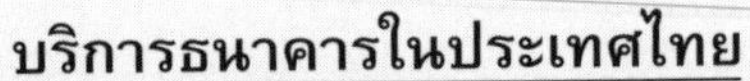
บริการธนาคารในประเทศไทย

ที่ทำการธนาคารในประเทศไทย ปกติเปิดให้บริการเฉพาะวันจันทร์ถึงวันศุกร์ เวลา 8 โมงครึ่ง ถึงบ่าย 3 โมงครึ่ง แต่เดี๋ยวนี้ ธนาคารส่วนมาก เปิดสาขาย่อยในศูนย์การค้าใหญ่ ๆ ด้วย ธนาคารในศูนย์การค้านี้ มักจะเปิดทุกวัน รวมทั้งวันเสาร์อาทิตย์ ตั้งแต่เวลา 11 โมงถึงราว ๆ หกโมงเย็น หรือ หนึ่งทุ่ม
สำหรับบริการแลกเปลี่ยนเงินต่างประเทศ ธนาคารส่วนมากจะมีเคาน์เตอร์พิเศษให้บริการทุกวัน เวลา 8 โมงครึ่ง ถึง หกโมงเย็น หรือ หนึ่งทุ่ม เหมือนกัน

bɔɔ-ri-kaan tha-naa-khaan nay pra-thêet thay

thîi tham-kaan tha-naa-khaan nay pra-thêet thay pà-ka-tì pə̀ət hây bɔɔ-ri-kaan cha-phɔ́ʔ wan can thʉ̌ŋ wan sùk wee-laa pɛ̀ɛt mooŋ khrʉ̂ŋ thʉ̌ŋ bàay sǎam mooŋ khrʉ̂ŋ. tɛ̀ɛ dǐaw-níi tha-naa-khaan sùan-mâak pə̀ət sǎa-khǎa yɔ̂y nay sǔun-kaan-kháa yày-yày dûay. tha-naa-khaan nay sǔun-kaan-kháa níi mák-ca pə̀ət thúk wan ruam-tháŋ wan sǎw ʔaa-thít tâŋ-tɛ̀ɛ wee-laa sìp-ʔet mooŋ thʉ̌ŋ raaw-raaw hòk mooŋ yen rʉ̌ʉ nʉ̀ŋ thûm.
sǎm-ràp bɔɔ-ri-kaan lɛ̂ɛk-plìan ŋən tàaŋ-pra-thêet tha-naa-khaan sùan-mâak ca mii kháw-tə̂ə phí-sèet hây bɔɔ-ri-kaan thúk wan wee-laa pɛ̀ɛt mooŋ khrʉ̂ŋ thʉ̌ŋ hòk mooŋ yen rʉ̌ʉ nʉ̀ŋ thûm mʉ̌an-kan.

Banking Services in Thailand

- Banks in Thailand usually only open for business from Monday to Friday, from 8.30 a.m. to 3.30 p.m. But nowadays, most banks open mini branches in big shopping centers too. Banks in these shopping centers are likely to open everyday, including weekends, from 11 a.m. until about 6 p.m. or 7 p.m. As for foreign currency exchange services, most banks have a special counter opening for service everyday from 8.30 a.m. until 6 p.m. or 7 p.m. as well.

Proverb ...สุภาษิต /su-phaa-sìt/

สอนจระเข้ให้ว่ายน้ำ sɔ̌ɔn cɔɔ-ra-khêe hây wâay-náam	to teach + crocodile + prep. purpose + to swim	To teach a crocodile to swim.

"To preach to the choir."

Idioms ...สำนวน /sǎm-nuan/

นอนกิน nɔɔn kin	to sleep + to eat	To have an income without working.
เสือนอนกิน sʉ̌a nɔɔn kin	tiger + to sleep + to eat	A tiger that has something to eat while reclining.

"A free rider; someone who gets something for nothing."

Vocabulary ...ศัพท์ /sàp/

พิเศษ	phí sèet	v. to be special, extra
ที่ทำการ	thîi tham-kaan	n. office (clf. แห่ง /hɛ̀ŋ/)
เหมา	mǎw	v. to take the whole lot
จำหน่าย	cam-nàay	v. to sell, be sold (formal)
ชำระ	cham-ráʔ	v. to pay (formal)
ห่อ	hɔ̀ɔ	v. to wrap, package
ของขวัญ	khɔ̌ɔŋ-khwǎn	v. gift, present
โปสการ์ด	póos-káat	n. postcard, card (clf. แผ่น /phɛ̀n/, ใบ /bay/)
ดวง	duaŋ	clf. classifier for the eyes and certain other round shapes or objects (seals, stamps, spots, stains)
ขึ้นอยู่กับ	khʉ̂n-yùu-kàp	v. depend on, hinge on; be decided by; rely on
น้ำหนัก	nám-nàk	n. weight
เดี๋ยวนี้	dǐaw-níi	n. now, at present
สาขา	sǎa-khǎa	n. branch; offshoot; subdivision; tributary (clf. สาขา /sǎa-khǎa/, แห่ง /hɛ̀ŋ/)
จึงจะ	cʉŋ-ca	aux. so that, in order to
รวมทั้ง	ruam-tháŋ	v. to include
สำหรับ	sǎm-ràp	1. prep. for; 2. conj. as for, regarding
เคาน์เตอร์	kháw-tɔ̂ɔ	n. counter (from English)

Language Notes

1. Mood particle: ไง /ŋay/

In Dialog 9.2.2, you see an example of use of another mood particle: ไง /ŋay/. This particle is used to show that the speaker thinks that the statement is self-evident, and directs the attention of the hearer to the statement or object. It can be followed with another mood particle of emphasis: **ล่ะ /lâ/, /là/** (See Unit7.1 Notes).

2. Purpose conjunction จึงจะ /cɯŋ-ca/, ถึงจะ /thɯ̌ŋ-ca/

In Dialog 9.2.7, จึงจะ/cɯŋ-ca/ "so that," "in order that," another purpose conjunction is introduced. It appears in the following pattern:

7b. Clause 1	Clause 2
	(Subject) + **จึงจะ /cɯŋ-ca/** + Verb Phrase

A more informal variant is **ถึงจะ /thɯ̌ŋ-ca/**.

Note that even though **จึงจะ /cɯŋ-ca/** looks similar and appears in a similar pattern with the consequence conjunction **จึง /cɯŋ/**, i.e., before the verb (see Unit 9.1 Structure Note 4), they are NOT the same.

Examples:

ส่งพัสดุกี่วัน sòŋ phát-sa-dù kìi wan	พัสดุ**จึงจะ**ถึงอเมริกา phát-sa-dù **cɯŋ-ca** thɯ̌ŋ ʔa-mee-ri-kaa
How many days in sending a parcel	in order for the parcel to arrive in America?

Culture Notes

1. Thai banks still use a passbook to keep a record of a bank account's transactions. It serves as a form of identification and proof of a bank account. Passbooks are required in conducting transactions on an account at the bank.

2. There are two types of so-called "express mail" services at the Thai post office:

- ไปรษณีย์ด่วน /pray-sa-nii dùan/, a regular "express delivery mail" which will deliver your mail as soon as the mail gets to the destination post office. This is equivalent to the Priority Mail service of the US Post Office.
- ไปรษณีย์ด่วนพิเศษ /pray-sa-nii dùan phí-sèet/, "super express mail," commonly known by its English abbreviation: อีเอ็มเอส /ʔii-ʔem-ʔées/, EMS Express Mail Service, handles the express mail all the way from the originating post office until the mail is delivered. This is the service that is equivalent to the US Post Office's Express Mail.

3. For international postal services, there are also a number of international courier services in Thailand such as UPS and DHL.

Unit 10

หน่วยที่ ๑๐

lesson 1

Obtain and provide information about planning a trip; learn about some popular tourist destinations in Thailand and modes of transportation to these places; and discuss the weather

lesson 2

Make reservations for a trip (transportation and accommodations)

บทที่ ๑

Lesson 1

Skills: To obtain and provide information about planning a trip; to learn about some popular tourist destinations in Thailand and modes of transportation to these places; and to discuss the weather

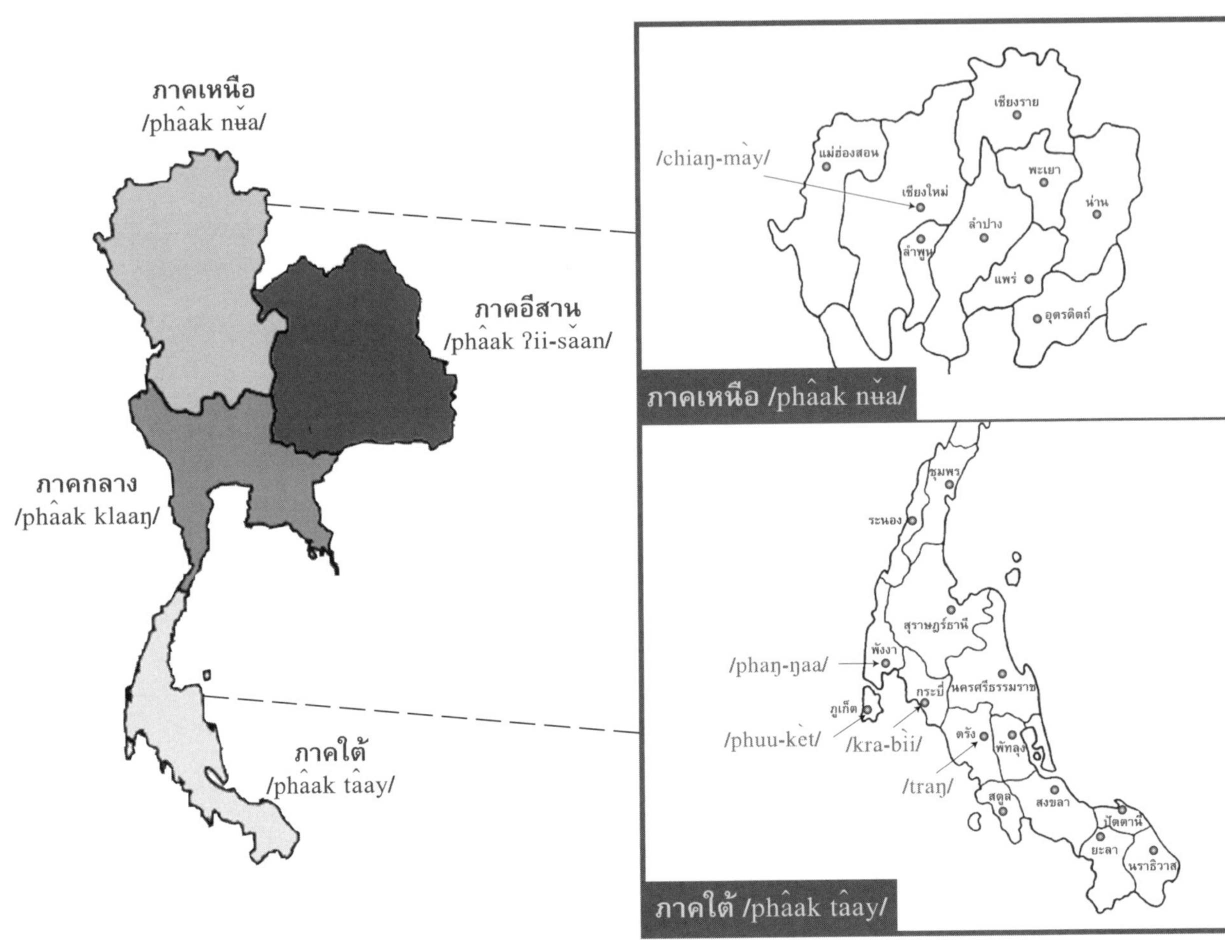

Dialogs ...บทสนทนา /bòt sǒn-tha-naa/

Dan (B) and Amy (C) ask Chai (A) to help plan a trip after the semester ends.

Dialog 10.1.1

A	แดน เอมี่ ปิดเทอมแล้ว จะไปเที่ยวที่ไหนก่อนกลับอเมริกา	dɛɛn. ʔee-mîi. pìt thəəm lɛ́ɛw ca pay thîaw thîi-nǎy kɔ̀ɔn klàp ʔa-mee-ri-kaa.	Dan and Amy, after the semester ends, where are you going sightseeing before returning to America?

B	ผมอยากไปภาคเหนือ ไปเที่ยวเชียงใหม่และจังหวัดแถว ๆ นั้น	phǒm yàak pay phâak nʉ̌a. pay thîaw chiaŋ-mày lɛ́ caŋ-wàt thɛ̌ɛw-thɛ̌ɛw nán.	I'd like to go to the northern region, to Chiangmai and provinces in that area.
C	เอมี่ อยากไปเที่ยวทะเลทางใต้ อยากไปเที่ยวเกาะต่าง ๆ ทางฝั่งอันดามัน ชัยช่วยแนะนำเรื่องที่พักการเดินทางให้เราได้ไหม	ʔee-mîi yàak pay thîaw tha-lee thaaŋ tâay. yàak pay thîaw kɔ̀ʔ tàaŋ-tàaŋ thaaŋ fàŋ ʔan-daa-man. chay chûay nɛ́-nam rʉ̂aŋ thîi-phák kaan dəən-thaaŋ hây raw dây-máy.	I want to go to the seaside in the southern region. I'd like to go to the islands along the Andaman coast. Can you advise us about accommodations and travel?
A	ได้เลยครับ ยินดีรับใช้	dây ləəy khráp. yin-dii ráp-cháy.	Of course. At your service.

Dialog 10.1.2

B ไปเชียงใหม่ ไปยังไงดี

pay chiaŋ-mày pay yaŋ-ŋay dii.

- How should I travel to Chiangmai?

A ไปรถไฟก็ได้ รถทัวร์ก็ได้ หรือ เครื่องบินก็ได้
ถ้านั่งรถไฟด่วน ใช้เวลาราว ๆ 12 ชั่วโมง
ถ้าไปรถทัวร์ ใช้เวลาราว ๆ 10 ชั่วโมง
ไปเครื่องบิน ใช้เวลาเพียงชั่วโมงเดียวเท่านั้น
ค่าตั๋วรถทัวร์ราว ๆเที่ยวละ 800 บาท
ค่าตั๋วรถไฟถูกกว่านิดหน่อย ราว ๆ เที่ยวละ 500-600 บาท
ค่าเครื่องบิน เที่ยวละ 1,500 บาท ถึง 2,000 บาท

pay rót-fay kɔ̂-dâay rót-thua kɔ̂-dâay rʉ̌ʉ khrʉ̂aŋ-bin kɔ̂-dâay. thâa nâŋ rót-fay dùan cháy wee-laa raaw-raaw sìp-sɔ̌ɔŋ chûa-mooŋ. thâa pay rót-thua cháy wee-laa raaw-raaw sìp chûa-mooŋ. pay khrʉ̂aŋ-bin cháy wee-laa phiaŋ chûa-mooŋ diaw thâw-nán. khâa-tǔa rót-thua raaw-raaw thîaw-la pɛ̀ɛt-rɔ́ɔy bàat. khâa-tǔa rót-fay thùuk kwàa nít-nɔ̀y raaw-raaw thîaw-la hâa-rɔ́ɔy thʉ̌ŋ hòk-rɔ́ɔy bàat. khâa-khrʉ̂aŋ-bin thîaw-la nʉ̀ŋ-phan-hâa-rɔ́ɔy bàat thʉ̌ŋ sɔ̌ɔŋ-phan bàat.

- You can go by train, or bus or plane. If you take an express train, it takes about 12 hours. If you go by bus, it takes about 10 hours. By plane, it only takes one hour. The bus fare is about 800 Baht one way. The train fare is a bit cheaper, around 500-600 Baht one way. The airfare is 1,500-2,000 Baht one way.

B ชัยคิดว่า ไปรถไฟกับรถทัวร์ อะไรสะดวกและปลอดภัย กว่ากัน

chay khít wâa pay rót-fay kap rót-thua ʔa-ray sa-dùak lɛ́ plɔ̀ɔt-phay kwàa kan.

- Which do you think is more convenient and safer, going by train or going by bus?

A ผมว่า รถไฟน่าจะปลอดภัยกว่านะ และนั่งสบายกว่าด้วย คุณเดินไปเดินมาได้

phǒm wâa rót-fay nâa-ca plɔ̀ɔt-phay kwàa ná lɛ́ nâŋ sa-baay kwàa dûay. khun dəən pay dəən maa dâay.

- I think the train should be safer and a more comfortable ride. You can walk around on the train.

B ถ้ายังงั้น ผมอยากนั่งรถไฟขาไป จะได้ดูวิว และจะนั่งเครื่องบินขากลับ

thâa-yaŋ-ŋán phǒm yàak nâŋ rót-fay khǎa pay ca-dây duu wiw lɛ́ ca nâŋ khrʉ̂aŋ-bin khǎa klàp.

- Then I'd like to take the train there so that I can see the scenery, and I'll take the plane on the return trip.

A แดนจะไปเที่ยวเชียงใหม่คนเดียว หรือมีเพื่อนไปด้วย

dɛɛn ca pay thîaw chiaŋ-mày khon diaw rʉ̌ʉ mii phʉ̂an pay dûay.

- Are you going sightseeing in Chiangmai by yourself or are you going with a friend?

B ผมไปเชียงใหม่คนเดียว แต่ผมมีเพื่อนอยู่ที่นั่น เราจะเช่ารถพร้อมคนขับไปเที่ยวกัน

phǒm pay chiaŋ-mày khon diaw. tɛ̀ɛ mii phʉ̂an yùu thîi-nân. raw ca châw rót phrɔ́ɔm khon-khàp pay thîaw kan.

- I'm going to Chiangmai alone, but I have a friend there. We will rent a car with a driver to go sightseeing.

Dialog 10.1.3

C แล้ว ทะเลทางใต้ล่ะ จะไปที่ไหนดี

lɛ́ɛw tha-lee thaaŋ tâay lâ. ca pay thîi-nǎy dii.

- And what about the southern seaside? Where should I go?

A นักท่องเที่ยวต่างประเทศส่วนมาก จะไปภูเก็ต หรือ พังงา แล้วก็ไปเที่ยวชายหาด และเกาะต่างๆ บริเวณนั้น แต่ค่าโรงแรมที่ภูเก็ตแพงมาก ผมว่า เอมี่ไปกระบี่ แล้วก็ไปเที่ยวจังหวัดแถวๆ นั้น เช่น ภูเก็ต ตรัง ดีกว่า ที่กระบี่ ค่าโรงแรมไม่ค่อยแพงเหมือนที่ภูเก็ต จากกระบี่ ไปเที่ยวเกาะต่างๆ เช่น เกาะพีพี ก็สะดวก

nák thɔ̂ŋ-thîaw tàaŋ-pra-thêet sùan-mâak ca pay phuu-kèt rʉ̌ʉ phaŋ-ŋaa lɛ́ɛw-kɔ̂ɔ pay thîaw chaay-hàat lɛ́ kɔ̀ʔ tàaŋ-tàaŋ bɔɔ-ri-ween nán. tɛ̀ɛ khâa rooŋ-rɛɛm thîi phuu-kèt phɛɛŋ mâak. phǒm wâa ʔee-mîi pay kra-bìi lɛ́ɛw-kɔ̂ɔ pay thîaw caŋ-wàt thɛ̌ɛw-thɛ̌ɛw nán chên phuu-kèt traŋ dii kwàa. thîi kra-bìi khâa rooŋ-rɛɛm mây-khɔ̂y phɛɛŋ mʉ̌an thîi phuu-kèt. càak kra-bìi pay thîaw kɔ̀ʔ tàaŋ-tàaŋ chên kɔ̀ʔ phii-phii kɔ̂ɔ sa-dùak.

- Most foreign tourists go to Phuket or Phang-nga, and to the beaches and islands in that area. But the hotels in Phuket are very expensive. I think you should go to Krabi and make a trip to see the provinces around there such as Phuket and Trang. At Krabi, the hotels are not as expensive as those in Phuket. From Krabi, you can conveniently travel to various islands such as Phi Phi Island.

C กระบี่อยู่ที่ไหนคะ แล้วจะไปกระบี่ยังไงดีคะ

kra-bìi yùu thîi-nǎy khá. lɛ́ɛw ca pay kra-bìi yaŋ-ŋay dii khá.

- Where is Krabi? And how should I travel to Krabi?

A กระบี่อยู่ทางตะวันออกของภูเก็ต ผมว่า สำหรับเอมี่ ไปเครื่องบินดีที่สุด ใช้เวลาเดินทางราวๆ 1 ชั่วโมง และค่าตั๋วราวๆ เที่ยวละ 2,500 บาท ถ้าเอมี่จะไปรถทัวร์ ใช้เวลาเดินทางราวๆ 13 ชั่วโมง ค่ารถราวๆ 800 บาท อ้อ ไม่มีรถไฟไปกระบี่นะ

kra-bìi yùu thaaŋ ta-wan-ɔ̀ɔk khɔ̌ɔŋ phuu-kèt. phǒm wâa sǎm-ràp ʔee-mîi pay khrʉ̂aŋ-bin dii thîi-sùt. cháy wee-laa dəən-thaaŋ raaw-raaw nʉ̀ŋ chûa-mooŋ lɛ́ khâa-tǔa raaw-raaw thîaw-la sɔ̌ɔŋ-phan-hâa-rɔ́ɔy bàat. thâa ʔee-mîi ca pay rót-thua cháy wee-laa dəən-thaaŋ raaw-raaw sìp-sǎam chûa-mooŋ. khâa rót raaw-raaw pɛ̀ɛt-rɔ́ɔy bàat. ʔɔ̂ɔ. mây mii rót-fay pay kra-bìi ná.

- Krabi is to the east of Phuket. I think, for you, going by plane would be the best way. It takes about an hour and the fare is about 2,500 Baht one way. If you go by bus, it takes 13 hours and the fare is about 800 Baht. By the way, there is no train to Krabi.

C เอมี่ คงไปเครื่องบิน ตามที่ชัยแนะนำ

ʔee-mîi khoŋ pay khrʉ̂aŋ-bin taam-thîi chay nɛ́-nam.

- I'll probably go by plane as you suggest.

A เอมี่ มีเพื่อนไปด้วยหรือเปล่า หรือว่าไปคนเดียวครับ

ʔee-mîi mii phʉ̂an pay dûay rʉ́-plàaw. rʉ̌ʉ-wâa pay khon diaw khráp.

- Are you going with a friend or are you going by yourself?

C เอมี่จะไปกับเจน เพื่อนจากวิสคอนซิน แล้วก็จะชวนตุ๊กไปด้วย

ʔee-mîi ca pay kàp ceen phʉ̂an càak "Wisconsin" lɛ́ɛw-kɔ̂ɔ ca chuan túk pay dûay.

- I'm going with Jane, a friend from Wisconsin. And I will ask Tuk to go along with us, too.

Vocabulary ...ศัพท์ /sàp/

เกาะ	kɔ̀ʔ	n. island (clf. เกาะ /kɔ̀ʔ/)
ฝั่ง	fàŋ	n. coast, shore
อันดามัน	ʔan-daa-man	Name. Andaman (Sea).
รับใช้	ráp-cháy	v. to serve, be in service of
ยินดีรับใช้	yin-dii ráp-cháy	At your service.
รถทัวร์	rót-thua	n. tour bus, coach; motor coach (clf. คัน /khan/) (from English "tour")
เที่ยว	thîaw	clf. classifier for a trip

ปลอด	plɔ̀ɔt	v. to be free from, lacking in, empty of
ปลอดภัย	plɔ̀ɔt-phay	v. to be safe, out of danger
ขา	khǎa	n. leg (of the body, of a piece of furniture, of a journey)
ขาไป	khǎa-pay	n. the trip going; (on) the way to, (on) the way there
ขากลับ	khǎa-klàp	n. the return trip
วิว	wiw	n. view (from English "view")
พร้อม	phrɔ́ɔm	1. v. to be ready, set, completed 2. conj. along with, to accompany (to be in company with)
เช่น	chên	conj. such as, for example
ตามที่	taam-thîi	conj. according to, following
ชวน	chuan	v. to invite, persuade (to do something)

Weather ...ดินฟ้าอากาศ /din fáa ʔaa-kàat/

อากาศ
/ʔaa-kàat/
• **n. climate, weather, air**

อุณหภูมิ
/ʔun-ha-phuum/
• **n. temperature**

องศา
/oŋ-sǎa/
• **clf. for degree of temperature or angles**

ฝน
/fǒn/
• **n. rain**

หิมะ
/hi-máʔ/
• **n. snow**

ลูกเห็บ
/lûuk-hèp/
• **n. hail**

แดด
/dɛ̀ɛt/
• **n. sunlight, sunshine**

รุ้ง
/rúŋ/
• **n. rainbow (clf. ตัว /tua/)**

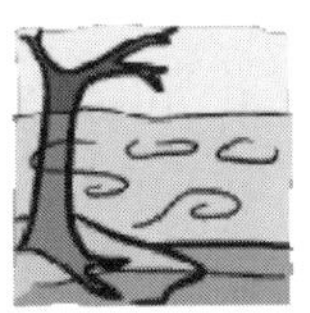

หมอก
/mɔ̀ɔk/
• **n. fog, mist**

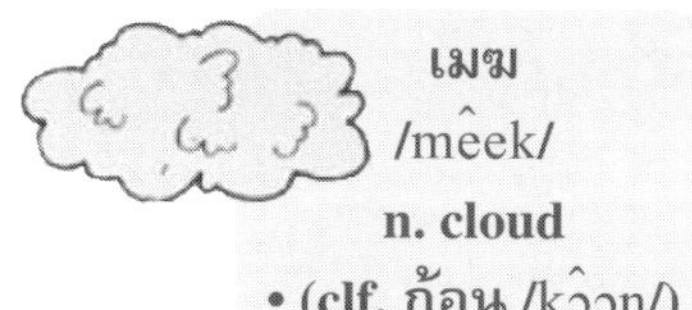

เมฆ
/mêek/
n. cloud
• (clf. ก้อน /kɔ̂ɔn/)

ลม
/lom/
• n. wind

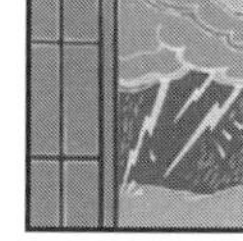

พายุ
/phaa-yúʔ/
• n. storm

แล้ง
/lɛ́ɛŋ/
• v. to be dry, lacking rain, arid

ครึ้ม
/khrɨ́m/
• v. to be cloudy, overcast, shady, gloomy

มรสุม
/mɔɔ-ra-sǔm/
• n. monsoon

อากาศเป็นยังไง	ʔaa-kàat pen yaŋ-ŋay	What's the weather like?
ฝนตก	fǒn tòk	It rains. (It's raining.)
หิมะตก	hi-máʔ tòk	It snows. (It's snowing.)
ลูกเห็บตก	lûuk-hèp tòk	It hails. (It's hailing.)
แดดออก	dɛ̀ɛt ʔɔ̀ɔk	The sun comes out. (The sun is coming out.)
หมอกลง	mɔ̀ɔk loŋ	It's foggy. (It's fogging up.)
ลมพัด	lom phát	The wind blows. (The wind is blowing.)
ฝนครึ้ม	fǒn khrɨ́m	It looks like rain.
ครึ้มฝน	khrɨ́m fǒn	It looks like rain.
ฝนแล้ง	fǒn lɛ́ɛŋ	There is a drought. There is a shortage of rain.
มีพายุ	mii phaa-yúʔ	There's a storm.
มีลมแรง	mii lom rɛɛŋ	There's a strong wind.
มีแดด	mii dɛ̀ɛt	It's sunny.
มีเมฆ	mii mêek	It's cloudy.
มีหมอก	mii mɔ̀ɔk	It's foggy.
มีฝน	mii fǒn	It's rainy.
มีมรสุม	mii mɔɔ-ra-sǔm	There's a monsoon.
ฟ้าร้อง	fáa rɔ́ɔŋ	n. thunder

ฟ้าแลบ
/fáa lɛ̂p/
• n. lightning,
v. light to flash lightning

ฟ้าผ่า
/fáa phàa/
• n. thunderbolt,
v. to be struck by lightning

Listening Practice ...ฝึกหัด ฟัง /fɨ̀k-hàt faŋ/

สถานที่ท่องเที่ยว

ทางภาคใต้ของไทย นักท่องเที่ยวนิยมไปเที่ยวทะเล เพราะภาคใต้อยู่ติดทะเลทั้ง 2 ด้าน คือ ทางฝั่งตะวันตก ติดกับทะเลอันดามัน ทางฝั่งตะวันออกติดกับทะเลจีนใต้ และอ่าวไทย ทางภาคใต้ มีลมมรสุมตะวันตกเฉียงใต้พัดผ่าน ตั้งแต่ราว ๆ เดือนพฤษภาคม ถึงเดือนพฤศจิกายน จึงมีฝนตกมาก และมีคลื่นลมในทะเลแรงในตอนนั้น เวลาที่นักท่องเที่ยวนิยมไปเที่ยวทะเลทางภาคใต้ คือ ในหน้าแล้ง ราว ๆ เดือนธันวาคมถึงเดือนเมษายน จังหวัดในภาคใต้ที่นักท่องเที่ยวต่างประเทศนิยมไปเที่ยวมากที่สุดคือจังหวัดภูเก็ต สำหรับในภาคเหนือ เชียงใหม่เป็นจังหวัดที่นักท่องเที่ยวนิยมไปมากที่สุด เวลาที่นักท่องเที่ยวนิยมไปเที่ยวเชียงใหม่ ก็คือในหน้าแล้งเหมือนกัน หน้าแล้งในเชียงใหม่ เริ่มตั้งแต่ราว ๆ เดือนตุลาคมถึงเดือนเมษายน ที่เชียงใหม่ นักท่องเที่ยวส่วนมากจะไปดูวัดต่าง ๆ และไปเที่ยวป่า หรือ เดินเขาไปดูหมู่บ้านชาวเขา ในเดือนเมษายน นักท่องเที่ยวก็จะนิยมไปเที่ยวงานเทศกาลสงกรานต์ของจังหวัดเชียงใหม่ที่มีชื่อเสียงมากด้วย

sa-thǎan thîi thɔ̂ŋ-thîaw

thaaŋ phâak tâay khɔ̌ŋ thay nák thɔ̂ŋ-thîaw ní-yom pay thîaw tha-lee phrɔ́ʔ phâak-tâay yùu tìt tha-lee tháŋ sɔ̌ɔŋ dâan khɨɨ thaaŋ fàŋ ta-wan- tòk tìt kàp tha-lee ʔan-daa-man thaaŋ fàŋ ta-wan- ʔɔ̀ɔk tìt kàp tha-lee ciin tâay lɛ́ ʔàaw thay. thaaŋ phâak-tâay mii lom mɔɔ-ra-sǔm ta-wan-tòk chǐaŋ tâay phát phàan tâŋ-tɛ̀ɛ raaw-raaw dɨan phrɨ́t-sa-phaa-khom thɨ̌ŋ dɨan phrɨ́t-sa-cì-kaa-yon cɨŋ mii fǒn tòk mâak lɛ́ mii khlɨ̂ɨn lom nay tha-lee rɛɛŋ nay tɔɔn nán. wee-laa thîi nák thɔ̂ŋ-thîaw ní-yom pay thîaw tha-lee thaaŋ phâak-tâay khɨɨ nay nâa lɛ́ɛŋ raaw-raaw dɨan than-waa-khom thɨ̌ŋ dɨan mee-sǎa-yon. caŋ-wàt nay phâak-tâay thîi nák thɔ̂ŋ-thîaw tàaŋ-pra-thêet ní-yom pay thîaw mâak thîi-sùt khɨɨ caŋ-wàt phuu-kèt.

sǎm-ràp nay phâak nɨ̌a chiaŋ-mày pen caŋ-wàt thîi nák thɔ̂ŋ-thîaw ní-yom pay mâak thîi-sùt. wee-laa thîi nák thɔ̂ŋ-thîaw ní-yom pay thîaw chiaŋ-mày kɔ̂ khɨɨ nay nâa lɛ́ɛŋ mɨ̌an-kan. nâa lɛ́ɛŋ nay chiaŋ-mày rɤ̂ɤm tâŋ-tɛ̀ɛ raaw-raaw dɨan tù-laa-khom thɨ̌ŋ dɨan mee-sǎa-yon. thîi chiaŋ-mày nák thɔ̂ŋ-thîaw sùan-mâak ca pay duu wát tàaŋ-tàaŋ lɛ́ pay thîaw pàa rɨ̌ɨ dəən-khǎw pay duu mùu-bâan chaaw-khǎw. nay dɨan mee-sǎa-yon nák thɔ̂ŋ-thîaw kɔ̂-ca ní-yom pay thîaw ŋaan thêet-sa-kaan sǒŋ-kraan khɔ̌ŋ caŋ-wàt chiaŋ-mày thîi mii chɨ̂ɨ-sǐaŋ mâak dûay.

Places to go Sightseeing

- In southern Thailand, tourists like to go to the seaside because the South is adjacent to the sea on both sides, i.e., the west coast is adjacent to the Andaman Sea, and the east coast is adjacent to the South China Sea and the Gulf of Thailand. In the southern region, there's a southwestern monsoon from around May to November, so there is a lot of rain and strong wind and waves at that time. The time that tourists like to visit the seaside in the south is in the dry season from around December to April. The southern province that foreign tourists like to visit the most is Phuket. As for the northern region, Chiangmai is the province that tourists like to visit the most. The time that tourists like to visit Chiangmai is also during the dry season. The dry season in Chiangmai lasts from October to April. In Chiangmai, tourists visit temples and go trekking in the forests or on the mountains to see hill tribe villages. In April most tourists also like to go to the Songkran Festival in Chiangmai which is very famous.

Proverb ...สุภาษิต /su-phaa-sìt/

น้ำพึ่งเรือ เสือพึ่งป่า náam phʉ̂ŋ rʉa sʉ̌a phʉ̂ŋ pàa	water + to rely on + boat tiger + to rely on + forest	The waterways depend on boats; tigers depend on the forest.

"Whether big or small, we are mutually dependent."

Idioms ...สำนวน /sǎm-nuan/

ยกเมฆ yók mêek	to raise + cloud	To cloud over; to obfuscate

"To trump up, lie; fib."
"To pull the wool over someone's eyes."

ปั้นน้ำเป็นตัว pân náam pen tua	To mold + water + into + body	To shape something out of water.

"To make up a story out of whole cloth."

Vocabulary ...ศัพท์ /sàp/

ดิน	din	n. earth, ground, soil, land
ฟ้า	fáa	n. sky
ดินฟ้าอากาศ	din fáa ʔaa-kàat	n. weather, climate
แรง	rɛɛŋ	adv. forcefully, hard, powerfully, strongly
พัด	phát	v. (the wind) to blow
แลบ	lɛ̂p	v. to flash (as lightning)
ผ่า	phàa	v. to split, cut, hew
อ่าว	ʔàaw	n. bay, gulf
ผ่าน	phàan	v. to pass
ร้อง	rɔ́ɔŋ	v. to cry out, bellow, shriek
นิยม	ní-yom	v. to like, to admire, to be popular
ด้าน	dâan	clf. side
ตั้งแต่	tâŋ-tɛ̀ɛ	prep. from (such and such a time or starting point), since
ป่า	pàa	n. forest, woods (clf. ผืน /phʉ̌ʉn/)
เริ่ม	rə̂əm	v. to begin
เขา	khǎw	n. mountain, hill (clf. ลูก /lûuk/)
เดินเขา	dəən-khǎw	v. to trek through the mountains
หมู่บ้าน	mùu-bâan	n. village (clf. หมู่บ้าน)
ชาวเขา	chaaw-khǎw	n. hill tribe member(s)
เทศกาล	thêet-sa-kaan	n. festival, festival season
สงกรานต์	sǒŋ-kraan	Name. Songkran. (see Culture Note)
พึ่ง	phʉ̂ŋ	v. to depend on (for help)
ยก	yók	v. to lift, raise
ปั้น	pân	v. to mold (e.g. things of clay, plaster, etc.)

Language Notes

1. Talking about weather in Thai

The general term for weather in that is a four-syllable compound: ดินฟ้าอากาศ from ดิน /din/ "earth" + ฟ้า /fáa/ "sky" + อากาศ /ʔaa-kàat/ "air". Note that all the words about weather in Thai such as ฝน /fǒn/ "rain", ลม /lom/ "wind," and พายุ /phaa-yúʔ/ "storm" are nouns. Therefore, in Thai, there are two ways to talk about a weather event:

a. by specifying an action of each weather entity, for example:

ลมพัด /lom phát/	wind + to blow	The wind blows.
ฝนตก /fǒn tòk/	rain + to fall	It rains.
หมอกลง /mɔ̀ɔk loŋ/	fog + to descend	It's foggy.

Especially for the terms referring to the lights and sounds of the sky, they are actually a compound of ฟ้า /fáa/ "sky" and a verb:

ฟ้าแลบ /fáa lɛ̂p/	sky + to flash, to spark	n. lightning
ฟ้าร้อง /fáa rɔ́ɔŋ/	sky + to call, make a sound	n. thunder
ฟ้าผ่า /fáa phàa/	sky + to split, to split open	n. lightning bolt

b. by using a presentational verb มี /mii/ or เกิด /kə̀ət/ (see Units 5.4 and 9.1) with the weather noun, or adding to a weather phrase, for example,

มีพายุ mii phaa-yúʔ	มี /mii/+ storm	There's a storm.
เกิดมรสุม kə̀ət mɔɔ-ra-sǔm	เกิด /kə̀ət/ + monsoon	There's a monsoon.
มีหมอกลง mii mɔ̀ɔk loŋ	มี /mii/+ fog + to descend	There's fog. It's foggy.

2. Repeated action with post-verbs ไป /pay/ and มา /maa/

In Dialog 10.1.2, we see an example of the verbs ไป and มา used as a series of secondary directional post-verbs to signify a repeated action/movement, equivalent to the "to and fro" or "back and forth" adverbial phrases in English.

The pattern is:

Verb + ไป /pay/ (+ Verb) + มา /maa/

เขาเดินไปเดินมาในรถไฟ kháw dəən pay dəən maa nay rót-fay	he + to walk + ไป /pay/ + to walk + มา /maa/ + in + train	He walks back and forth in the train.
เขาเดินทางไปมาระหว่างกรุงเทพฯ กับเชียงใหม่ kháw dəən-thaaŋ pay maa ra-wàaŋ kruŋ-thêep kàp chiaŋ-mày	he + to travel+ ไป /pay/ + มา /maa/ + between + Bangkok + and + Chiangmai	He travels back and forth between Bangkok and Chiangmai.

Culture Note

สงกรานต์ /sǒŋ-kraan/ is an annual celebration of the Thai traditional New Year, which starts on April 13th every year and lasts for three days. Songkran is traditionally celebrated with water. The celebration rituals include sprinkling water on Buddha images; pouring scented water into the palms of the hands of the elders and parents as a sign of respect and to wish them well, with the elders giving blessings in return; and sprinkling water on each other for good luck. However, in modern days, the sprinkling of water has turned into a water fight. Since Songkran occurs during the hottest month of the year, people seem to enjoy incorporating the water fight into the Songkran activities. This festival is also known among visitors to Thailand as the "Water Festival."

The Songkran festival is also an occasion for family members to get together and celebrate, much like Christmas or Thanksgiving in the United States. In B.E. 2532 (1989 A.D.), the Thai government declared the 14th of April, the second day of the Songkran festival, a "Family Day" วันครอบครัว /wan khrɔ̂ɔp-khrua/.

Skill: To make reservations for a trip (transportation) and accommodations

Vocabulary ...ศัพท์ /sàp/

จอง	cɔɔŋ	v. to reserve, make a reservation
ค่าโดยสาร	khâa dooy-sǎan	n. fare, cost of passage
ค่าธรรมเนียม	khâa tham-niam	n. fee
ผู้โดยสาร	phûu dooy-sǎan	n. passenger
บัตรโดยสาร	bàt dooy-sǎan	n. (bus, train, boat) ticket (clf. ใบ /bay/, ฉบับ cha-bàp)
ตั๋วโดยสาร	tǔa dooy-sǎan	n. (bus, train, boat) ticket (clf. ใบ /bay/, ฉบับ cha-bàp)
เที่ยวเดียว	thîaw diaw	n. one way (Lit. a single trip)
ไปกลับ	pay klàp	n. round trip
สายการบิน	sǎay kaan-bin (clf. สาย /sǎay/)	n. an airline (system or company)
รถไฟ	rót-fay	n. train (clf. ขบวน /kha-buan/)
ขบวน	kha-buan	clf. classifier for processions, lines, trains
รถนั่ง	rót nâŋ	n. passenger car
รถนอน	rót nɔɔn	n. sleeping car, sleeper
ชานชาลา	chaan chaa-laa	n. (railroad) station platform
รถเก๋ง	rót-kěŋ	n. sedan (car, automobile)
รถตู้	rót-tûu	n. van

Commonly used phrases in making a reservation

ขอจอง _____	khɔ̌ɔ cɔɔŋ _____	May I reserve _____
ฉันอยากจะจอง _____	chán yàak-ca cɔɔŋ _____	I'd like to reserve _____

Dialogs ...บทสนทนา /bòt sǒn-tha-naa/

Dialog 10.2.1

Dan (A) makes a reservation at the train station with an agent (B).

A ผมขอจองตั๋วรถนั่งด่วนพิเศษจากสถานีรถไฟหัวลำโพงไปเชียงใหม่ 1 ที่ วันศุกร์หน้า
phǒm khɔ̌ɔ cɔɔŋ tǔa rót nâŋ dùan phí-sèet càak sa-thǎa-nii rót-fay hǔa-lam-phooŋ pay chiaŋ-mày nʉ̀ŋ thîi wan sùk nâa.
- I'd like to reserve a seat on the Special Express train from Hualamphong to Chiangmai for next Friday.

สถานีรถไฟหัวลำโพง
/sa-thǎa-nii rót-fay hǔa-lam-phooŋ/

B มี 2 ขบวนนะครับ ขบวนเช้า ออกจากสถานีหัวลำโพง 8.30 น. ถึงเชียงใหม่ 19.45 น. ขบวนเย็น ออกจากกรุงเทพฯ 19.25 น. ถึงเชียงใหม่ 7.20 น. ทั้งสองขบวนเป็นรถนั่งด่วนพิเศษ ชั้น 2 ปรับอากาศ
mii sɔ̌ɔŋ kha-buan ná khráp. kha-buan cháaw ʔɔ̀ɔk-càak sa-thǎa-nii hǔa-lam-phooŋ pɛɛt naa-li-kaa sǎam-sìp naa-thii thʉ̌ŋ chiaŋ-mày sìp-kâaw naa-li-kaa sìi-sìp-hâa naa-thii. kha-buan yen ʔɔ̀ɔk-càak kruŋ-thêep sìp-kâaw naa-li-kaa yîi-sìp-hâa naa-thii thʉ̌ŋ chiaŋ-mày cèt naa-li-kaa yîi-sìp naa-thii. tháŋ sɔ̌ɔŋ kha-buan pen rót nâŋ dùan phí-sèet chán sɔ̌ɔŋ pràp-ʔaa-kàat.
- There are two trains. The morning train leaves Hualamphong station at 8.30 a.m. and arrives in Chiangmai at 7.45 p.m. The evening train leaves Bangkok at 7.25 p.m. and arrives in Chiangmai at 7.20 a.m. Both are special express, second class, air-conditioned passenger cars only.

A ผมขอจองขบวนเช้าครับ ยังมีที่นั่งไหมครับ
phǒm khɔ̌ɔ cɔɔŋ kha-buan cháaw khráp. yaŋ mii thîi nâŋ máy khráp.
- I'd like to make a reservation on the morning train. Do you still have seats available?

รถนั่งด่วนพิเศษชั้นสองปรับอากาศ
/rót nâŋ dùan phí-sèet chán sɔ̌ɔŋ pràp-ʔaa-kàat/

B มีครับ ขอทราบชื่อครับ

mii khráp. khɔ̌ɔ sâap chʉ̂ʉ khráp.

- Yes. May I have your name, please?

A ผมชื่อ แดน นามสกุล คิม ครับ ชื่อสะกด D-A-N นามสกุล สะกด K-I-M ค่าตั๋วเท่าไหร่ครับ

phǒm chʉ̂ʉ dɛɛn naam-sa-kun khim khráp. chʉ̂ʉ sa-kòt 'D-A-N' naam-sa-kun sa-kòt 'K-I-M'. khâa tǔa thâw-rày khráp.

- My name is Dan, last name Kim. The name is spelled D-A-N and the family name K-I-M. What is the fare?

B ค่าโดยสารและค่าธรรมเนียม รวมทั้งหมด 711 บาท เรียบร้อยแล้วครับ คุณจะมาจ่ายเงินและรับตั๋วได้ที่สถานีหัวลำโพง ก่อนเวลารถออกอย่างน้อยหนึ่งชั่วโมง

khâa dooy-saan lɛ́ khâa tham-niam ruam tháŋ-mòt cèt rɔ́ɔy sìp-ʔèt bàat. rîap-rɔ́ɔy lɛ́ɛw khráp. khun ca maa càay ŋən lɛ́ ráp tǔa dâay thîi sa-thǎa-nii hǔa-lam-phooŋ kɔ̀ɔn wee-laa rót ʔɔ̀ɔk yàaŋ nɔ́ɔy nʉ̀ŋ chûa-mooŋ.

- The total fare and fee altogether is 711 Baht. It's all in order. You can pay and pick up the ticket at Hualamphong Station at least one hour before the train departure time.

Dialog 10.2.2

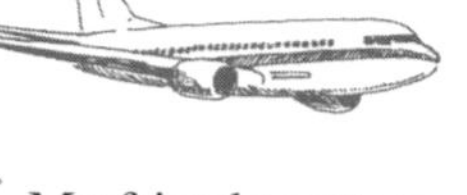

Amy (A) and Suda (C) make a reservation with a travel agent (B).

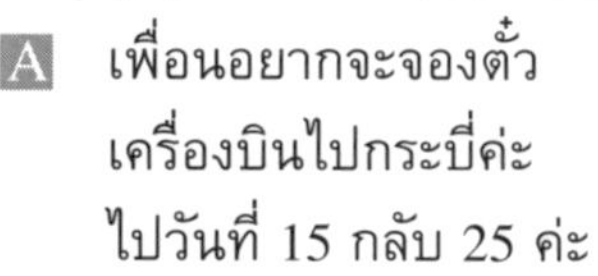

A	เพื่อนอยากจะจองตั๋วเครื่องบินไปกระบี่ค่ะ ไปวันที่ 15 กลับ 25 ค่ะ	phʉ̂an yàak-ca cɔɔŋ tǔa khrʉ̂aŋ-bin pay kra-bìi khâ. pay wan-thîi sìp-hâa. klàp yîi-sìp-hâa khâ.	My friend wants to reserve a seat on a flight to Krabi. She leaves on the 15th and returns on the 25th.
B	เครื่องบินไปกระบี่มีการบินไทย พีบีแอร์ แล้วก็ ภูเก็ตแอร์ค่ะ จะไปสายการบินอะไรดีคะ	khrʉ̂aŋ-bin pay kra-bìi mii kaan-bin thay phi-bii ʔɛɛ lɛ́ɛw-kɔ̂ phuu-kèt ʔɛɛ khâ. ca pay sǎay kaan-bin ʔa-ray dii khá.	Airlines that fly to Krabi are Thai Airways, PB Air and Phuket Air. What airline do you want?
A	อะไรก็ได้ ที่ราคาถูกที่สุดน่ะค่ะ	ʔa-ray kɔ̂-dâay thîi ra-khaa thùuk thîi-sùt nâ khâ.	Any airline is fine as along as it has the cheapest price.
B	ถ้ายังงั้น ดิฉันจะจองสายการบินพีบีแอร์นะคะ ค่าตั๋วไปกลับ 4,000 บาทค่ะ กี่ที่คะ	thâa-yaŋ-ŋán di-chán ca cɔɔŋ sǎay kaan-bin phi-bii ʔɛɛ ná khá. khâa tǔa pay klàp sìi-phan bàat khâ. kìi thîi khá.	In that case, I'll reserve PB Air. The roundtrip fare is 4,000 Baht. How many seats?
C	ที่เดียวค่ะ	thîi diaw khâ.	One.
B	ขอชื่อ และนามสกุลผู้โดยสาร และเบอร์โทรติดต่อด้วยค่ะ	khɔ̌ɔ chʉ̂ʉ lɛ́ naam-sa-kun phûu-dooy-sǎan lɛ́ bəə thoo tìt-tɔ̀ɔ dûay khâ.	May I have the full name of the passenger and contact telephone number.

C	Amy Johnson ค่ะ เบอร์โทรศัพท์ 02-224-3564 สำหรับค่าตั๋วเครื่องบินคุณรับเป็นบัตรเครดิตหรือเปล่าคะ	Amy Johnson khâ. bɔɔ thoo-ra-sàp sǔun sɔ̌ɔŋ sɔ̌ɔŋ sɔ̌ɔŋ sìi sǎam hâa hòk sìi. sǎm-rap khâa tǔa khrʉ̂aŋ-bin khun ráp pen bàt khree-dìt rʉ̌-plàaw khá.	Amy Johnson. Phone number 02-224-3564. For the airfare, do you take credit cards or not?
A	ไม่รับค่ะ ขอเป็นเงินสดนะคะ	mây ráp khâ. khɔ̌ɔ pen ŋən-sòt ná khá.	No, we don't. Please pay in cash.

Dialog 10.2.3

At a guest house in Chiangmai, Dan (A) asks a hotel receptionist (B) about the room.

A	ที่นี่มีห้องว่างไหมครับ	thîi-nîi mii hɔ̂ŋ wâaŋ máy khráp.	Is there a room available here?
B	มีครับ ต้องการกี่ห้องครับ	mii khráp. tɔ̂ŋ-kaan kìi hɔ̂ŋ khráp.	Yes. How many rooms do you want?
A	ห้องเดียวครับ พัก 2 คน มีห้องเตียงเดี่ยว 2 เตียงไหมครับ	hɔ̂ŋ diaw khráp. phák sɔ̌ɔŋ khon. mii hɔ̂ŋ tiaŋ-dìaw sɔ̌ɔŋ tiaŋ máy khráp.	One, for two guests. Do you have a double room with two beds?
B	มีครับ	mii khráp.	Yes.
A	ค่าห้องราคาคืนละเท่าไหร่ครับ	khâa hɔ̂ŋ ra-khaa khʉʉn-la thâw-rày khráp.	What is the room rate?
B	700 บาท ไม่รวมอาหารเช้าครับ	cèt-rɔ́ɔy bàat. mây ruam ʔaa-hǎan cháaw khráp.	700 Baht, not including breakfast.
A	มีแอร์กับ ห้องน้ำในห้องใช่ไหม	mii ʔɛɛ kàp hɔ̂ŋ-náam nay hɔ̂ŋ chây-máy.	The room's air-conditioned with a bathroom inside, isn't it?
B	ครับ แล้วก็มีเคเบิ้ลทีวีและตู้เย็นด้วย	khráp. lɛ́ɛw-kɔ̂ɔ mii khee-bɔ̂n thii-wii lɛ́ tûu-yen dûay.	Yes, and there's cable TV and a refrigerator as well.
A	ตกลงครับ เราจะพัก 2 คืน	tòk-loŋ khráp. raw ca phák sɔ̌ɔŋ khʉʉn.	Okay. We'll stay two nights.

Dialog 10.2.4

Dan (B) calls to reserve a rental car from an agent (A).

A	ฮัลโหล บริษัทล้านนารถเช่าครับ	han-lǒo bɔɔ-ri-sàt láan-naa rót châw khráp.	Hello. Lanna Car Rental Company.
B	ผมอยากจะเช่ารถพร้อมคนขับ 2 วัน ตั้งแต่พรุ่งนี้ครับ มีรถไหมครับ	phǒm yàak-ca châw rót phrɔ́ɔm khon khàp sɔ̌ɔŋ wan tâŋ-tɛ̀ɛ phrûŋ-níi khráp. mii rót máy khráp.	I'd like to rent a car and driver for two days starting tomorrow. Do you have a car available?

A	รถตู้ไม่มีว่างเลยครับ แต่รถเก๋งว่าง	rót tûu mây mii wâaŋ ləəy khráp. tɛ̀ɛ rót kěŋ wâaŋ.	We don't have any vans free, but a sedan is available.
B	ดีครับ มีผมกับเพื่อนแค่ 2 คน ค่าเช่าวันละเท่าไหร่ครับ	dii khráp. mii phom kàp phʉ̂an khɛ̂ɛ sɔ̌ɔŋ khon. khâa châw wan la thâw-rày khráp.	Good. There are just two of us, me and a friend. What is the charge per day?
A	วันละ 1,200 บาทครับ	wan la nʉ̀ŋ-phan sɔ̌ɔŋ-rɔ́ɔy bàat khráp.	1,200 baht a day.
B	โอเคครับ	ʔoo-khee khráp.	OK.
A	ผมขอชื่อคุณ และชื่อโรงแรมที่คุณพัก และเบอร์โทรศัพท์ติดต่อ พรุ่งนี้คุณจะต้องการให้รถไปรับคุณกี่โมงครับ	phǒm khɔ̌ɔ chʉ̂ʉ khun lɛ́ chʉ̂ʉ rooŋ-rɛɛm thîi khun phák lɛ́ bəə thoo-ra-sàp tìt-tɔ̀ɔ. phrûŋ-níi khun ca tɔ̂ŋ-kaan hây rót pay ráp khun kìi mooŋ khráp.	May I have your name and the name of the hotel where you are staying, and a phone number? Tomorrow, what time do you want the car to pick you up?
B	ผมชื่อ แดน นามสกุล คิม ผมพักที่กาแลเกสต์เฮาส์ อยู่ถนนห้วยแก้ว เบอร์โทรศัพท์ 053-210000 พรุ่งนี้ คุณช่วยส่งรถมาตอน 8 โมงเช้านะครับ	phǒm chʉ̂ʉ dɛɛn naam-sa-kun khim. phǒm phák thîi kaa-lɛɛ kés-háws. yùu tha-nǒn hûay-kɛ̂ɛw bəə thoo-ra-sàp sǔun hâa sǎam sɔ̌ɔŋ nʉ̀ŋ sǔun sǔun sǔun sǔun. phrûŋ-níi khun chûay sòŋ rót maa tɔɔn pɛ̀ɛt mooŋ cháaw ná khráp.	My name is Dan, family name Kim. I'm staying at Kalae Guesthouse on Huaykaew Road. The phone number here is 053-210000. Tomorrow, please send a car to pick us up at 8:00 a.m.

Proverbs ...สุภาษิต /su-phaa-sìt/

วัวหายล้อมคอก wua hǎay lɔ́ɔm khɔ̂ɔk	cattle + to disappear + to fence in + pen	To put up a pen after the cattle has been stolen.

"It's too late to shut the stable door after the horse has bolted."

เสียน้อยเสียยาก เสียมากเสียง่าย sǐa nɔ́ɔy sǐa yâak sǐa mâak sǐa ŋâay	to spend + little + to spend + to be difficult to spend + a lot + to spend + to be easy	It's difficult to spend a little, easy to spend a lot.

"Penny wise, pound foolish."

Vocabulary ...ศัพท์ /sàp/

◂ เรียบร้อย	rîap-rɔ́ɔy	v. to be ready, all set
◂ เรียบร้อยแล้ว	rîap-rɔ́ɔy lɛ́ɛw	All set.
◂ ต้องการ	tɔ̂ŋ-kaan	v. to want, need, require (formal) = อยาก /yàak/
◂ ล้อม	lɔ́ɔm	v. to surround, encircle
◂ คอก	khɔ̂ɔk	n. pen, sty (for animals); stable, cowbarn

Language Note

Some noun compounds in Thai are the "mirror image" of their corresponding verb phrases. Some examples that we see in this lesson and the previous units are:

Noun Compound (N + V)	Verb Phrase (V + N)
รถเช่า /rót châw/ "rental car, car for hire"	เช่ารถ /châw rót / "to rent" + "car"
เงินทอน /ŋən-thɔɔn/ "change"	ทอนเงิน /thɔɔn-ŋən/ "to change" + "money"

Culture Notes

1. หัวลำโพง /hǔa-lam-phooŋ/ is the name of the main train station in Bangkok. It also is adjacent to a subway station of the same name.

2. Thai trains have three classes: first, second, and third. Only sleeping cars on overnight trains have first class. Second class seats are available in both passenger and sleeping cars, in air-conditioned cars and regular cars. Only regular non air-conditioned cars have third class seats. For the second class seats on air-conditioned special express trains that Dan buys a ticket for in Dialog 10.2.1, the fare includes light meals and refreshments.

3. Car rental daily rates at local car rental companies in popular tourist destinations in the provinces typically include the chauffeurs' fee.

Song ...เพลง /phleeŋ/

ผู้ใหญ่ลี /phûu-yày lii/

พ.ศ. 2504 ผู้ใหญ่ลี ตี กลอง ประชุม	phɔɔ-sɔ̌ɔ sɔ̌ɔŋ-phan-hâa-rɔ́ɔy-sìi phûu-yày lii tii klɔɔŋ pra-chum.	In the year 1961, Village Chief Lee hit the drum to call a meeting.
ชาวบ้าน ต่าง มา ชุมนุม มา ประชุม ที่ บ้าน ผู้ใหญ่ลี	chaaw-bâan tàaŋ maa chum-num. maa pra-chum thîi bâan phûu-yày lii.	Each villager went to gather At the meeting at Village Chief Lee's house.
ต่อไปนี้ ผู้ใหญ่ลี จะ ขอ กล่าว ถึง เรื่องราว ที่ ได้ ประชุม มา	tɔ̀ɔ-pay-níi phûu-yày lii ca khɔ̌ɔ klàaw thʉ̌ŋ rʉ̂aŋ-raaw thîi dâay pra-chum maa.	Then Village Chief Lee asked to speak About the subject of the meeting that he had just attended.
ทางการ เขา สั่ง มา ว่าให้ ชาวนา เลี้ยง เป็ด และ สุกร	thaaŋ-kaan kháw sàŋ maa wâa hây chaaw-naa líaŋ pèt lɛ́ sù-kɔɔn.	The government had ordered that The villagers were to raise ducks and "sukorn."
ฝ่าย ตาสี หัวคลอน ถามว่า สุกร นั้น คืออะไร	fàay taa sǐi hǔa khlɔɔn thǎam wâa sù-kɔɔn nán khʉʉ ʔa-ray.	Then Old Man See, with the shaking head, asked, "What's that 'sukorn'?"
ผู้ใหญ่ลี ลุก ขึ้น ตอบ ทันใด	phûu-yày lii lúk khʉ̂n tɔ̀ɔp than-day	Village Chief Lee got up at once and replied,
สุกร นั้น ไซร้ คือ หมาน้อย ธรรมดา	sù-kɔɔn nán sáy khʉʉ mǎa nɔ́ɔy tham-ma-daa	"Those 'sukorn' are just ordinary little dogs,
หมาน้อย หมาน้อย ธรรมดา	mǎa nɔ́ɔy mǎa nɔ́ɔy tham-ma-daa	Just ordinary little dogs."

Vocabulary ...ศัพท์ /sàp/

ผู้ใหญ่บ้าน	phûu-yày bâan	n. elected head of a village, headman (clf. คน /khon/)
กลอง	klɔɔŋ	n. drum (clf. ใบ /bay/, ลูก /lûuk/)
ประชุม	pra-chum	v. to meet (in a group), assemble; to hold a meeting

◂ ชาวบ้าน	chaaw-bâan	n. villager, commoner; the common folk
◂ ต่าง	tàaŋ	quant. each
◂ ชุมนุม	chum-num	v. to gather together, assemble, congregate, concentrate (in one place)
◂ ต่อไปนี้	tɔ̀ɔ-pay-níi	conj. from now on, as follows
◂ กล่าวถึง	klàaw thɯ̌ŋ	v. to talk about
◂ เรื่องราว	rɯ̂aŋ-raaw	n. story, account; matter; happening; case (clf. เรื่อง /rɯ̂aŋ/)
◂ ทางการ	thaaŋ-kaan	n. government, authorities
◂ เลี้ยง	líaŋ	v. to raise, breed
◂ สุกร	sù-kɔɔn	n. pig (clf. ตัว /tua/) (formal)
◂ ฝ่าย	fàay	conj. as for, regarding
◂ คลอน	khlɔɔn	v. to be shaky, unstable, unsteady
◂ ลุก	lúk	v. to get up, to get to one's feet
◂ ตอบ	tɔ̀ɔp	v. to reply, answer
◂ ทันที	than-thii	adv. promptly, immediately, at once, instantly
◂ ทันใด	than-day	adv. suddenly, immediately (formal) = ทันที
◂ ไซร้	sáy	prt. marking a topic. (literary use)

Language Notes

1. The word ผู้ใหญ่ /phûu-yày/ in this song is used as a title before a name; it is shortened from ผู้ใหญ่บ้าน /phûu-yày bâan/. The title means "village chief/ headman."

2. สุกร /sù-kɔɔn/ is an Indic loanword, meaning "pig." The commonly used Thai word for pig is /muu/. Indic loanwords typically are considered "prestige" forms and used in government formal announcements and documents. The incident depicted in this song arises from the villagers' confusion of this Indic loanword for pig with a very similar Indic loanword สุนัข /sù-nák/ "dog."

Culture Notes

1. About the song (ผู้ใหญ่ลี Village Chief Lee)

This is one of the most famous Thai "country" songs, one that everybody seems to know by heart. The song was written by พิพัฒน์ บริบูรณ์ /phí-phát bɔɔ-ri-buun/, and first performed by ศักดิ์ศรี ศรีอักษร /sàk-sǐi sǐi-ʔàk-sɔ̌ɔn/ around 1960. The song takes a humorous look at the implementation of the First National Economic Development Plan which took place in 1961 (B.E. 2504) during the beginning of the economic development era of Thailand with aid and loans from the World Bank. At that time, development programs used the "top down" approach in which all policies, plans and decisions were made by the government or by "the authorities" and passed down to the villagers to carry out.

In the song, Lee, the headman of the village, has just received orders from "the authorities" for the villagers to carry out. Hilarious misunderstanding arises from the government's use of "high" (Pali-Sanskrit loan) vocabulary in the order.

The "full version" of the lyrics has three parts. Here, we only present the first of the three parts, which is the part that is most widely known.

2. To view and listen to a sing-along karaoke style presentation of this song, visit the following website: http://www.hawaii.edu/thai/thaisongs/

Appendices

Appendix 1

Songs and Poems of Thailand

Songs can be regarded as a cultural expression of a society. A number of commonly known children's songs and popular songs are introduced in the lessons in this volume (Book 2) as well as in Book 1. In this section of this volume, we present additional songs that are of cultural importance in three categories:

a. Songs for Special Cultural Occasions

1. Loy Krathong

2. The New Year Blessing

b. Songs and Thai Life

3. Krungthep Maha Nakhon

c. Songs from Poems

4. Eating Rice

1. รำวงลอยกระทง /ram-wong lɔɔy-kra-thoŋ/ Ramwong Loy Krathong

This is a song synonymous with the ลอยกระทง Loy Krathong Festival, a festival celebrated on the full moon night of the twelfth lunar month, which usually falls on some day in November. ลอย /lɔɔy/ means "to float" and กระทง /kra-thoŋ/ refers to a banana leaf cup. The กระทง used in this festival is lotus-shaped decorated with flowers, candles, incense sticks, coins etc. It is believed that the floating of a กระทง is intended to float away ill fortune as well as to express apologies to Khongkha or Ganga, the River Goddess. The Loy Krathong Festival is celebrated nationwide in Thailand, especially where there are rivers, canals or sources of water.

As for the song, it was originally composed as a sound track for a Thai movie in 1950. The lyrics were composed by แก้ว อัจฉริยะกุล /kɛ̂ɛw ʔat-cha-rí-ya-kun/ and the music composed by เอื้อ สุนทรสนาน /ʔɨ̂a sǔn-thɔɔn-sa-nǎan/ of the famed สุนทราภรณ์ sǔn-tha-raa-phɔɔn/ Big Band. It is also a song meant for accompanying a รำวง /ram-woŋ/. รำวง /ram-woŋ/ is a popular Thai folk dance in which men and women dance in pairs in a circle, hence the name รำวง "dance in circle," from รำ /ram/ "to dance (with hands)" and วง /woŋ/ "circle."

Ramwong is modified from the traditional Central Thai folk dance called รำโทน /ram-thoon/, a dance to the beat of a โทน /thoon/, a Thai drum. The ramwong songs and dance patterns as known today were set during 1938-1944 as part of the promotion of nationalism by Field Marshall Plaek Pibulsongkram, the Prime Minister then, who aimed to create the Thai National Identity. Ramwong was then promoted as the national dance. A set of ramwong songs and dance patterns were commissioned by the government as the "standard" of ramwong. There are altogether 10 so – called "standard ramwong" songs and dance patterns.

The Ramwong Loy Krathong is probably the best known of all the ramwong type songs, and has become the song of the Loy Krathong Festival.

The accompanying audio file is from the version of the song recorded by the สุนทราภรณ์ Band.

วันเพ็ญเดือนสิบสอง wan-phen dɯan sìp-sɔ̌ɔŋ	On the full moon day of the twelfth lunar month
น้ำก็นองเต็มตลิ่ง náam kɔ̂ɔ nɔŋ tem ta-lìŋ	When the water overflows the river bank,
เราทั้งหลายชายหญิง raw tháŋ-lǎay chaay yǐŋ	All of us, men and women,
สนุกกันจริงวันลอยกระทง sa-nùk kan ciŋ wan lɔɔy kra-thoŋ.	Have great fun on the Loy Krathong day.
ลอย ลอยกระทง ลอย ลอยกระทง lɔɔy lɔɔy kra-thoŋ. lɔɔy lɔɔy kra-thoŋ.	Float, float the Krathong. Float, float the Krathong.
ลอยกระทงกันแล้ว lɔɔy kra-thoŋ kan lɛ́ɛw	After we float the Krathong,
ขอเชิญน้องแก้วออกมารำวง khɔ̌ɔ chəən nɔ́ɔŋ-kɛ̂ɛw ʔɔ̀ɔk maa ram-woŋ	May I invite my beloved to come out to dance the ramwong with me.
รำวงวันลอยกระทง ram-woŋ wan lɔɔy kra-thoŋ.	Dance the ramwong on Loy Krathong day.
รำวงวันลอยกระทง ram-woŋ wan lɔɔy kra-thoŋ.	Dance the ramwong on Loy Krathong day.
บุญจะส่งให้เราสุขใจ bun ca sòŋ hây raw sùk-cay.	The meritorious deed will make us happy.
บุญจะส่งให้เราสุขใจ bun ca sòŋ hây raw sùk-cay.	The meritorious deed will make us happy.

2. พรปีใหม่ /phɔɔn pii-mày/ The New Year Blessing

This is a song composed by King Bhumibhol in 1951 as a New Year blessing to all Thais. The lyrics were composed by Prince Chakkraphanphensiri. It was first performed by the Chulalongkorn University Band and Suntharaporn Big Band on January 1st, 1952. The accompanying audio file is from the official website of the King's activities: http://kanchanapisek.or.th/royal-music/pornpeemai.html

สวัสดีวันปีใหม่พา sa-wàt-dii wan pii mày phaa	Greetings on the New Year day
ให้บรรดาเราท่านรื่นรมย์ hây ban-daa raw thâan rʉ̂ʉn-rom.	Which brings us joy
ฤกษ์ยามดีเปรมปรีดิ์ชื่นชม rə̂ək-yaam dii preem-prii chʉ̂ʉn-chom	An auspicious time to rejoice,
ต่างสุขสมนิยมยินดี tàaŋ sùk-sǒm ní-yom yin-dii.	And be merry.
ข้าวิงวอนขอพรจากฟ้า khâa wiŋ-wɔɔn khɔ̌ɔ phɔɔn càak fáa	I pray for celestial blessings
ให้บรรดาปวงท่านสุขศรี hây ban-daa puaŋ thân sùk-sǐi.	For happiness to all of you.
โปรดประทานพรโดยปรานี pròot pra-thaan phɔɔn dooy praa-nii	For kind grace
ให้ชาวไทยล้วนมีโชคชัย hây chaw-thay lúan mii chôok-chay.	That brings good luck and victory to all Thais
ให้บรรดาปวงท่านสุขสันต์ hây ban-daa puaŋ thân sùk-sǎn	And jubilation to all of you
ทุกวันทุกคืนชื่นชมให้สมฤทัย thúk wan thúk khʉʉn chʉ̂ʉn-chom hây sǒm rʉ́-thay	Each and everyday. May your wishes come true.
ให้รุ่งเรืองในวันปีใหม่ hây rûŋ-rʉaŋ nay wan pii-mày	May you prosper on the New Year occasion.
ผองชาวไทยจงสวัสดี phɔ̌ɔŋ chaw-thay coŋ sa-wàt-dii.	May all Thais be well
ตลอดปีจงมีสุขใจ ta-lɔ̀ɔt pii coŋ mii sùk-cay	And merry through out the year
ตลอดไปนับแต่บัดนี้ ta-lɔ̀ɔt pay náp tɛ̀ɛ bàt-níi	And always from now on.
ให้สิ้นทุกข์สุขเกษมเปรมปรีดิ์ hây sîn thúk sùk ka-sěem preem-prii	May you be free of sorrow and full of joy and happiness.
สวัสดีวันปีใหม่เทอญ sa-wàt-dii wan pii-mày thəən.	Happy New Year!

3. กรุงเทพมหานคร /kruŋ-thêep ma-hǎa ná-khɔɔn/ The Great City of Angels

The lyrics of this song is the full ceremonial name of Bangkok as given by King Rama I who established this city as the capital of the kingdom in 1782. Nowadays Thais call it by its abbreviated name “Krungthep.” Foreigners however still refer to the city by its old name: บางกอก /baaŋ-kɔ̀ɔk/ “place of olive plums.”

The melody was composed by the brothers อัสนี-วสันต์ โชติกุล (Asanee and Wasan Chotikul) in 1989.

The name is composed mostly from Pali-Sanskrit words with meanings that glorify the city as a divine capitol befitting a deva-raja (god-king).

The full name of the city is said to be listed by the Guinness Book of Records as the world’s longest place name.

กรุงเทพ มหา นคร kruŋ-thêep ma-hǎa ná-khɔɔn	The great city of angels,
อมร รัตนโกสินทร์ ʔa-mɔɔn rát-ta-ná koo-sǐn	the gem of Indra,
มหินทรายุทธยา มหา ดิลก ภพ ma-hǐn-tha-raa-yút-tha-yaa ma-hǎa di-lòk phóp	the supreme unconquerable city (Ayuthaya) of the great immortal divinity (Indra),
นพรัตน์ ราชธานี บุรีรมย์ nóp-pha-rát râat-cha-thaa-nii bù-rii rom	the royal capital of nine noble gems, the pleasant city,
อุดม ราชนิเวศน์ มหาสถาน ʔù-dom râat-cha-ní-wêet ma-hǎa sa-thǎan	with plenty of grand royal palaces,
อมร พิมาน อวตาร สถิต ʔa-mɔɔn phí-maan ʔa-wa-taan sa-thìt	and divine paradises for the reincarnated deity (Vishnu),
สักกะ ทัตติย วิษณุกรรม ประสิทธิ์ sàk-kà thát-ti-yá wít-sa-nú-kam pra-sìt	given by Indra and created by the god of crafting (Visnukarma)

4. เปิบข้าว /pə̀əp khâaw/ **Eating Rice**

This poem was composed by จิตร ภูมิศักดิ์ Jit Phumisak, a progressive Thai intellectual and writer in the 1960's who posthumously became a culture-hero to the Thai students' political movement during the 1970's. He composed this piece in 1964 while imprisoned along with other progressive intellectuals, writers and politicians under the dictatorial regime of Sarit Thanarat.

This poem was written using the กาพย์ ยานี 11 /kàap yaa-nii/ versification shown below. One stanza of this type of poetry consists of two lines, called บาท /bàat/. The ยานี meter of this type has eleven syllables per บาท divided into two วรรค /wák/ of five and six syllables respectively.

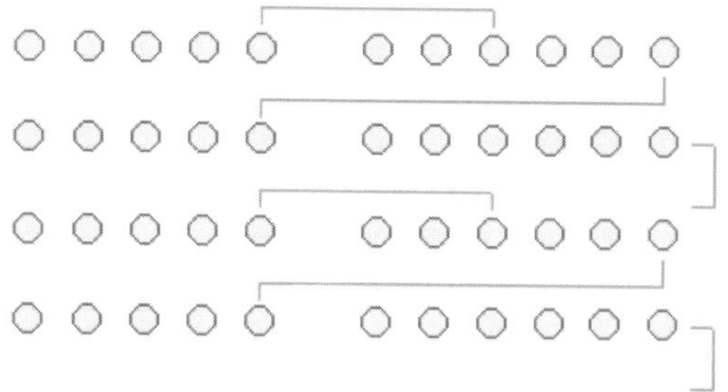

The poem was put into a song by a pioneer "Song for Life" band called คาราวาน Caravan and performed during student political rallies in the 70's. The song is one of the best known Thai "Song for Life" songs for the way in which it calls attention to the hardship of the farmers and the working class.

There are two versions of accompanying audio files of this song. One is performed by the original Caravan band. The other version that is set to orchestral music was produced by the Committee of the 30th Anniversary of October 14th, 1973 Event, and sung by เอกชัย ศรีวิชัย /ʔeek-ka-chay sǐi-wí-chay/.

The English translation is by Yuangrat Wedel (Wedel and Wedel (1987: 85).

เปิบข้าวทุกคราวคำ จงสู้จำเป็นอาจิณ เหงื่อกูที่สูกิน จึงก่อเกิดมาเป็นคน pə̀əp khâaw thúk khraaw kham coŋ sǔu cam pen ʔaa-cin ŋʉ̀a kuu thîi suu kin cʉŋ kɔ̀ɔ kə̀ət maa pen khon	Each time you grab a fistful of rice, Remember it is my sweat you swallow. To keep on living.

ข้าวนี้นะมีรส ให้ชนชิมทุกชั้นชน เบื้องหลังสิทุกข์ทน และขมขื่นจนเขียวคาว khâaw nii ná mii rót hây chon chim thúk chán chon bʉ̂aŋ-lǎŋ sì thúk-thon lɛ́ khǒm-khʉ̀ʉn con khǐaw khaaw	This rice has the taste To please the tongue of every class, But to grow rice is the bitter work That only we farmers must taste.
จากแรงมาเป็นรวง ระยะทางนั้นเหยียดยาว จากรวงเป็นเม็ดพราว ล้วนทุกข์ยากลำบากเข็ญ càak rɛɛŋ maa pen ruaŋ rá-yá-thaaŋ nán yìat-yaaw càak ruaŋ pen mét phraaw lúan thúk-yaak lam-bàak khěn	From my labor the rice becomes stalks It takes a long, long time From sprouts to grain And it is full of misery.
เหงื่อหยดสักกี่หยาด ทุกหยดหยาดล้วนยากเย็น ปูดโปนกี่เส้นเอ็น จึงแปรรวงมาเป็นกิน ŋʉa yot sák kìi yàat thúk yòt-yàat lúan yâak-yen pùut poon kìi sên ʔen cʉŋ prɛɛ ruaŋ maa pen kin	Every drop of my sweat Reflects this hard life. My veins strain and bulge So you can eat
น้ำเหงื่อที่เรื่อแดง และน้ำแรงอันหลั่งริน สายเลือดกูทั้งสิ้น ที่สูซดกำซาบฟัน náam-ŋʉa thîi rʉ̀a dɛɛŋ lɛ́ nám-rɛɛŋ ʔan làŋ-rin sǎay-lʉ̂at kuu tháŋ-sîn thîi sǔu sót kam-sâap fan	The red sweat of my labor Is really my life's blood That delights your teeth.

Reference

Wedel, Yuangrat and Paul Wedel. 1987. *Radical Thoughts, Thai mind: the Development of Revolution any ideas in Thailand.* Bangkok: Assumption Business Administration College.

Appendix 2

Summary of Structural Patterns

Sentence Pattern #	Unit/Lesson
1. Subject + Copula Verb + Noun เขาเป็นนักเรียน /kháw pen nák-rian/	Unit 1.2
2. Subject + Verb (+ Object) (+ Adverb) สุดาเรียนอะไร /su-daa rian ʔa-ray/	Unit 1.2
2a. Subject + Verb+ Object + (***ไม่*** mây)+ Evaluative Post-verb + (Adverb-degree) เขาพูดภาษาไทยได้นิดหน่อย /kháw phûut pha-săa-thay dâay nít-nɔ̀y/ ฉันอ่านภาษาไทยไม่ได้ /chán ʔàan pha-săa-thay mây dâay/	Unit 1.3/1.4
2b. Subject + Pre-verb + Verb + (Object) + (Adverb) แดนเคย ไป เมืองไทย 2 ครั้ง /dɛɛn khəəy pay mɯaŋ-thay sɔ̌ɔŋ khráŋ/	Unit 2.1
2c. Subject + กำลัง /kam-laŋ/ + Verb + (Object) + (อยู่ /yùu/) เขากำลังหาอพาร์ตเมนต์อยู่ /kháw kam-laŋ hăa ʔa-pháat-mén yùu/	Unit 2.2
2d. Subject + NEG + Verb (+ Object) (+ [degree]-Adverb) เงินเดือนไม่มากเท่าไร /ŋən-dɯan mây mâak thâw-rày/	Unit 2.1/2.4
2e. Subject + ***ใช้*** /cháy/ + Instrument Noun + Verb + Object + Adverb คนไทยใช้ช้อนกินข้าว /khon thay cháy chɔ́ɔn kin khâaw/	Unit 3.4
2f. Subject + Verb + Object + Adverb + ***ด้วย*** /dûay/ + Instrument Noun คนไทยกินข้าวด้วยช้อน /khon thay kin khâaw dûay chɔ́ɔn/	Unit 3.4
2g. Subject + Verb (+ Object) + Post-verb (+ Adverb) เขาเอาหนังสือไปที่ห้องสมุด /kháw ʔaw năŋ-sɯ̌ɯ pay thîi hɔ̂ŋ-sa-mùt/	Unit 4.1
3. Statement + Yes/no Question particle คุณเข้าใจไหม /khun khâw-cay máy/	Unit 1.3
4a. **A** + Verb (attributive) + ***กว่า*** /kwàa/ + **B** + (Adverb-degree) กรุงเทพฯใหญ่กว่าโฮโนลูลูมาก /kruŋ-thêep yày kwàa hoo-noo-luu-luu mâak/	Unit 2.1
4b. **A** + Verb (attributive) + (Adverb-degree) + ***ที่สุด*** /thîi-sùt/ เดือนเมษายนร้อนมากที่สุด /dɯan mee-săa-yon rɔ́ɔn mâak thîi-sùt/	Unit 4.4
5a. Time Conjunction + Clause 1, Clause 2 **ตอน**แดนอยู่อเมริกา เขาทำงานโรงแรม /tɔɔn dɛɛn yùu ʔa-mee-ri-kaa kháw tham-ŋaan rooŋ-rɛɛm/	Unit 2.4

Sentence Pattern #	Unit/Lesson
5b. Clause 1, Time Conjunction + Clause 2 แดนทำงานโรงแรม **ตอน**เขาอยู่อเมริกา /dɛɛn tham-ŋaan rooŋ-rɛɛm tɔɔn kháw yùu ʔa-mee-ri-kaa/	Unit 3.4
6. Conditional Conjunction + Clause 1, ***ก็*** /kɔ̂/ Clause 2 ***ถ้า***ซื้อ 2 กิโล ***ก็***คิดราคา 50 บาท /thâa sɨ́ɨ sɔ̌ɔŋ ki-loo kɔ̂ khít raa-khaa hâa-sìp bàat/	Unit 3.1
7a. Clause 1 + Purpose Conjunction + Clause 2 with จะได้ เอมี่ น่าจะดูรายการนี้ เพื่อ (เอมี่) จะได้ฟังภาษาไทยเก่ง /ʔee-mîi nâa-cà duu raay-kaan níi phɨ̂a ʔee-mîi cà-dâay faŋ phaa-sǎa thay kèŋ/	Unit 7.1
7b. Clause 1 + Clause 2 with จึงจะ ส่งพัสดุกี่วัน พัสดุ**จึงจะ**ถึงอเมริกา /sòŋ phát-sa-dù kìi wan phát-sa-du cɨŋ-ca thɨ̌ŋ ʔa-mee-ri-kaa/	Unit 9.2
8. Affected Subject + **ถูก** /thùuk/ (+Agent) + Verb Phrase (+ Adverb) เด็กถูกหมากัด /dèk thùuk mǎa kàt/	Unit 9.1
9. Cause Conjunction + Clause 1, จึง + Clause 2 ***เพราะ***เขาสนใจเรื่องเมืองไทย เขา**จึง**เรียนภาษาไทย /phrɔ́ʔ kháw sǒn-cay rɨ̂aŋ mɨaŋ-thay kháw cɨŋ rian pha-sǎa thay/	Unit 9.1

Noun Phrase Pattern #	Unit/Lesson
1a. Noun + Classifier + Demonstrative นักศึกษาคนนี้ /nák-sɨk-sǎa khon níi/	Unit 1.4
1b. Noun + (Classifier + Specifier) + (Classifier + Demonstrative) เสื้อตัวสีแดงตัวนี้ /sɨ̂a tua sǐi-dɛɛŋ tua níi/	Unit 6.2
1c. Noun + Classifier + ไหน /nǎy/ นักศึกษาคนไหน /nák-sɨ̀k-sǎa khon nǎy/	Unit 6.2
2. Noun + Quantity + Classifier นักศึกษา 3 คน /nák-sɨ̀k-sǎa sǎam khon/	Unit 1.4
2a. Noun + attitude adverb + Quantity + classifier หนังสือเพียง 2 เล่ม /naŋ-sɨ̌ɨ phiaŋ sɔ̌ɔŋ lêm/	Unit 3.4

Noun Phrase Pattern #	Unit/Lesson
3. Noun +(ของ /khɔ̌ɔŋ/)+ Possessor Noun บ้านของชัย /bâan khɔ̌ɔŋ chay/	Unit 2.2
4a. Noun + ที่ /thîi/ + relative clause เดือน ที่ ร้อน ที่สุด /dɨan thîi rɔ́ɔn thîi-sùt/ 4b. Noun + ซึ่ง /sɨ̂ŋ/ + relative clause กรุงเทพ ซึ่ง เป็น เมืองหลวงของ ประเทศไทย /kruŋ-thêep sɨ̂ŋ pen mɨaŋ-lǔaŋ khɔ̌ɔŋ pra-thêet thay/	Unit 4.4 Unit 5.3

Word Formation Patterns	Unit/Lesson
นัก /nák/ + Verb	Unit 1.2
ชาว /chaw/ + Noun	Unit 1.4
ต่าง /tàaŋ/ + location Noun	Unit 2.2
ค่า /khâa/ + Verb/Noun	Unit 2.2
ความ /khwaam/ + State Verb	Unit 4.1
การ /kaan/ + Action verb	Unit 4.3
น่า /nâa/+ Verb	Unit 7.1
Verb + ใจ /cay/	Unit 7.2
ใจ /cay/ + Verb	Unit 7.2

Alphabetical Order of the IPA Transcription of the Thai

The following section provides vocabulary indices of the words and phrases introduced in each lesson, with a reference to the unit/lesson number.

For the Thai to English Vocabulary Index, the main entries in IPA transcription are listed in the following order (from left to right):

Consonants

ʔ	b	c	ch	d	f	h	k	kh	l	m	n
ŋ	p	ph	r	s	t	th	w	y			

Vowels

a	e	ɛ	i	o	ɔ	u	ʉ	ə

Tones

mid (no tone mark), low (`), falling (ˆ), high (´), rising (ˇ)

Vocabulary Index

ʔ

ʔa-pháat-mén อพาร์ตเมนต์ n. apartment *Unit 2.2*

ʔa-ray อะไร n., q. what? *Unit 1.2*

ʔa-ray-kɔ̂-dâay อะไรก็ได้ Anything will do. Anything whatever. *Unit 6.1*

ʔa-rɔ̀y อร่อย v. to be delicious, tasty (as food) *Unit 3.4*

ʔàk-sèep อักเสบ v. to be inflamed, infected *Unit 8.2*

ʔan อัน clf. for object *Unit 3.1*

ʔàt-traa อัตรา n. rate *Unit 9.2*

ʔàt-traa lɛ̂ɛk-plìan อัตราแลกเปลี่ยน n. exchange rate *Unit 9.2*

ʔaw เอา v. to take *Unit 2.4*

ʔay ไอ v. to cough *Unit 8.2*

ʔay-sa-khriim, ʔay-sa-kriim ไอศกรีม n. ice cream *Unit 3.4*

ʔaa อา n. younger paternal uncle or aunt *Unit 2.3*

ʔâa อ้า v. to open (e.g. the mouth) *Unit 8.2*

ʔaa-caan, ʔa-caan อาจารย์ n. professor, teacher *Unit 1.1*

ʔaa-cian อาเจียน v. to vomit (formal) *Unit 8.2*

ʔaa-chîip อาชีพ n. occupation, profession *Unit 2.4*

ʔaa-hǎan, ʔa-hǎan อาหาร n. food, meal *Unit 2.4*

ʔaa-kaan อาการ n. symptom *Unit 8.1*

ʔaa-kàat อากาศ n. weather, air, climate *Unit 4.4*

ʔaa-thít อาทิตย์ n. week *Unit 4.3*

ʔaa-yát อายัด v. to seize, detain *Unit 9.1*

ʔaa-yúʔ อายุ n. age (in years) *Unit 2.1*

ʔàan อ่าน v. to read *Unit 1.3*

ʔàap náam อาบน้ำ v. to bathe, take a bath, shower *Unit 4.2*

ʔàaw อ่าว n. bay, gulf *Unit 10.1*

ʔéʔ เอ๊ะ excl. expressing surprise, wonder. *Unit 3.2*

ʔèek-ka-sǎan เอกสาร n. document *Unit 9.1*

ʔeeŋ เอง adv. alone, by oneself; without company *Unit 5.4*

ʔeew เอว n. waist *Unit 8.1*

ʔɛɛ แอร์ n. air-conditioner *Unit 3.2*

ʔìm อิ่ม v. to be full (from eating) *Unit 3.2*

ʔin-thɔɔ-nèt อินเทอร์เน็ต n. Internet *Unit 7.1*

ʔii-sǎan อีสาน n. the northeast *Unit 2.2*

ʔìik อีก adv. another *Unit 1.3*

ʔòk อก n. chest (of body) *Unit 8.1*

ʔoŋ-sǎa องศา clf. degree *Unit 4.4*

ʔòp อบ v. to bake, to roast *Unit 3.3*

ʔôo-hoo โอ้โฮ excl. Gosh! Wow! Oh! *Unit 6.1*

ʔoo-líaŋ โอเลี้ยง n. iced coffee *Unit 3.3*

ʔoon ŋən โอนเงิน v. to transfer money *Unit 9.2*

ʔɔ̂ɔ อ้อ excl. Oh! Oh, yes! *Unit 3.3*

ʔɔ̀ɔk ออก v. to exit, to go out *Unit 4.2*

ʔɔ̀ɔk kam-laŋ-kaay ออกกำลังกาย v. to exercise *Unit 4.2*

ʔɔ̀ɔk-ŋən ออกเงิน v. to pay *Unit 3.4*

ʔɔɔm-sáp ออมทรัพย์ n. savings (account) *Unit 9.2*

ʔɔ̀ɔn อ่อน v. to be light (of color) *Unit 6.2*

ʔɔ̂ɔy อ้อย n. sugarcane *Unit 3.3*

ʔù-bàt-tì-hèet,ʔu-bàt-ti-hèet อุบัติเหตุ n. accident *Unit 9.1*

ʔûak อ้วก v. to vomit (informal) *Unit 8.2*

ʔûan อ้วน v. to be fat *Unit 2.1*

ʔun-ha-phuum อุณหภูมิ n. temperature *Unit 10.1*

ʔɨ̀ʔ อึ v. to poo-poo, n. poop *Unit 3.2*

ʔɨ̀ɨn อื่น n. other, others *Unit 3.3*

ʔɨ̀ɨn-ʔɨ̀ɨn อื่น ๆ n. other, other ones, others *Unit 3.3*

ʔɨ̀ɨt อืด n. to be swollen *Unit 8.2*

b

ba-mìi บะหมี่ n. egg noodles *Unit 3.3*

ban-chii บัญชี n. account *Unit 9.2*

ban-chii ʔɔɔm-sáp บัญชีออมทรัพย์ n. savings account *Unit 9.1*

ban-chii fàak pra-cam บัญชีฝากประจำ n. fixed account *Unit 9.2*

ban-chii kra-sɛ̌ɛ-raay-wan บัญชีกระแสรายวัน n. current account *Unit 9.2*

ban-day บันได n. staircase *Unit 5.4*

ban-thəəŋ บันเทิง n. entertainment *Unit 7.1*

baŋ บัง v. to obstruct one's view *Unit 7.1*

bàt บัตร n. card, ticket *Unit 3.4*

bàt ʔee-thii-ʔem บัตรเอทีเอ็ม n. ATM card *Unit 9.1*

bàt khree-dìt บัตรเครดิต n. credit card *Unit 3.4*

bay ใบ clf. for container, fruit *Unit 3.1*

bâan บ้าน n. house, home *Unit 2.2*

baaŋ บาง quant. some *Unit 4.4*

baaŋ บาง v. to be thin *Unit 6.2*

baaŋ-thii บางที adv. sometimes, at times *Unit 4.4*

bâaŋ บ้าง prt. in part, somewhat, to some extent *Unit 1.4*

báas-kêt-bɔɔn บาสเก็ตบอล n. basketball *Unit 7.1*

bàat บาด v. to cut (as of a sharp object) *Unit 8.1*

bàat-cèp บาดเจ็บ v. to be injured, wounded *Unit 9.1*

bàay บ่าย n. afternoon *Unit 4.1*

bɛ̀ŋ แบ่ง v. to divide, to share *Unit 3.4*

bɛ́ŋ แบงค์ n. banknote (from English "bank") *Unit 3.1*

bɛ́ŋ-yɔ̂y แบงค์ย่อย n. small denomination banknotes *Unit 3.1*

bèt-min-tân แบดมินตัน n. badminton *Unit 7.1*

bɛɛn แบน v. to be flat *Unit 6.3*

bɛ̀ɛp แบบ clf. for types, styles *Unit 7.1*

bɛ̀ɛp-fɔɔm แบบฟอร์ม n. form (from English "form") *Unit 9.2*

bia เบียร์ n. beer *Unit 3.4*

bin บิน v. to fly *Unit 5.1*

bin บิล n. bill *Unit 3.4*

bɔ̀ɔk บอก v. to tell (something) (to), inform *Unit 3.2*

bon บน prep. on *Unit 5.2*

bɔ̀y-bɔ̀y บ่อย ๆ adv. often, frequently *Unit 2.3*

bɔɔ-ri-kaan บริการ n. service, v. to serve *Unit 4.3*

bɔɔ-ri-sàt บริษัท n. company, firm *Unit 2.4*

bɔɔ-ri-ween บริเวณ n. area, vicinity *Unit 2.2*

bu-rìi บุหรี่ n. cigarette *Unit 3.4*

bûan-pàak บ้วนปาก v. to rinse one's mouth *Unit 8.1*

bun-tham บุญธรรม v. to be adopted *Unit 2.3*

búu บู๊ v. to fight *Unit 7.1*

bəə เบอร์ n. number (from English word "number") *Unit 2.2*

C

ca-mùuk จมูก n. nose; snout *Unit 2.1*

ca-raa-cɔɔn จราจร n. traffic *Unit 5.2*

câ จ้ะ prt. particle used to show affection/familiarity *Unit 1.1*

càk-kra-yaan, càk-ka-yaan จักรยาน n. bicycle *Unit 4.2*

càk-ka-yaan-yon จักรยานยนต์ n. motorcycle *Unit 5.3*

cam-nàay จำหน่าย v. to sell, be sold (formal) *Unit 9.2*

caŋ จัง adv. very much, extremely (colloquial) *Unit 3.1*

caŋ-wàt จังหวัด n. changwat, i.e. township *Unit 2.1*

càp จับ v. to catch *Unit 1.2*

cay ใจ n. heart, mind *Unit 4.2*

cay-dam ใจดำ to be mean, unkind *Unit 7.2*

cay-dii ใจดี to be kind, good-hearted *Unit 7.2*

cay-kwâaŋ ใจกว้าง to be generous, open-minded *Unit 7.2*

cay-khɛ̂ɛp ใจแคบ to be narrow-minded, ungenerous *Unit 7.2*

cay-lɔɔy ใจลอย to be absent-minded *Unit 7.2*

cay-ráay ใจร้าย to be cruel, mean, vicious *Unit 7.2*

cay-rɔ́ɔn ใจร้อน to be impatient *Unit 7.2*

cay-yen ใจเย็น to be patient *Unit 7.2*

cǎa จ๋า prt. particle to show affection/familiarity *Unit 1.1*

càak จาก prep. from *Unit 1.2*

càak จาก v. to leave, depart, go away *Unit 7.2*

caam จาม v. to sneeze *Unit 8.2*

caan จาน n., clf. plate *Unit 3.1*

câaw เจ้า clf. for a selling enterprise as identified with the occupation of its owner *Unit 3.1*

càay จ่าย v. to spend, pay, disburse *Unit 3.2*

càay-ŋən จ่ายเงิน v. to pay *Unit 3.2*

cèp เจ็บ to hurt, to feel piercing pain, to feel sore (from wound, infection etc.) *Unit 8.1*
cee เจ n. vegetarian food *Unit 3.3*
cɛ̂ɛŋ แจ้ง v. to report, inform *Unit 9.1*
cɛ̂ɛŋ-khwaam แจ้งความ v. to report to police *Unit 9.1*
ciŋ จริง v. to be true, real *Unit 3.4*
ciŋ-cay จริงใจ v. to be sincere, heartfelt *Unit 7.2*
ciŋ-ciŋ จริง ๆ adv. really, very *Unit 6.1*
ciŋ-dûay จริงด้วย It's true. I agree. *Unit 3.4*
còp จบ v. to finish, end *Unit 2.4*
còt-mǎay จดหมาย n. letter *Unit 9.2*
còt-mǎay ráp-rɔɔŋ จดหมายรับรอง n. reference letter, recommendation letter *Unit 9.2*
cɔɔ-ra-khêe จระเข้ n. crocodile *Unit 9.1*
cɔɔŋ จอง v. to reserve, make a reservation *Unit 10.2*
cɔ̀ɔt จอด v. to stop, park (a car) *Unit 5.3*
cùt จุด n. spot, dot, point *Unit 6.1*
cɯŋ จึง conj. so, therefore, as a consequence *Unit 9.1*
cɯŋ-ca จึงจะ aux. so that, in order to *Unit 9.2*
cɯ̀ɯt จืด v. to be tasteless, to be bland *Unit 3.3*
cəə เจอ v. to meet *Unit 1.1*

ch

cha-bàp ฉบับ clf. for newspaper, book, document *Unit 3.1*
cha-lǐaŋ เฉลียง n. porch, terrace *Unit 5.4*
cha-nít ชนิด clf. kind, type *Unit 8.2*
cha-phɔ́ʔ เฉพาะ v. especially, exclusively *Unit 6.3*
cham-ráʔ ชำระ v. to pay (formal) *Unit 9.2*
chán ชั้น n. level; floor *Unit 5.2*
chán ชั้น n. shelf *Unit 5.4*
chán ชั้น n. layer *Unit 6.1*
chǎn, chán ฉัน pron. I *Unit 1.2*
chây ใช่ v. to be so, to be it; yes. *Unit 1.3*
cháy ใช้ v. to use, spend *Unit 2.4*
chaa ชา n. tea (leaves) *Unit 3.1*
chaa ชา v. to feel numb *Unit 8.1*
cháa ช้า v. to be slow *Unit 1.3*
chaam ชาม n., clf. bowl *Unit 3.1*
chaan chaa-laa ชานชาลา n. (railroad) station platform *Unit 10.2*
cháaŋ ช้าง n. elephant *Unit 2.1*
châat ชาติ n. nation *Unit 4.1*
chaaw ชาว n. (prefix) person *Unit 1.4*
chaaw-bâan ชาวบ้าน n. villager, commoner; the common folk *Unit 10.2*
chaaw-khǎw ชาวเขา n. hill tribe, member (s) *Unit 10.1*
cháaw เช้า n. morning (time) *Unit 4.2*
chaay ชาย n. edge, border, rim *Unit 5.1*
chaay-hàat ชายหาด n. beach *Unit 5.1*
chaay-tha-lee ชายทะเล n. seaside *Unit 7.1*
chék เช็ค v. to check (from English) *Unit 3.4*
chên เช่น conj. such as, for example *Unit 1.2*
chên-kan เช่นกัน adv. also, as well; too; likewise *Unit 4.1*
chɛm-phuu แชมพู n. shampoo *Unit 8.1*
chǐaŋ เฉียง v. to be aslant, diagonal *Unit 5.1*
chii-wít ชีวิต n. life *Unit 7.1*
chìi ฉี่ v. to urinate (especially to or of a child) *Unit 3.2*
chìit ฉีด v. to inject, inoculate *Unit 8.2*
chín ชิ้น clf. for "piece" of anything whole *Unit 3.1*
chom-phuu ชมพู n. pink *Unit 6.1*
chom-phûu ชมพู่ n. rose apple *Unit 6.3*
chon ชน v. to collide *Unit 9.1*
chɔ́p-pîŋ ช็อปปิ้ง n. shopping (from English) *Unit 7.1*
chɔ̂ŋ ช่อง n. hole, cavity *Unit 2.2*
chɔ̂ŋ ช่อง n. channel *Unit 7.1*
chɔ́ɔn ช้อน n. spoon *Unit 3.4*
chɔ́ɔn-klaaŋ ช้อนกลาง n. serving spoon *Unit 3.4*
chɔ̂ɔp ชอบ v. to like, be fond of *Unit 2.4*
chûa ชั่ว v. to be bad, evil *Unit 1.3*
chûa-mooŋ ชั่วโมง n. hour *Unit 4.3*
chuan ชวน v. to invite, persuade (to do something) *Unit 10.1*
chûay ช่วย v. to help, assist *Unit 3.3*

chûay-dûay ช่วยด้วย Help! *Unit 9.1*

chùk-chɔ̌ɔn ฉุกเฉิน v. to be of an emergency nature *Unit 9.1*

chum-num ชุมนุม v. to gather together, congregate *Unit 10.2*

chút ชุด clf. for a suit, dress (e.g. of clothing) *Unit 6.1*

chʉ́a เชื้อ n. germ, bacteria *Unit 8.2*

chʉ́a-sǎay เชื้อสาย n. lineage, descendants *Unit 1.4*

chʉ̂ʉ ชื่อ n. name, v. to be named *Unit 1.2*

chʉ̂ʉ-lên ชื่อเล่น n. nickname, v. to be nicknamed *Unit 1.2*

chʉ̂ʉ-sǐaŋ ชื่อเสียง n. fame, reputation *Unit 2.4*

chəən เชิญ Please do. Go ahead. *Unit 1.1*

chəən เชิญ v. to invite *Unit 4.1*

d

dam ดำ v. to be black, n. black *Unit 2.1*

daŋ ดัง v. to be loud *Unit 1.3*

dâay-máy ได้ไหม Could you? Could it? *Unit 1.3*

dâay tháŋ-nán ได้ทั้งนั้น Anything will do. Anything is acceptable. *Unit 7.1*

dâay-yin ได้ยิน v. to hear *Unit 1.3*

dâam ด้าม clf. for pens *Unit 3.1*

dâan ด้าน n., clf. side *Unit 5.4*

dâay, dây ได้ v. can, could *Unit 1.3*

dâay ได้ v. to get, obtain *Unit 2.3*

dèk เด็ก n. child, young person *Unit 2.1*

dɛɛŋ แดง n. red *Unit 5.2*

dɛ̀ɛt แดด n. sunlight *Unit 10.1*

di-chǎn, di-chán ดิฉัน pron. I (for female) *Unit 1.2*

diaw เดียว v. to be single, sole; to be alone *Unit 2.3*

dìaw เดี่ยว v. to be single, sole *Unit 6.1*

dǐaw-níi เดี๋ยวนี้ n. now, at present *Unit 9.2*

dii ดี v. to be good *Unit 1.1*

dii-kwàa ดีกว่า adv. to be better, better than *Unit 1.4*

din ดิน n. soil, land *Unit 10.1*

din fáa ʔaa-kàat ดินฟ้าอากาศ n. weather, climate *Unit 10.1*

din-sɔ̌ɔ ดินสอ n. pencil *Unit 1.3*

don-trii ดนตรี n. music *Unit 4.2*

doon โดน aux. used in making passive construction *Unit 8.1*

doon-cay โดนใจ v. to be pleased, to be satisfactory *Unit 7.2*

dooy-sǎan โดยสาร v. to travel by a vehicle (as a passenger) *Unit 5.3*

dɔ̀ɔk ดอก clf. for flowers *Unit 6.1*

dɔ̀ɔk-can ดอกจัน n. asterisk *Unit 7.2*

dùan ด่วน v. to be urgent, hasty *Unit 9.1*

duaŋ ดวง clf. for lights, seals, stamps, stains *Unit 9.2*

dûay ด้วย adv. also, too, prep. with, prt. request *Unit 3.4*

dûay-khon ด้วยคน adv. along, together with *Unit 7.1*

duu ดู v. to look *Unit 4.2*

duu naŋ-sʉ̌ʉ ดูหนังสือ v. to self study, to review *Unit 4.2*

dʉan เดือน n. month *Unit 2.2*

dʉ̀k ดึก n. late at night *Unit 4.2*

dʉ̀ʉm ดื่ม v. to drink *Unit 3.2*

dəən เดิน v. to walk *Unit 3.2*

dəən-khǎw เดินเขา v. to trek through the montains *Unit 10.1*

dəən-thaaŋ เดินทาง v. to travel *Unit 5.3*

f

fa-ràŋ ฝรั่ง n. Westerner (Caucasian) *Unit 1.4*

fa-ràŋ ฝรั่ง n. guava *Unit 3.3*

fan ฟัน n. teeth *Unit 8.1*

faŋ ฟัง v. to listen *Unit 1.3*

fàŋ ฝั่ง n. coast, shore *Unit 10.1*

fay ไฟ n. light *Unit 5.2*

fay mây ไฟไหม้ Fire! *Unit 9.1*

fay-dɛɛŋ ไฟแดง n. red light *Unit 5.2*

fay-fáa ไฟฟ้า n. electricity *Unit 5.2*

fáa ฟ้า n. sky blue (color) *Unit 6.1*
fáa ฟ้า n. sky *Unit 7.2*
fáa lɛ̂ɛp ฟ้าแลบ n., v. lightning *Unit 10.1*
fáa phàa ฟ้าผ่า n. thunderbolt, v. to be struck by lightning *Unit 10.1*
fáa rɔ́ɔŋ ฟ้าร้อง n. thunder *Unit 10.1*
fǎa ฝา n. wall, partition *Unit 5.4*
fǎa-fɛ̀ɛt ฝาแฝด n. twin *Unit 2.3*
fàak ฝาก v. to entrust, leave (something) (with someone) *Unit 7.2*
fàak khɔ̂ɔ-khwaam ฝากข้อความ v. to leave a message *Unit 7.2*
fàak ŋən ฝากเงิน v. to deposit money *Unit 9.2*
fàay ฝ่าย conj. as for, regarding *Unit 10.2*
fâay ฝ้าย n. cotton *Unit 6.2*
fɛɛn แฟน n. girlfriend, boyfriend (slang) *Unit 2.3*
fít ฟิต v. to be tight, tight-fitting *Unit 6.2*
fǒn ฝน n. rain *Unit 4.4*
fǒn tòk ฝนตก It's raining. It rains. *Unit 4.4*
fút ฟุต clf. the English foot (length) *Unit 2.1*
fʉ̀k ฝึก v. to practice, drill *Unit 4.3*
fʉ̌ʉn-cay ฝืนใจ v. to force oneself (to do something) against one's will *Unit 7.2*
fɔ̂ə เฟ้อ v. to be in excess *Unit 8.2*
fəə-ni-cə̂ə เฟอร์นิเจอร์ n. furniture *Unit 5.4*

h

hây ให้ prep. for *Unit 3.4*
hǎa หา v. to look for, search for *Unit 2.2*
hàak หาก conj. if, in case, provided that *Unit 7.2*
hâam ห้าม v. to forbid, prohibit, It's forbidden *Unit 5.4*
haaŋ หาง n. tail *Unit 2.1*
hàaŋ ห่าง v. to be far *Unit 5.1*
hàat หาด n. beach *Unit 5.1*
hǎay หาย v. to recover, to get well, to be healed *Unit 8.2*
hǎay-cay หายใจ v. to breath *Unit 8.2*
hǎay-pùay หายป่วย v. to recover, get well *Unit 8.2*
hěn เห็น v. to see *Unit 2.1*
hɛ̀ŋ แห่ง clf. for place, location *Unit 1.2*
hɛ̂ɛŋ แห้ง v. to be dry, dried *Unit 3.3*
hi-ma หิมะ n. snow *Unit 4.4*
hǐw หิว v. to be hungry *Unit 3.2*
hǐw khâaw หิวข้าว v. to be hungry *Unit 3.2*
hǒn หน clf. for counting event *Unit 1.3*
hòt หด v. to shrink *Unit 6.2*
hɔ̂ŋ ห้อง n., clf. room *Unit 1.3*
hɔ̂ŋ kèp-khɔ̌ɔŋ ห้องเก็บของ n. storage room, closet *Unit 5.4*
hɔ̂ŋ kin-khâaw ห้องกินข้าว n. dining room *Unit 5.4*
hɔ̂ŋ khrua ห้องครัว n. kitchen *Unit 5.4*
hɔ̂ŋ-lɔɔŋ ห้องลอง n. fitting room *Unit 6.2*
hɔ̂ŋ nâŋ-lên ห้องนั่งเล่น n. living room *Unit 5.4*
hɔ̂ŋ-náam ห้องน้ำ n. bathroom *Unit 3.2*
hɔ̂ŋ nɔɔn ห้องนอน n. bedroom *Unit 5.4*
hɔ̂ŋ ráp-khɛ̀ɛk ห้องรับแขก n. drawing room *Unit 5.4*
hɔ̂ŋ ráp-pra-thaan ʔaa-hǎan ห้องรับประทานอาหาร n. dining room *Unit 5.4*
hɔ̂ŋ-sa-mùt ห้องสมุด n. library *Unit 2.4*
hɔ̂ŋ sûam ห้องส้วม n. toilet *Unit 5.4*
hɔ̂ŋ tham-ŋaan ห้องทำงาน n. study room, office *Unit 5.4*
hɔ̌y หอย n. shellfish *Unit 3.3*
hɔ̀ɔ ห่อ v. to wrap, package *Unit 9.2*
hɔ̌ɔ-phák หอพัก n. dormitory *Unit 2.2*
hǔa หัว n. head *Unit 5.2*
hǔa láan หัวล้าน v. to be bald-headed *Unit 6.2*
hǔa mum หัวมุม n. corner *Unit 5.2*
hǔa-rɔ́ʔ หัวเราะ to laugh *Unit 8.1*
hǔu หู n. ear *Unit 2.1*

k

ka-phraw กะเพรา n. Thai holy basil *Unit 3.3*
kà-rú-naa, ka-ru-naa กรุณา v. to be so kind as to, please (do such and such) *Unit 6.1*
ka-thí กะทิ n. coconut milk *Unit 3.4*

ka-wii กวี n. poet *Unit 2.4*

kam-laŋ กำลัง aux. progressive *Unit 2.2*

kam-laŋ กำลัง n. power, energy, force *Unit 4.2*

kam-laŋ-ca กำลังจะ v. be about to, be on the point of, on the verge of *Unit 2.4*

kam-laŋ-dii กำลังดี v. to be just right (in size, amount, etc.) *Unit 6.2*

kan กัน pron. each other, one another, mutually, together *Unit 3.2*

kaŋ-keeŋ khǎa-sân กางเกงขาสั้น n. shorts, short pants *Unit 6.1*

kaŋ-keeŋ khǎa-yaaw กางเกงขายาว n. long pants, trousers *Unit 6.1*

kaŋ-keeŋ yiin กางเกงยีน n. jeans *Unit 6.1*

kàp-khâaw กับข้าว n. food that is eaten with rice *Unit 3.3*

kaw-lǎw เกาเหลา n. soup without noodles *Unit 3.3*

kàw เก่า v. to be old *Unit 5.1*

kâw-ʔîi เก้าอี้ n. chair *Unit 1.3*

kâw-ʔîi-yaaw เก้าอี้ยาว n. sofa *Unit 5.4*

kày ไก่ n. chicken *Unit 3.3*

kaa-fɛɛ กาแฟ n. coffee *Unit 3.1*

kaa-tuun การ์ตูน n. cartoon *Unit 7.1*

kaan- การ n. affairs of ..., matters of ...; prefix to form noun derivatives *Unit 2.4*

kaaŋ-keeŋ กางเกง n. pants, trousers *Unit 3.1*

kaan-kháa การค้า n. business, trade *Unit 5.1*

kaan-mʉaŋ การเมือง n. politics; political affairs *Unit 2.4*

kaay กาย n. body *Unit 4.2*

kèŋ เก่ง adv. proficiently, skillfully *Unit 1.3*

kèp เก็บ v. to keep, to store *Unit 5.4*

kés-háws เกสต์เฮาส์ n. guest house *Unit 5.3*

keem-choo เกมโชว์ n. game show *Unit 7.1*

kɛ̀ɛ แก่ v. to be dark (of color) *Unit 6.2*

kɛ̂ɛ แก้ v. to undo (an error), correct *Unit 6.2*

kɛ̂ɛ แก้ v. to remedy, relieve (an illness) Unit 8.2

kɛɛŋ แกง n. soup/curry dish *Unit 3.3*

kɛɛŋ-cʉ̀ʉt แกงจืด n. clear soup *Unit 3.3*

kɛɛŋ-phèt แกงเผ็ด n. spicy curry *Unit 3.3*

kɛ̂ɛw แก้ว n., clf. glass *Unit 3.1*

ki-loo-kram กิโลกรัม clf. kilogram *Unit 2.1*

kíaw เกี๊ยว n. wonton *Unit 3.3*

kìaw-kàp เกี่ยวกับ prep. about, regarding; concerning *Unit 2.4*

kìi กี่ q. how many *Unit 2.3*

kii-laa กีฬา n. sports *Unit 7.1*

kin กิน v. to eat, consume *Unit 3.2*

kin khâaw กินข้าว v. to eat (one's meal) *Unit 3.2*

kìt-ca-wát กิจวัตร n. routine *Unit 8.1*

klàp กลับ v. to go back *Unit 4.2*

klay ไกล v. to be far, distant *Unit 5.1*

klây ใกล้ v. to be near, close, nearby *Unit 2.1*

klâam กล้าม n. muscle *Unit 6.1*

klaaŋ กลาง n. middle, center *Unit 2.2*

klaaŋ กลาง n. medium *Unit 6.2*

klaaŋ-khʉʉn กลางคืน n. at night, in the night *Unit 4.1*

klaaŋ-wan กลางวัน n. in the daytime, by day *Unit 4.1*

klàaw thʉ̌ŋ กล่าวถึง v. to talk about *Unit 10.2*

klom กลม v. to be round *Unit 6.3*

klɔɔŋ กลอง n. drum *Unit 10.2*

klɔ̀ŋ กล่อง n., clf. box, carton *Unit 3.1*

klûay กล้วย n. banana *Unit 6.3*

klʉa เกลือ n. salt *Unit 3.3*

kôn ก้น n. the bottom (of anything) *Unit 3.3*

kòp กบ n. frog *Unit 2.1*

kòt กด v. to press on (something), push *Unit 7.2*

kòt-mǎay กฎหมาย n. law *Unit 2.4*

koon โกน v. to shave *Unit 8.1*

kɔ̀ɔn ก่อน adv. first (before doing something else) *Unit 1.1*

kɔ̀ɔn ก่อน conj. before *Unit 2.4*

kɔ̀ʔ เกาะ v. to cling to *Unit 6.1*

kɔ̀ʔ เกาะ n. island *Unit 10.1*

kɔ̂-dâay ก็ได้ prt. also will do *Unit 1.2*

kra-cùk-kra-cìk กะจุกกะจิก v. to be trifling, insignificant *Unit 7.1*

kra-daan กระดาน n. board *Unit 1.3*

kra-dàat กระดาษ n. paper *Unit 1.3*
kra-pɔ̌ŋ กระป๋อง n., clf. can *Unit 3.1*
kra-pǎw กระเป๋า n. pocket, bag *Unit 9.1*
kra-pǎw ʔèek-ka-sǎan กระเป๋าเอกสาร n. brief-case, portfolio *Unit 9.1*
kra-pǎw sa-taaŋ กระเป๋าสตางค์ v. purse, wallet *Unit 9.1*
kra-prooŋ chút กระโปรงชุด n. dress *Unit 6.1*
krà-prooŋ, kra-prooŋ กระโปรง n. skirt *Unit 6.1*
kra-thǎaŋ กระถาง n. earthen flower-pot *Unit 5.4*
krom-ma-thâa กรมท่า n. navy blue *Unit 6.1*
krɔ̀ɔk กรอก v. to fill, fill out, fill in *Unit 9.2*
krɔ̀ɔp กรอบ n. frame *Unit 6.3*
kuan กวน v. to trouble, bother, disturb *Unit 7.2*
kuan-cay กวนใจ v. to disturb, bother, agitate *Unit 7.2*
kǔay-tǐaw ก๋วยเตี๋ยว n. noodles *Unit 3.3*
kûŋ กุ้ง n. shrimp, prawn, lobster *Unit 3.3*
kùt กุด v. to cut off, to be truncated *Unit 6.1*
kɨ̀ap เกือบ aux. almost, nearly, about *Unit 2.3*
kəən เกิน v. to exceed, be in excess of *Unit 9.2*
kəən-pay เกินไป adv. excessively, too *Unit 6.1*
kə̀ət เกิด v. to be born *Unit 2.1*
kə̀ət เกิด v. to arise, occur, happen, take place *Unit 9.1*
kwàa กว่า adv. more (to a greater degree) *Unit 2.1*
kwâaŋ กว้าง v. to be broad, wide *Unit 8.2*

kh

kha-mooy ขโมย v. to steal, pilfer, n. thief *Unit 9.1*
kha-náʔ คณะ n. faculty, college, group, team *Unit 7.2*
kha-nàat ขนาด n. size *Unit 6.2*
kha-nǒm ขนม n. candy, dessert *Unit 1.3*
kha-nǒm-ciin ขนมจีน n. Thai rice noodles *Unit 3.3*
kha-nǔn ขนุน n. jackfruit *Unit 3.1*
khâa ฆ่า v. to kill, execute, destroy *Unit 8.2*
khâa châw ค่าเช่า n. the rental fee *Unit 2.2*
khâa dooy-sǎan ค่าโดยสาร n. fare *Unit 5.3*
khâa-râat-cha-kaan ข้าราชการ n. government official *Unit 2.4*
khâa rót ค่ารถ n. fare *Unit 5.3*
khâa tham-niam ค่าธรรมเนียม n. fee *Unit 10.2*
kháa ค้า v. to do business (in), trade (in), sell, engage in trade *Unit 5.1*
khǎa ขา n. leg (of the body, of a piece of furniture, of a journey) *Unit 6.1*
khǎa-klàp ขากลับ n. the return trip *Unit 10.1*
khǎa-pay ขาไป n. the trip going *Unit 10.1*
khâam ข้าม v. to cross *Unit 5.2*
khaaŋ คาง n. chin *Unit 8.1*
khâaŋ ข้าง n. side *Unit 5.2*
khâaŋ ข้าง prep. aside *Unit 5.4*
khâaŋ-bon, khâŋ-bon ข้างบน n. (location) upstairs *Unit 5.2*
khâaŋ-lâaŋ, khâŋ-lâaŋ ข้างล่าง n. (location) downstairs *Unit 5.2*
khâaŋ-lǎŋ, khâŋ-lǎŋ ข้างหลัง n. (location) in the back *Unit 5.2*
khâaŋ-nâa, khâŋ-nâa ข้างหน้า n. (location) in front *Unit 5.2*
khâaŋ-nɔ̂ɔk, khâŋ-nɔ̂ɔk ข้างนอก n. (location) outside *Unit 5.2*
khâaŋ-nay, khâŋ-nay ข้างใน n. (location) inside *Unit 5.2*
khâat คาด v. to belt, to strap *Unit 6.1*
khàaw ข่าว n. news *Unit 7.1*
khâaw ข้าว n. rice *Unit 3.2*
khâaw klɔ̂ŋ ข้าวกล้อง n. brown rice (unpolished rice) *Unit 3.3*
khâaw nǐaw ข้าวเหนียว n. sticky rice *Unit 3.3*
khâaw phàt ข้าวผัด n. fried rice *Unit 3.3*
khâaw plàaw ข้าวเปล่า n. plain (white) rice *Unit 3.3*
khâaw tôm ข้าวต้ม n. rice soup *Unit 3.3*
khǎaw ขาว v. to be white, fair (of complexion) *Unit 2.1*
khǎaw ขาว n. white (color) *Unit 6.1*
khǎay ขาย v. to sell *Unit 3.1*
khâm ค่ำ n. late evening *Unit 4.2*

khan คัน v. to itch, to be itchy *Unit 8.2*

khàp rót ขับรถ v. to drive *Unit 5.3*

kháp คับ v. to be tight, tight-fitting *Unit 6.2*

khaw-róp เคารพ v. to respect *Unit 4.1*

khàw เข่า n. knee *Unit 8.1*

khâw เข้า v. to enter *Unit 3.2*

khâw-cay เข้าใจ v. to understand *Unit 1.3*

khâw-hɔ̂ŋ-náam เข้าห้องน้ำ v. to use the rest-room *Unit 3.2*

khâw nɔɔn เข้านอน v. to retire, go to bed *Unit 4.2*

kháw เขา pron. he, she, they *Unit 1.2*

kháw-tɔ̂ɔ เคาน์เตอร์ n. counter (from English) *Unit 9.2*

khǎw เขา n. mountain, hill *Unit 10.1*

khày ไข่ n. egg *Unit 3.3*

khày-ciaw ไข่เจียว n. omelette *Unit 3.3*

khày-daaw ไข่ดาว n. fried egg *Unit 3.3*

khây ไข้ v. fever *Unit 8.2*

khây-wàt ไข้หวัด n. fever due to a common cold *Unit 8.2*

khem เค็ม v. to be salty *Unit 3.3*

khêm เข้ม v. to be dark (of color) *Unit 6.2*

khěm-khàt เข็มขัด n. belt *Unit 6.1*

khéek เค้ก n. cake *Unit 3.1*

khěŋ แข็ง v. to be hard, firm *Unit 3.3*

khèɛk แขก n. guest, visitor *Unit 5.4*

khěɛn แขน n. arm, sleeve *Unit 6.1*

khǐan เขียน v. to write, draw *Unit 1.3*

khîaw เขี้ยว n. fang, canine tooth, eyetooth *Unit 2.1*

khǐaw เขียว n. green *Unit 6.1*

khìi ขี่ v. to ride, to straddle *Unit 4.2*

khîi ขี้ v. to defecate, n. excrement *Unit 3.2*

khîi-rèe ขี้เหร่ v. to be ugly, unattractive *Unit 2.1*

khìit ขีด clf. 100 grams, n. line, v. to mark with line *Unit 3.1*

khít คิด v. to think, figure, calculate *Unit 2.1*

khít-raa-khaa คิดราคา v. to charge; appraise; value *Unit 3.1*

khít-thǔŋ คิดถึง v. to think of, to miss *Unit 2.3*

khít wâa คิดว่า v. to think that *Unit 2.1*

khíw คิ้ว n. eye-brow *Unit 8.1*

khlám คล้ำ v. to be dark (of complexion) *Unit 2.1*

khlɔ̂ŋ คล่อง v. to be fluent *Unit 7.1*

khlɔɔn คลอน v. to be shaky *Unit 10.2*

khlɔɔŋ คลอง n. canal *Unit 5.2*

khlûun คลื่น n. wave *Unit 7.1*

khlûun-sây คลื่นไส้ v. to be sick (in the stomach), to feel nauseated *Unit 8.2*

khon คน n., clf. person *Unit 1.4*

khon laʔ คนละ per person, a person *Unit 2.3*

khon-la คนละ n. mod. different, each different *Unit 5.4*

khón-khwáa ค้นคว้า v. to do research *Unit 2.4*

khǒn ขน n. hair (on body), fur *Unit 6.1*

khǒn-sòŋ ขนส่ง v. to transport *Unit 5.1*

khoŋ-ca คงจะ aux. most likely will, probably will *Unit 2.1*

khoom-fay โคมไฟ n. lamp, lighting fixture *Unit 5.4*

khóoŋ โค้ง v. to be curved *Unit 6.3*

khóp คบ v. to associate with, be friends with *Unit 7.2*

khóp-hǎa คบหา v. to associate with, be friends with *Unit 7.2*

khɔm-phiw-tɔ̂ɔ คอมพิวเตอร์ n. computer *Unit 2.4*

khɔ̌ŋ ของ prep. of, owned by, belonging to *Unit 2.2*

khɔɔ คอ n. neck *Unit 8.1*

khɔɔ-sɔ̌ɔ ค.ศ. n. Christian era *Unit 2.1*

khɔ̂ɔ-khwaam ข้อความ n. statement, message *Unit 7.2*

khɔ̂ɔ-sɔ̀ɔk ข้อศอก n. elbow *Unit 8.1*

khɔ̌ɔ ขอ v. to ask for, beg, request *Unit 3.3*

khɔ̌ɔ pay dûay khon ขอไปด้วยคน May I join in (going)? *Unit 7.1*

khɔ̌ɔ-thôot, khɔ̌-thôot ขอโทษ I apologize. I'm sorry. *Unit 1.1*

khɔ̌ɔŋ kra-cùk-kra-cìk ของกระจุกกระจิก n. odds and ends, knick-knacks *Unit 7.1*

khɔ̌ɔŋ-khwǎn ของขวัญ v. gift, present *Unit 9.2*

khɔ̌ɔŋ-wǎan ของหวาน n. dessert, sweetstuffs *Unit 3.4*

khɔ̀ɔp-cay ขอบใจ v. to thank (someone) *Unit 6.1*

khɔ̀ɔp-khun ขอบคุณ Thank you. *Unit 1.1*

khɔ̂ɔk คอก n. pen, sty (for animals); stable *Unit 10.2*

khɔ̂y-yaŋ-chûa ค่อยยังชั่ว v. to feel better, to get better *Unit 8.2*

khrân-nʉ́a khrân-tua ครั่นเนื้อครั่นตัว v. to feel feverish, to have a chill *Unit 8.2*

khráp ครับ prt. polite particle for men (neutral) *Unit 1.1*

khray ใคร pron. who *Unit 1.2*

khriim koon-nùat ครีมโกนหนวด n. shaving cream *Unit 8.1*

khrɔ̂ɔp-khrua ครอบครัว n. family *Unit 2.2*

khruu ครู n. teacher *Unit 2.4*

khrûu ครู่ n. moment *Unit 7.2*

khrʉ̂aŋ เครื่อง n., clf. for electronic appliances *Unit 3.1*

khrʉ̂aŋ-bɛ̀ɛp เครื่องแบบ n. uniform *Unit 6.1*

khrʉ̂aŋ-bin เครื่องบิน n. airplane (formal) *Unit 5.3*

khrʉ̂aŋ-cháy เครื่องใช้ n. utensils, appliances, equipment *Unit 3.4*

khrʉ̂aŋ-dʉ̀ʉm เครื่องดื่ม n. beverage, drink; refreshment *Unit 3.3*

khrʉ̂aŋ-fɛ̀k เครื่องแฟ็กซ์ n. fax (informal) *Unit 5.4*

khrʉ̂aŋ-mǎay เครื่องหมาย n. sign, mark, symbol, signal *Unit 7.2*

khrʉ̂aŋ pràp ʔaa-kàat เครื่องปรับอากาศ n. air-conditioner (formal) *Unit 5.4*

khrʉ̂aŋ-pruŋ เครื่องปรุง n. seasoning, condiment; ingredient *Unit 3.3*

khrʉ̂aŋ-rʉan เครื่องเรือน n. furniture *Unit 5.4*

khrʉ́m ครึ้ม v. to be cloudy, overcast, shady, gloomy *Unit 10.1*

khrʉ̂ŋ ครึ่ง n. half *Unit 3.1*

khuan-ca ควรจะ aux. ought to, should *Unit 6.3*

khùat ขวด n., clf. bottle, jar *Unit 3.1*

khúk-kîi คุกกี้ n. cookie *Unit 3.1*

khun คุณ pron. you *Unit 1.2*

khûu คู่ clf. for pairs (of anything), n. couples. *Unit 3.4*

khuy คุย v. to chat, talk, converse *Unit 2.3*

khʉ̂n ขึ้น v. to be upward *Unit 5.2*

khʉ̂n-yùu-kàp ขึ้นอยู่กับ v. to depend on *Unit 9.2*

khʉʉ คือ v. to be *Unit 2.1*

khʉʉn คืน n. night, night-time; nightfall, v. to return *Unit 4.1*

khəəy เคย aux. to be used to V, to have done V in the past *Unit 2.1*

khə̌əy เขย n. a male in-law *Unit 2.3*

khwǎn ขวัญ n. spirits, morale *Unit 7.1*

khwǎa ขวา n. right (direction) *Unit 2.1*

khwaam ความ n. "state of" or "quality of," prefixed to verbs to form abstract nouns *Unit 4.1*

khwɛ̌ɛn แขวน v. to hang, suspend *Unit 5.4*

l

lâ ล่ะ prt. particle of emphasis *Unit 7.1*

la-khɔɔn ละคร n. play, soap opera *Unit 7.1*

la-mút ละมุด n. sopadilla *Unit 6.3*

láan ล้าน n. million *Unit 2.2*

lǎan หลาน n. grandchild *Unit 2.3*

lǎan-chaay หลานชาย n. grandson *Unit 2.3*

lǎan-sǎaw หลานสาว n. granddaughter *Unit 2.3*

laaŋ-sàat ลางสาด n. lansa (fruit) *Unit 6.3*

lâaŋ ล่าง v. to be below *Unit 5.2*

laay ลาย n. design, pattern *Unit 6.1*

lǎay หลาย quant. many, several *Unit 6.2*

lam-yay ลำไย n. longan (fruit) *Unit 3.1*

lǎŋ-càak หลังจาก conj., prep. after, also shortened to หลัง /lǎŋ/ *Unit 4.2*

lǎy ไหล v. to flow *Unit 8.2*

lee-khǎa-nú-kaan เลขานุการ n. secretary *Unit 2.4*

lêek-thîi เลขที่ n. number *Unit 2.2*

leen เลน v. lane (from English) *Unit 9.1*

lèk เหล็ก n. iron (the metal) *Unit 6.3*

lék เล็ก v. to be small, little (in size) *Unit 3.3*

lêm เล่ม clf. for sharp-pointed objects (e.g. knives,needles); for candles, books *Unit 3.1*

lên เล่น v. to play *Unit 4.2*

lép เล็บ n. nail (of a finger) *Unit 8.1*

léʔ และ conj. and *Unit 1.2*

lɛ̂ɛk ŋən แลกเงิน v. to exchange money *Unit 9.2*

lɛ̂ɛk-plìan แลกเปลี่ยน v. to exchange *Unit 1.2*

lɛ́ɛŋ แล้ง v. to be dry (as of the season), lacking rain, arid *Unit 4.4*

lɛ̀p แล็บ n. lab (from English) *Unit 4.3*

lɛ̂p แลบ v. to flash (as lightning) *Unit 10.1*

lìam เหลี่ยม n. angle, v. to be angular *Unit 6.3*

líaŋ เลี้ยง v. to treat (i.e. provide a treat for) *Unit 3.4*

líaŋ เลี้ยง v. to raise, breed *Unit 10.2*

líaw เลี้ยว v. to turn (and proceed in another direction); to veer *Unit 5.2*

lín-chák ลิ้นชัก n. a chest of drawers, a dresser Unit 5.4

lín-cìi ลิ้นจี่ n. lychee *Unit 6.3*

lom ลม n. wind *Unit 10.1*

loŋ ลง v. to release, drop, v. dir. down *Unit 4.1*

lót ลด v. to lower, reduce, decrease, discount *Unit 3.1*

lót-raa-khaa ลดราคา v. to reduce the price, to give a discount; to have a sale *Unit 3.1*

lɔ́ɔ ล้อ n. wheel *Unit 5.3*

lɔ̀ɔ หล่อ v. to be handsome (of males only) *Unit 2.1*

lɔ́ɔm ล้อม v. to surround, encircle *Unit 10.2*

lɔɔŋ ลอง v. to try, try out, try on *Unit 3.4*

lɔɔŋ-duu ลอง_ดู v. to try, try out, try and see (what something is like). *Unit 3.4*

lɔɔŋ-dii ลองดี v. to test, challenge, to put to the test *Unit 3.4*

lɔɔŋ-kɔɔŋ ลองกอง n. longkong (fruit) *Unit 6.3*

lûak ลวก v. to scald, to blanch (vegetables), to parboil *Unit 3.3*

lǔam หลวม v. to be loose (of clothing) *Unit 6.2*

lúaŋ ล้วง v. to reach into (e.g. a pocket, deep drawer, hole) *Unit 9.1*

lúaŋ kra-pǎw ล้วงกระเป๋า v. to pick a pocket, to put one's hand in a pocket or bag *Unit 9.1*

lúk ลุก v. to get up, to get to one's feet *Unit 10.2*

luŋ ลุง n. elder uncle (older brother of father or mother) *Unit 2.3*

lûuk ลูก n. offspring, child *Unit 2.3*

lûuk ลูก clf. for round and small objects such as fruits, balls *Unit 3.1*

lûuk-chaay ลูกชาย n. son *Unit 2.3*

lûuk-chín ลูกชิ้น n. meatball *Unit 3.3*

lûuk-hèp ลูกเห็บ n. hail *Unit 10.1*

lûuk-khon-diaw ลูกคนเดียว n. only child *Unit 2.3*

lûuk-khon-sùt-thɔ́ɔŋ ลูกคนสุดท้อง n. last-born, youngest child *Unit 2.3*

lûuk-phîi lûuk-nɔ́ɔŋ ลูกพี่ลูกน้อง n. cousin *Unit 2.3*

lûuk ra-bə̀ət ลูกระเบิด n. bomb *Unit 6.3*

lûuk-sǎaw ลูกสาว n. daughter *Unit 2.3*

lûup ลูบ v. to stroke, pat, pet *Unit 8.1*

lɨ̂ak เลือก v. to choose, elect, select *Unit 6.3*

lɨ̌aŋ เหลือง n. yellow *Unit 6.1*

lɨ̂at เลือด n. blood *Unit 3.3*

lɨ́k-láp ลึกลับ v. to be mysterious *Unit 7.1*

lɨɨm ลืม v. to forget *Unit 9.1*

lə̂ək เลิก v. to quit, finish; be over; to end; to discontinue; to give up; to break up *Unit 7.2*

lə̂ək-raa เลิกรา v. to break up, to separate, to end *Unit 7.2*

ləəy เลย adv. really, indeed *Unit 3.4*

ləəy เลย v. to go beyond, to pass *Unit 5.2*

m

ma-fɨaŋ มะเฟือง n. star fruit *Unit 6.3*

ma-hǎa-wít-tha-yaa-lay มหาวิทยาลัย n. university *Unit 1.2*

ma-la-kɔɔ มะละกอ n. papaya *Unit 6.3*

ma-mûaŋ มะม่วง n. mango *Unit 6.3*

ma-naaw มะนาว n. lime/lemon *Unit 3.3*

ma-phráaw มะพร้าว n. coconut *Unit 6.3*
ma-rʉʉn มะรืน n. day after tomorrow *Unit 4.3*
maa มา v. to come *Unit 1.2*
maa-càak มาจาก v. to come from *Unit 1.2*
máa ม้า n. bench *Unit 5.4*
man มัน pron. it, they, them *Unit 2.1*
man มัน v. to be oily, to be rich in flavor *Unit 3.3*
maŋ-khút มังคุด n. mangosteen *Unit 6.3*
maŋ-sa-wí-rát มังสวิรัติ n. vegetarian food *Unit 3.3*
mǎw เหมา v. to take the whole lot *Unit 9.2*
may-khroo-wéep ไมโครเวฟ n. microwave *Unit 5.4*
mây ไม่ neg. no, not *Unit 1.1*
mây ไหม้ v. to be burned, charred *Unit 9.1*
mây-baw ไม่เบา adv. very, extremely *Unit 2.1*
mây-chây ไม่ใช่ No, it's not! No! *Unit 1.3*
mây-khɔ̂y ไม่ค่อย adv. scarcely, hardly, not quite, not very *Unit 1.4*
mây-pen-ray ไม่เป็นไร That's alright. It doesn't matter. *Unit 1.1*
mây-thâw-rày ไม่___เท่าไหร่ neg. not very, not too much, many *Unit 2.4*
mǎy, máy ไหม prt. yes/no question particle *Unit 1.3*
mǎy ไหม n. silk *Unit 6.2*
mǎy khàt-fan ไหมขัดฟัน n. dental floss *Unit 8.1*
mee-nuu เมนู n. menu (from English) *Unit 3.3*
mêek เมฆ n. cloud *Unit 10.1*
mét เม็ด n., clf. seed, kernel, grain *Unit 6.3*
mɛ̂ɛ แม่ n. mother *Unit 2.3*
mɛ̂ɛ-bâan แม่บ้าน n. housekeeper, housewife *Unit 2.4*
mɛ̂ɛ-kháa แม่ค้า n. female street vendor *Unit 2.4*
mɛ̂ɛ-náam แม่น้ำ n. river *Unit 5.2*
mɛ̂ɛ-yaay แม่ยาย n. mother-in-law, wife's mother *Unit 2.3*
mɛ́ɛ แม้ conj. even though, even if *Unit 7.2*
mɛ̌ɛ แหม excl. Say! Well! Oh my goodness! *Unit 2.3*
mɛ́k-kaa-siin แมกกาซีน n. magazine *Unit 7.1*
mia เมีย n. wife *Unit 2.3*
mii มี v. to have, possess, v. there is, there are *Unit 2.1, 5.4*
mii chʉ̂ʉ-sǐaŋ มีชื่อเสียง v. to be well-known, famous, famed *Unit 2.4*
mii thú-rá มีธุระ v. to be busy, occupied *Unit 3.2*
mìi หมี่ n. a type of thin rice noodles *Unit 3.3*
mîit มีด n. knife *Unit 3.4*
mooŋ โมง clf. o'clock *Unit 4.1*
mooŋ cháaw โมงเช้า 7:00 a.m., seven o'clock in the morning *Unit 4.1*
mòt หมด v. to be used up, exhausted (in supply) *Unit 8.2*
mɔɔ-ra-sǔm มรสุม n. monsoon *Unit 10.1*
mɔɔ-tɔɔ-say มอเตอร์ไซค์ n. motorcycle *Unit 5.3*
mɔ̌ɔ หมอ n. doctor *Unit 2.4*
mɔ̀ɔk หมอก n. fog, mist *Unit 10.1*
mùak หมวก n. hat, cap *Unit 6.1*
mûaŋ ม่วง n. purple *Unit 6.1*
mum มุม n. corner *Unit 5.2*
mǔn หมุน v. to turn, rotate, spin *Unit 7.2*
mǔn thoo-ra-sàp หมุนโทรศัพท์ v. to dial a number *Unit 7.2*
múŋ มุ้ง n. mosquito net *Unit 5.4*
mùu-bâan หมู่บ้าน n. village *Unit 10.1*
mǔu หมู n. pig, pork *Unit 2.1*
mǔu-dɛɛŋ หมูแดง n. Chinese-style barbecued pork *Unit 3.3*
mʉ̂a เมื่อ conj. when *Unit 4.1*
mʉ̂a-ray เมื่อไร adv., q. When? At what time? *Unit 2.1*
mʉ̂a-waan เมื่อวาน n. yesterday *Unit 4.3*
mʉ̂a-waan-sʉʉn เมื่อวานซืน n. day before yesterday *Unit 4.3*
mʉ̌an-kan เหมือนกัน conj. likewise *Unit 1.2*
mʉaŋ-lǔaŋ เมืองหลวง n. capital (of a country or state) *Unit 5.1*
mʉ̂ay เมื่อย v. to be tired, stiff (of muscles) *Unit 3.2*
mʉʉ มือ n. hand *Unit 1.2*
mʉʉ-thʉ̌ʉ มือถือ n. cellular phone *Unit 2.2*

mʉ̀ʉn **หมื่น** n. ten thousand *Unit 2.2*

mʉ̂ʉt **มืด** v. to be dark (of hue) *Unit 6.2*

n

ná **นะ** prt. end of a statement, used to make an utterance gentler *Unit 1.1*

naa-li-kaa **นาฬิกา** n. clock, watch, timepiece *Unit 1.3*

naa-thii **นาที** n. minute (of time) *Unit 4.1*

naa-yók **นายก** n. prime official, chairman *Unit 2.4*

naa-yók rát-tha-mon-trii **นายกรัฐมนตรี** n. prime minister; premier *Unit 2.4*

nâa **หน้า** n. next; fore, front *Unit 4.3*

nâa **หน้า** n. season, prep. ahead, in front *Unit 4.4*

nâa **น่า** v. prefix. placed before verbs to make new verb derivatives *Unit 7.1*

nâa-ca **น่าจะ** aux. ought to, might like to *Unit 7.1*

nâa-klìat **น่าเกลียด** v. to be ugly, unsightly *Unit 2.1*

nâa-phàak **หน้าผาก** n. forehead *Unit 8.1*

nâa-rák **น่ารัก** v. to be lovable, lovely, cute *Unit 2.1*

nâa-sǒn-cay **น่าสนใจ** v. to be interesting *Unit 7.1*

nâa-taa **หน้าตา** n. look, appearance *Unit 2.1*

nâa-tàaŋ **หน้าต่าง** n. window *Unit 2.2*

náa **น้า** n. younger maternal uncle or aunt *Unit 2.3*

nǎa **หนา** v. to be thick *Unit 6.2*

naam-sa-kun **นามสกุล** n. family name, v. to be surnamed *Unit 1.2*

náam ʔàt-lom **น้ำอัดลม** n. carbonated beverage *Unit 3.3*

náam phǒn-la-máay **น้ำผลไม้** n. juice *Unit 3.3*

náam thûam **น้ำท่วม** n. flood; floodwaters *Unit 9.1*

naan **นาน** adv. a long time *Unit 5.3*

naaŋ-bὲɛp **นางแบบ** n. a female model *Unit 2.1*

nǎaw **หนาว** v. to be cold (of the weather, of personal sensation) *Unit 3.2*

nák **นัก** n. prefix. a person who- *Unit 2.1*

nák-sʉ̀k-sǎa **นักศึกษา** n. student (used for university or college student) *Unit 1.2*

nàk **หนัก** v. to be heavy *Unit 2.1*

nám-khěŋ **น้ำแข็ง** n. ice *Unit 3.3*

nám-mûuk **น้ำมูก** n. nasal mucus, nasal discharge *Unit 8.2*

nám-nàk **น้ำหนัก** n. weight *Unit 9.2*

nám-ŋən **น้ำเงิน** n. dark blue *Unit 6.1*

nám-plaa **น้ำปลา** n. fish sauce *Unit 3.3*

nám-sôm sǎay-chuu **น้ำส้ม (สายชู)** n. vinegar *Unit 3.3*

nám-taan **น้ำตาล** n. sugar *Unit 3.3*

nám-taan **น้ำตาล** n. brown *Unit 6.1*

nám-tòk **น้ำตก** waterfall *Unit 7.1*

nám-yaa **น้ำยา** n. chemical solution (non-technical term) *Unit 8.1*

nám-yaa bûan-pàak **น้ำยาบ้วนปาก** n. mouthwash *Unit 8.1*

nân **นั่น** n. that one *Unit 4.4*

nân-ŋay **นั่นไง** There it is. *Unit 9.2*

nâŋ **นั่ง** v. to sit *Unit 3.2*

nǎŋ **หนัง** n. movie *Unit 4.2*

nǎŋ **หนัง** n. leather *Unit 6.2*

nǎŋ-sʉ̌ʉ, naŋ-sʉ̌ʉ **หนังสือ** n. book *Unit 1.2*

nát **นัด** v. to make an appointment, set a date, set the time, n. appointment, date *Unit 4.2*

nay **ใน** prep. in *Unit 1.2*

nǎy **ไหน** q. Where? *Unit 1.1*

nék-thay **เนคไท** n. necktie *Unit 6.1*

nèp **เหน็บ** n. numbness *Unit 8.2*

nɛ́ʔ-nam **แนะนำ** v. to introduce *Unit 1.2*

nɛɛw **แนว** n. line, row *Unit 6.3*

nɛɛw nɔɔn **แนวนอน** v. to be horizontal *Unit 6.3*

nɛɛw tâŋ **แนวตั้ง** v. to be vertical *Unit 6.3*

ní-yaay **นิยาย** n. novel, fiction *Unit 7.1*

ní-yom **นิยม** v. to like, to admire, to be popular *Unit 10.1*

nǐaw **เหนียว** v. to be sticky, viscous *Unit 3.3*

nîi **นี่** Here it is. Here you are. *Unit 1.1*

nîi-khʉʉ **นี่คือ** This is___. *Unit 2.1*

nǐi **หนี** v. to flee, escape *Unit 9.1*

nít-nɔ̀y **นิดหน่อย** adv. little, tiny, small *Unit 1.4*

nít-ta-yá-sǎan **นิตยสาร** n. magazine *Unit 7.1*

níw **นิ้ว** clf. inch *Unit 2.1*

níw **นิ้ว** n. finger *Unit 8.1*

nók **นก** n. bird *Unit 2.3*

nóon **โน้น** d.a. over there *Unit 6.2*

nɔ̂ɔk **นอก** v. to be outside *Unit 5.2*

nɔ̂ɔk-chaan **นอกชาน** n. porch, terrace *Unit 5.4*

nɔɔn **นอน** v. to lie, recline *Unit 3.2*

nɔ́ɔŋ **น้อง** n. younger sibling, i.e. younger brother or sister *Unit 2.1*

nɔ́ɔŋ-khɤ̌ɤy **น้องเขย** n. brother-in-law who is the husband of one's younger sister *Unit 2.3*

nɔɔnɔ́ɔŋ-sǎaw **น้องสาว** n. younger sister *Unit 2.3*

nɔ́ɔy **น้อย** v. to be little, less, small, slight (in quantity) *Unit 3.4*

nɔ́ɔy-nàa **น้อยหน่า** n. custard apple *Unit 6.3*

nùat **หนวด** moustache *Unit 8.1*

nûŋ **นุ่ง** v. to dress, put on, wear (lower garment) *Unit 6.1*

nùm **หนุ่ม** n. young man; adolescent boy; guy *Unit 2.1*

nǔu **หนู** 1. pron. I, 2. n. mouse *Unit 3.4*

nʉ́a **เนื้อ** n. meat, flesh *Unit 3.3*

nʉ̌a **เหนือ** n. the north, northern *Unit 2.2*

nʉ̌a **เหนือ** n. prep. above, over *Unit 5.4*

nʉ̀ay **เหนื่อย** v. to be tired, fatigued *Unit 3.2*

nʉ̂ŋ **นึ่ง** v. to steam *Unit 3.3*

ŋ

ŋaa **งา** n. tusk, ivory *Unit 2.1*

ŋaam **งาม** v. to be beautiful *Unit 6.1*

ŋaan **งาน** n. work, task, job *Unit 2.4*

ŋaan ʔà-di-rèek **งานอดิเรก** n. hobby *Unit 7.1*

ŋán **งั้น** shortened from **ถ้ายังงั้น** /thâa yaŋ-ŋán/ if so, in that case. *Unit 4.1*

ŋay **ไง** prt. used to show that the speaker thinks that the statement is self-evident *Unit 9.2*

ŋɔ́ʔ **เงาะ** n. rambutan *Unit 6.3*

ŋuaŋ **งวง** n. trunk (of elephant) *Unit 2.1*

ŋûaŋ-nɔɔn **ง่วงนอน** v. to be sleepy, drowsy *Unit 3.2*

ŋuu **งู** n. snake *Unit 5.1*

ŋən **เงิน** n. money *Unit 2.4*

ŋən-dʉan **เงินเดือน** n. salary, monthly salary *Unit 2.4*

ŋən-sòt **เงินสด** n. cash *Unit 3.4*

ŋən-thɔɔn **เงินทอน** n. change (money returned) *Unit 3.1*

p

pà **ปะ** v. to meet, encounter *Unit 8.1*

pa-rin-yaa **ปริญญา** n. academic degree, diploma *Unit 2.4*

pa-rin-yaa-trii **ปริญญาตรี** n. bachelor's degree *Unit 2.4*

pa-tì-chii-wa-ná **ปฏิชีวนะ** n. antibiotic *Unit 8.2*

pàa **ป่า** n. forest, woods *Unit 10.1*

pàak **ปาก** n. mouth, beak, lips *Unit 5.4*

pàak-kaa, pàk-kaa **ปากกา** n. pen *Unit 1.3*

pâay **ป้าย** n. sign, placard *Unit 5.1*

pâay-rót-mee **ป้ายรถเมล์** n. bus stop *Unit 5.1*

pân **ปั้น** v. to mold (e.g. things of clay, plaster, etc.) *Unit 10.1*

pay **ไป** v. to go *Unit 1.1*

pay klàp **ไปกลับ** n. round trip *Unit 10.2*

pay thîaw **ไปเที่ยว** v. to go around (here and there for pleasure); to go out (as for an evening) *Unit 4.2*

pay-nǎy **ไปไหน** Where are you going? *Unit 1.1*

pay-nǎy-maa **ไปไหนมา** Where have you been? *Unit 1.1*

pen **เป็น** v. to be able to, know how to *Unit 7.1*

pen-lom **เป็นลม** v. to swoon, faint *Unit 8.2*

pèt **เป็ด** n. duck (animal and meat) *Unit 3.3*

pɛ̂ɛŋ **แป้ง** n. powder, flour *Unit 8.1*

pii **ปี** n. year *Unit 1.2*

pîŋ **ปิ้ง** v. to grill, to broil *Unit 3.3*

pìt **ปิด** v. to close *Unit 4.1*

pìt **ปิด** v. to cover, to cover up *Unit 8.1*

plaa ปลา n. fish *Unit 1.2*

plaa mʉ̀k ปลาหมึก n. squid, cuttlefish *Unit 3.3*

plàaw เปล่า v. to be bare, empty, blank *Unit 3.3*

plaay ปลาย n. end (of anything); tip *Unit 4.4*

plɛɛ แปล v. to translate, interpret *Unit 2.4*

plɛ̀ɛk แปลก v. to be strange, unusual *Unit 7.2*

plɛ̀ɛk-cay แปลกใจ to be surprised, amazed *Unit 7.2*

plìan เปลี่ยน v. to change, vary *Unit 6.1*

plôn ปล้น v. to commit a robbery *Unit 9.1*

plɔ̀ɔt ปลอด v. to be free from, lacking in, empty of *Unit 10.1*

plɔ̀ɔt-phay ปลอดภัย v. to be safe, out of danger *Unit 10.1*

plʉ̀ak เปลือก n. peel, skin, rind (of fruit), shell (of egg, nut) *Unit 6.3*

póʔ-tɛ̀ɛk โป๊ะแตก n. assorted seafood *Unit 3.4*

pòk-ka-tì, pà-ka-tì ปกติ v. to be normal, routine, usual *Unit 3.4*

póos-káat โปสการ์ด n. postcard, card *Unit 9.2*

pɔ̀ɔk ปอก v. to peel *Unit 6.3*

pɔɔn ปอนด์ clf. pound (weight) *Unit 2.1*

pə̀ət เปิด v. to open; to be open, opened *Unit 4.1*

pra-cam ประจำ v. constantly, regularly, habitually *Unit 6.1*

pra-cam wan ประจำวัน daily; everyday, routine *Unit 6.1*

pra-chum ประชุม v. to meet (in a group), assemble; to hold a meeting *Unit 10.2*

pra-dǐaw ประเดี๋ยว adv. for a moment, in a moment *Unit 7.2*

pra-kàat ประกาศ v. to announce *Unit 9.1*

pra-maan ประมาณ prep. about; approximately *Unit 4.2*

pra-thêet ประเทศ n. country, nation *Unit 1.4*

pra-tuu ประตู n. door *Unit 2.2*

pra-yàt ประหยัด v. to economize, to save, to be thrifty *Unit 7.2*

pray-sa-nii ไปรษณีย์ n. post office *Unit 9.2*

pray-sa-nii dùan ไปรษณีย์ด่วน n. express mail *Unit 9.2*

pray-sa-nii loŋ tha-bian ไปรษณีย์ลงทะเบียน n. registered mail *Unit 9.2*

pray-sa-nii ráp pra-kan ไปรษณีย์รับประกัน n. certified mail *Unit 9.2*

prɛɛŋ แปรง v. to brush *Unit 8.1*

prɛɛŋ-fan แปรงฟัน v. to brush one's teeth *Unit 8.1*

prɛɛŋ-sǐi-fan แปรงสีฟัน n. toothbrush *Unit 8.1*

proo-krɛm โปรแกรม n. program *Unit 4.4*

pròot โปรด v. please (do such and such) *Unit 6.1*

pruŋ ปรุง v. to season, flavor *Unit 3.3*

prʉ̀k-sǎa ปรึกษา v. to consult with *Unit 1.3*

pùat ปวด v. to ache, to be in (aching) pain *Unit 8.1*

pùay ป่วย v. to be sick, ill, unwell *Unit 8.2*

puu ปู n. crab *Unit 3.3*

pùu ปู่ n. paternal grandfather, father's father *Unit 2.3*

ph

pha-con ผจญ v. to encounter, meet, face, fight *Unit 7.1*

pha-con phay ผจญภัย v. to encounter danger, face danger *Unit 7.1*

pha-nák-ŋaan พนักงาน n. officer, person in charge *Unit 2.4*

pha-nǎŋ ผนัง n. wall *Unit 5.4*

pha-ya-baan พยาบาล n. nurse *Unit 2.4*

phaa พา v. to take along, bring along *Unit 4.3*

phaa-sǎa, pha-sǎa ภาษา n. language *Unit 1.3*

phaa-yúʔ พายุ n. storm *Unit 10.1*

phàa ผ่า v. to split, cut, hew *Unit 10.1*

phâa ผ้า n. cloth *Unit 4.2*

phâa-bay ผ้าใบ n. canvas, sailcloth *Unit 6.1*

phâa yʉ̂ut ผ้ายืด n. stretchable fabric *Unit 6.2*

phâak ภาค n. region (an administrative unit) *Unit 2.2*

phâak kaan-sʉ̀k-sǎa ภาคการศึกษา n. term, semester (of school) *Unit 4.3*

phàan ผ่าน v. to pass through *Unit 5.2*

phák พัก v. to rest, stay over (as at someone's home, at a hotel) *Unit 2.2*

phák-phɔ̀n **พักผ่อน** v. to rest, take a rest *Unit 5.4*
phàk **ผัก** n. vegetable *Unit 3.3*
phàk-chii **ผักชี** n. coriander *Unit 3.4*
phan-ra-yaa, phan-yaa **ภรรยา** n. wife *Unit 2.3*
phàp **ผับ** n. pub; bar; tavern (from British English) *Unit 7.1*
phát **พัด** v. (the wind) to blow *Unit 10.1*
phát-lom **พัดลม** n. electric fan *Unit 5.4*
phát-sa-dù? **พัสดุ** n. package, parcel *Unit 9.2*
phàt **ผัด** n. stir fried dishes *Unit 3.3*
phay **ภัย** n. danger, peril *Unit 7.1*
phây **ไพ่** n. playing cards *Unit 7.1*
phee-daan **เพดาน** n. ceiling *Unit 5.4*
phèt **เผ็ด** v. to be spicy; to be peppery *Unit 3.3*
phɛ́ɛ **แพ้** v. to be allergic to *Unit 8.2*
phɛ́ɛ ʔaa-kàat **แพ้อากาศ** v. to have hay fever *Unit 8.2*
phɛ̌ɛn-thîi **แผนที่** n. map *Unit 1.3*
phɛɛŋ **แพง** v. to be expensive, high in price *Unit 2.2*
phɛ̀n **แผ่น** clf. for thin, flat objects *Unit 3.1*
phí-sèet **พิเศษ** v. to be special, extra *Unit 3.4*
phîi **พี่** n. older sibling, i.e. older brother or sister *Unit 2.3*
phîi-chaay **พี่ชาย** n. older brother *Unit 2.3*
phîi-nɔ́ɔŋ **พี่น้อง** n. brothers, sisters, brother and sister, brothers and sisters; cousins *Unit 2.3*
phîi-sǎaw **พี่สาว** n. older sister *Unit 2.3*
phǐi **ผี** n. ghost, spirit *Unit 7.1*
phǐw **ผิว** n. complexion *Unit 2.1*
phláas-tə̂ə **พลาสเตอร์** n. adhesive bandage *Unit 8.1*
phlɛ̌ɛ **แผล** n. wound, cut *Unit 8.1*
phǒm **ผม** pron. I (polite first person pronoun for male) *Unit 1.2*
phǒm **ผม** n. hair *Unit 7.1*
phǒn-la-máay **ผลไม้** n. fruit *Unit 3.3*
phǒŋ chuu rót **ผงชูรส** n. monosodium glutamate *Unit 3.3*
phòt **ผด** n. prickly heat, heat rash *Unit 8.2*
phɔɔ **พอ** v. to be enough, sufficient *Unit 2.4*
phɔɔ-dii **พอดี** v. to be just right (in size, amount, etc.) *Unit 6.2*
phɔɔ-sɔ̌ɔ **พ.ศ.** n. Buddhist Era *Unit 2.1*
phɔ̂ɔ **พ่อ** n. father *Unit 2.3*
phɔ̂ɔ-kháa **พ่อค้า** n. merchant, male street vendor *Unit 2.4*
phɔ̂ɔ-líaŋ **พ่อเลี้ยง** n. stepfather; foster father *Unit 2.3*
phɔ̂ɔ-taa **พ่อตา** n. (man's) father-in-law *Unit 2.3*
phɔ̌ɔm **ผอม** v. to be thin (not fat), lean *Unit 2.1*
phə̂əm **เพิ่ม** v. to add, increase, augment *Unit 9.2*
phə̂ŋ **เพิ่ง** adv. just, just now *Unit 9.1*
phrá **พระ** 1. n. lord, god, 2. n. priest, 3. n. Buddha image *Unit 4.1*
phrík **พริก** n. chili pepper *Unit 3.3*
phrík-thay **พริกไทย** n. pepper *Unit 3.3*
phrom **พรม** n. carpet, rug *Unit 5.4*
phrɔ́? **เพราะ** conj. because *Unit 5.3*
phrɔ́ɔm **พร้อม** v. to be ready, set, completed, conj. along with, to accompany (to be in company with) *Unit 10.1*
phrûŋ-níi **พรุ่งนี้** tomorrow *Unit 4.3*
phǔa **ผัว** n. husband *Unit 2.3*
phûak **พวก** n. group, party *Unit 8.2*
phuu-khǎw **ภูเขา** n. mountain *Unit 7.1*
phûu dooy-sǎan **ผู้โดยสาร** n. passenger *Unit 5.3*
phûu-yày bâan **ผู้ใหญ่บ้าน** n. elected head of a village, headman *Unit 10.2*
phùuk **ผูก** v. tie, bind, fasten *Unit 6.1*
phûut **พูด** v. to speak, say *Unit 1.3*
phûut sǎay **พูดสาย** v. to telephone, to speak (with) *Unit 7.2*
phɨ̂a **เพื่อ** prep. for (the sake of) *Unit 4.1*
phɨ̂a ca-dâay **เพื่อจะได้** conj. in order to, in order that *Unit 7.1*
phɨ̂an-bâan **เพื่อนบ้าน** n. neighbor *Unit 1.4*
phɨ̂ŋ **พึ่ง** v. to depend on (for help) *Unit 10.1*
phɨ̀ɨn **ผื่น** n. rash *Unit 8.2*
phɨ́ɨn **พื้น** n. floor *Unit 5.4*

r

ra-biaŋ ระเบียง n. lanai, balcony *Unit 5.4*

ra-bə̀ət ระเบิด v. to explode, burst, blast *Unit 6.3*

ra-hàt รหัส n. code *Unit 7.2*

ra-wàaŋ ระหว่าง prep. between, among *Unit 5.4*

ra-waŋ ระวัง Watch out! Be careful! *Unit 9.1*

raa-khaa ราคา n. price *Unit 3.1*

raa-khaa mǎw ราคาเหมา n. flat rate, all inclusive price *Unit 9.2*

ráan ร้าน n. store, shop *Unit 2.4*

ráan ʔaa-hǎan ร้านอาหาร n. restaurant *Unit 5.1*

ráan khǎay-nǎŋ-sʉ̌ʉ ร้านขายหนังสือ n. bookstore *Unit 5.1*

raaŋ-wan รางวัล n. prize, reward, award *Unit 9.1*

râat-cha-kaan ราชการ n. government service *Unit 4.1*

raaw-raaw ราว ๆ adv. around, about; approximately *Unit 2.1*

raay-kaan รายการ n. list, list of items *Unit 7.1*

ráay ร้าย v. to be fierce, cruel, wicked, bad *Unit 4.4*

rák รัก v. to love *Unit 7.1*

rák-sǎa รักษา v. to treat (illness), cure; remedy; heal *Unit 8.2*

ram รำ v. to dance (with hand, in Thai fashion) *Unit 4.2*

ráp รับ v. to receive, accept, take on *Unit 3.1*

ráp รับ v. to pick up *Unit 5.3*

ráp sǎay รับสาย v. to answer the phone, pick up the phone *Unit 7.2*

ráp thoo-ra-sàp รับโทรศัพท์ v. to answer the phone, pick up the phone *Unit 7.2*

ráp-cháy รับใช้ v. to serve, be in service of *Unit 10.1*

ráp-pra-thaan รับประทาน v. to eat (something) (formal) *Unit 5.4*

ráp-rɔɔŋ รับรอง v. to certify, guarantee, vouch *Unit 9.2*

rát รัฐ n. state *Unit 1.4*

rát-tha-mon-trii รัฐมนตรี n. minister (of the government) *Unit 2.4*

raw เรา pron. we *Unit 1.1*

rêŋ เร่ง v. to hurry, speed up, urge, urge on *Unit 3.4*

rɛɛŋ แรง adv. forcefully, strongly *Unit 10.1*

rɛ̂ɛk แรก v. to be first *Unit 2.3*

rîak เรียก v. to call *Unit 1.3*

rîak-wâa เรียกว่า v. to be called *Unit 1.3*

rian เรียน v. to study (in a class) *Unit 1.2*

rian เรียน v. to inform, tell (particularly when speaking to a superior) *Unit 7.2*

rian-rúu เรียนรู้ v. to learn *Unit 7.2*

rian-tɔ̀ɔ เรียนต่อ v. study further, continue to study *Unit 2.4*

rǐan เหรียญ n. coin; medal; dollar *Unit 3.1*

rîap-rɔ́ɔy เรียบร้อย v. to be ready, all set *Unit 10.2*

rii รี v. to be oval-shaped *Unit 6.3*

rîit รีด v. to press, iron *Unit 5.4*

rim ริม n. edge, rim *Unit 5.4*

rooŋ-ʔaa-hǎan โรงอาหาร n. cafeteria *Unit 5.1*

rooŋ-nǎŋ โรงหนัง n. movie theater *Unit 5.1*

rooŋ-pha-yaa-baan โรงพยาบาล n. hospital *Unit 2.4*

rooŋ-rɛɛm โรงแรม n. hotel *Unit 2.2*

rooŋ-rian โรงเรียน n. school *Unit 5.1*

rooŋ-rót โรงรถ n. garage *Unit 5.4*

rooy โรย v. to sprinkle *Unit 3.4*

rót รส n. taste *Unit 3.3*

rót รถ n. vehicle *Unit 5.1*

rót-fay รถไฟ n. train *Unit 5.1*

rót-fay tâay-din รถไฟใต้ดิน n. subway, underground train *Unit 5.3*

rót-kěŋ รถเก๋ง n. sedan (car, automobile) *Unit 10.2*

rót-mee รถเมล์ n. city bus *Unit 5.1*

rót nâŋ รถนั่ง n. passenger car *Unit 10.2*

rót nɔɔn รถนอน n. sleeping car, sleeper *Unit 10.2*

rót pha-yaa-baan รถพยาบาล n. ambulance *Unit 9.1*

rót sɔ̌ɔŋ-thɛ̌ɛw รถสองแถว n. jeepney, minibus taxi *Unit 5.3*

rót tìt รถติด n. traffic jam *Unit 5.3*

rót túk-túk **รถตุ๊กๆ** n. motorized tricycle *Unit 5.3*

rót-tûu **รถตู้** n. van *Unit 10.2*

rót thɛ́k-sîi **รถแท็กซี่** n .taxi *Unit 5.3*

rót-thua **รถทัวร์** n. tour bus, coach; motor coach (from English "tour") *Unit 10.1*

rót-yon **รถยนต์** n. motorcar *Unit 5.3*

rɔɔ **รอ** v. to wait, wait for, await *Unit 7.2*

rɔ̀ɔk, rɔ̀k **หรอก** prt. used with statements of negation, contradiction *Unit 6.1*

rɔ́ɔn **ร้อน** v. to be hot *Unit 3.2*

rɔɔŋ-tháaw, rɔŋ-tháaw **รองเท้า** n. footware *Unit 6.1*

rɔ́ɔŋ **ร้อง** v. to sing *Unit 2.4*

rɔ́ɔŋ **ร้อง** v. to cry out, bellow, shriek *Unit 10.1*

rɔ́ɔŋ-hâay **ร้องไห้** to weep, cry *Unit 8.1*

rɔŋ-tháaw kii-laa **รองเท้ากีฬา** n. sports shoes *Unit 6.1*

rɔŋ-tháaw-tɛ̀ **รองเท้าแตะ** n. slippers, sandals *Unit 6.1*

ruam **รวม** v. to combine, add, add up, sum up, include *Unit 3.4*

ruam-tháŋ **รวมทั้ง** v. to include *Unit 9.2*

rúŋ **รุ้ง** n. rainbow *Unit 10.1*

rúu-càk **รู้จัก** v. to be acquainted with *Unit 1.2*

rúu-rʉ̂aŋ **รู้เรื่อง** v. to understand *Unit 7.1*

rûup **รูป** n. picture *Unit 5.4*

rûup **รูป** n. form, shape *Unit 6.3*

rûup khày **รูปไข่** v. to be egg-shaped (vertical) *Unit 6.3*

rûup-râaŋ **รูปร่าง** n. appearance, form, figure, shape *Unit 2.1*

rʉ́-duu **ฤดู** n. season *Unit 4.4*

rʉa **เรือ** n. boat, ship *Unit 5.1*

rʉa-bay **เรือใบ** n. sailing, sailboat *Unit 7.1*

rʉa-bin **เรือบิน** n. airplane (informal) *Unit 5.3*

rʉ̂aŋ **เรื่อง** n., clf. story, subject, subject matter *Unit 6.3*

rʉ̂aŋ-raaw **เรื่องราว** n. story, account; matter *Unit 10.2*

rʉ̂aŋ-sân **เรื่องสั้น** n. short story *Unit 7.1*

rʉ̌ʉ **หรือ** conj. or *Unit 1.4*

rʉ̌ʉ-plàaw, rʉ́-plàaw **หรือเปล่า** prt. for yes-no question, asking for confirmation *Unit 2.1*

rə̌ə **เหรอ** excl. Is that so? (expressing surprise at what was said) *Unit 6.1*

rə̂əm **เริ่ม** v. to begin *Unit 10.1*

S

sa-ʔàat **สะอาด** v. to be clean *Unit 4.2*

sa-baay **สบาย** v. to be comfortable *Unit 1.1*

sa-baay dii **สบายดี** I'm fine. *Unit 1.1*

sa-bùu **สบู่** n. soap *Unit 8.1*

sa-dɛɛŋ **แสดง** v. to put on a show, to play (act) *Unit 2.1*

sa-dùak **สะดวก** v. to be convenient *Unit 2.2*

sa-kii **สกี** n. skiing, ski *Unit 7.1*

sa-kɔ́t **สก็อต** n. Scottish, Scotland (from English Scot) *Unit 6.1*

sa-kun (ŋən) **สกุล (เงิน)** currency *Unit 9.2*

sa-mùt **สมุด** n. notebook, folio *Unit 1.3*

sa-mùt ban-chii **สมุดบัญชี** n. passbook *Unit 9.2*

sa-mùt fàak **สมุดฝาก** n. passbook *Unit 9.2*

sa-nǎam **สนาม** n. field, lawn *Unit 5.1*

sa-nǎam bin **สนามบิน** n. airport *Unit 5.1*

sa-nǎam kii-laa **สนามกีฬา** n. stadium *Unit 5.1*

sa-pháy **สะใภ้** n. a female relative by marriage *Unit 2.3*

sà phǒm **สระผม** to wash one's hair *Unit 8.1*

sa-tɛm **แสตมป์** n. stamp (from English "stamp") *Unit 9.2*

sa-thǎa-ban **สถาบัน** n. institute *Unit 6.1*

sa-thǎa-nii **สถานี** n. station *Unit 4.1*

sa-thǎa-nii khǒn-sòŋ **สถานีขนส่ง** n. bus terminal *Unit 5.1*

sa-thǎa-nii rót-fay **สถานีรถไฟ** n. train station *Unit 5.1*

sa-thǎa-nii tam-rùat **สถานีตำรวจ** n. police station *Unit 5.1*

sa-thǎan-thîi **สถานที่** n. place, site *Unit 4.1*

sa-thǎan-thûut **สถานทูต** n. embassy *Unit 2.4*

sa-wàaŋ สว่าง v. to be bright (of hue) *Unit 6.2*

sa-wàt-dii สวัสดี Hello. (neutral, formal) *Unit 1.1*

sa-yɔ̌ɔŋ สยอง v. to terrify, frighten; scare *Unit 7.1*

sa-yɔ̌ɔŋ khwǎn สยองขวัญ v. to be terrified, frightened *Unit 7.1*

sǎa-khǎa สาขา n. branch; subdivision *Unit 9.2*

sǎa-mii สามี n. husband *Unit 2.3*

sǎa-rá-kha-dii สารคดี n. documentary *Unit 7.1*

sǎam-lìam สามเหลี่ยม n. triangle, v. to be triangular *Unit 6.3*

sâap ทราบ v. to know; to learn of (formal) *Unit 7.2*

sǎaw สาว n. young woman; adolescent girl *Unit 2.1*

sáay ซ้าย n. left (direction) *Unit 2.1*

sǎay สาย n. late morning, v. to be late *Unit 4.2*

sǎay สาย n. line (in the sense of a channel), route *Unit 5.1*

sǎay kaan-bin สายการบิน n. an airline (system or company) *Unit 10.2*

sàk, sák สัก adv. just; about; around; approximately; only *Unit 3.4*

sák ซัก v. to wash (clothes) *Unit 4.2*

sák phâa ซักผ้า v. to launder *Unit 4.2*

sǎm-phâat สัมภาษณ์ n. interview, v. to interview *Unit 7.1*

sǎm-ràp สำหรับ prep. for *Unit 4.4*

sǎm-ràp สำหรับ 1. prep. for 2. conj. as for, regarding *Unit 9.2*

sân สั้น v. to be short (in length) *Unit 2.1*

sǎn-ya-lák สัญลักษณ์ n. symbol *Unit 5.2*

sàp-daa สัปดาห์ n. week *Unit 4.3*

sàp-pa-rót สับปะรด n. pineapple *Unit 3.1*

sày ใส่ v. to put on, to put in, insert *Unit 6.1*

sáy ไซร้ prt. marking a topic (literary use) *Unit 10.2*

sěem-hàʔ เสมหะ n. phlegm, sputum *Unit 8.2*

sèet-tha-sàat เศรษฐศาสตร์ n. economics (as a science) *Unit 7.2*

sen เซ็น v. to sign *Unit 9.2*

sen-ti-méet เซนติเมตร clf. centimeter *Unit 2.1*

sên เส้น clf. for strands of hair, thread; for string, wire, bracelets *Unit 3.3*

sên-phǒm เส้นผม n. strand of hair *Unit 7.1*

sèt เสร็จ v. to be finished, ready *Unit 4.2*

sɛ̌ɛn แสน n. hundred thousand *Unit 2.2*

si ซิ prt. used to indicate the imperative mood *Unit 2.3*

sǐa เสีย v. to lose *Unit 5.3*

sǐa-cay เสียใจ v. to be sorry, to feel sorry, to feel badly, to regret *Unit 7.2*

sǐa-daay เสียดาย v. to feel sorry (about something lost, about a lost opportunity), to regret *Unit 7.2*

sìat-thɔ́ɔŋ เสียดท้อง v. to feel a sharp pain in the stomach, to have heartburn *Unit 8.2*

sìi-lìam สี่เหลี่ยม n. rectangle, v. to be rectangular *Unit 6.3*

sǐi สี n. color *Unit 6.1*

sǐi-fan สีฟัน v. to brush the teeth *Unit 8.1*

sǐi tòk สีตก v. to be non colorfast *Unit 6.2*

sôm ส้ม n. orange *Unit 3.1*

sôm-ʔoo ส้มโอ n. pomelo *Unit 6.3*

sôn ส้น n. heel (of the foot or shoes) *Unit 6.2*

sǒn-cay สนใจ v. to be interested (in) *Unit 6.1*

sòŋ ส่ง v. to send *Unit 3.3*

sòŋ ส่ง v. to drop off *Unit 5.3*

soo-faa โซฟา n. sofa *Unit 5.4*

sòot โสด n. single, unmarried state *Unit 2.3*

sòt สด v. to be fresh, raw, uncooked *Unit 3.4*

sòt สด v. to be bright (of hue) *Unit 6.2*

sɔ̂m ส้อม n. fork *Unit 3.4*

sɔ̌ɔn สอน v. to teach *Unit 2.4*

sɔɔŋ ซอง n. envelope *Unit 9.2*

sɔ̌ɔŋ yaam สองยาม n. midnight *Unit 4.1*

sù-phâap สุภาพ v. to be polite, respectable *Unit 6.1*

sù-kɔɔn สุกร n. pig (formal) *Unit 10.2*

sù-khǎa สุขา v. toilet, lavatory *Unit 3.2*

sǔam สวม v. to put on, wear *Unit 6.1*

sùan-mâak ส่วนมาก adv. mostly, the greater part *Unit 6.1*

sùan-tua **ส่วนตัว** n. private, personal, individual *Unit 8.1*

sǔan **สวน** n. garden *Unit 5.4*

sǔay **สวย** v. to be pretty (of things that are seen) *Unit 2.1*

sùk **สุข** v. to be happy; to be content *Unit 7.2*

sùt **สุด** n. the end *Unit 4.3*

sùt-thɔ́ɔŋ **สุดท้อง** n. last-born, youngest *Unit 2.3*

sǔun **ศูนย์** n. center (of activity) *Unit 5.1*

sǔun-kaan-kháa **ศูนย์การค้า** n. shopping center *Unit 5.1*

sǔuŋ **สูง** v. to be tall *Unit 2.1*

sùut **สูท** n. suit *Unit 6.1*

sʉ̂a **เสื้อ** n. shirt, blouse *Unit 3.1*

sʉ̂a-chə́ət **เสื้อเชิ้ต** n. shirt *Unit 6.1*

sʉ̂a haa-waay **เสื้อฮาวาย** n. aloha shirt *Unit 6.1*

sʉ̂a klâam **เสื้อกล้าม** n. men's undershirt *Unit 6.1*

sʉ̂a kɔ̀-ʔòk **เสื้อเกาะอก** n. a tube top *Unit 6.1*

sʉ̂a khɛ̌ɛn kùt **เสื้อแขนกุด** n. sleeveless blouse *Unit 6.1*

sʉ̂a khɛ̌ɛn sân **เสื้อแขนสั้น** n. short-sleeved top *Unit 6.1*

sʉ̂a khɛ̌ɛn yaaw **เสื้อแขนยาว** n. long-sleeved top *Unit 6.1*

sʉ̂a-nɔ̂ɔk **เสื้อนอก** n. suitcoat, jacket *Unit 6.1*

sʉ̂a-phâa **เสื้อผ้า** n. clothes, clothing *Unit 6.1*

sʉ̂a poo-loo **เสื้อโปโล** n. polo shirt *Unit 6.1*

sʉ̂a sǎay-dìaw **เสื้อสายเดี่ยว** n. a spaghetti strap tank top *Unit 6.1*

sʉ̂a-yʉ̂ʉt **เสื้อยืด** n. T-shirt, singlet; tee-shirt *Unit 6.1*

sʉ̌a **เสือ** n. tiger *Unit 9.1*

sʉ̀k-sǎa **ศึกษา** v. to learn, study *Unit 4.3*

sʉ̂ŋ **ซึ่ง** pron. which, that, who (as a relative pronoun) *Unit 5.3*

sʉ́ʉ **ซื้อ** v. to buy *Unit 3.1*

sʉ́ʉ-khɔ̌ɔŋ **ซื้อของ** v. to shop *Unit 3.2*

sʉ̀ʉp **สืบ** v. to search for the facts, seek clues *Unit 7.1*

sʉ̀ʉp-sǔan **สืบสวน** v. to investigate *Unit 7.1*

sə̀əp **เสิร์ฟ** v. to serve, wait on a table (English loan) *Unit 2.4*

t

ta-kìap **ตะเกียบ** n. chopsticks *Unit 3.4*

ta-krɔ̂ɔ **ตะกร้อ** n. sepak-takraw, foot volleyball *Unit 7.1*

ta-khriw **ตะคริว** n. cramp, painful spasmodic muscular contraction *Unit 8.2*

ta-làat **ตลาด** n. market *Unit 1.3*

ta-lòk **ตลก** v. to be funny, comical, farcical *Unit 7.1*

ta-lɔ̀ɔt **ตลอด** prep. through, all over, throughout *Unit 6.3*

ta-wan-ʔɔ̀ɔk **ตะวันออก** n. east *Unit 5.1*

ta-wan-ʔɔ̀ɔk-chǐaŋ-nʉ̌a **ตะวันออกเฉียงเหนือ** n. northeast *Unit 5.1*

ta-wan-ʔɔ̀ɔk-chǐaŋ-tâay **ตะวันออกเฉียงใต้** n. southeast *Unit 5.1*

ta-wan-tòk **ตะวันตก** n. west *Unit 5.1*

ta-wan-tòk-chǐaŋ-nʉ̌a **ตะวันตกเฉียงเหนือ** n. northwest *Unit 5.1*

ta-wan-tòk-chǐaŋ-tâay **ตะวันตกเฉียงใต้** n. southwest *Unit 5.1*

taa **ตา** n. eye *Unit 2.1*

taa **ตา** n. maternal grandfather, mother's father *Unit 2.3*

taa bɔ̀ɔt **ตาบอด** v. to be blind *Unit 6.2*

taam **ตาม** v. to follow *Unit 3.2*

taam tham-ma-daa **ตามธรรมดา** adv. usually, ordinarily, commonly, normally *Unit 4.1*

taam-thîi **ตามที่** conj. according to, following *Unit 10.1*

tàaŋ **ต่าง** quant. each *Unit 10.2*

tàaŋ-caŋ-wàt **ต่างจังหวัด** n. out-of-town, provincial *Unit 2.2*

tàaŋ-tàaŋ **ต่าง ๆ** d.a. different, various *Unit 8.2*

taay **ตาย** v. to die *Unit 8.1*

tâay **ใต้** prep. to be under, underneath, below *Unit 2.1* tâay ใต้ n. south, southern *Unit 2.2*

taay-lɛ́ɛw ตายแล้ว excl. expressing dismay or alarm; "My goodness." *Unit 8.1*

tam-rùat ตำรวจ n. policeman *Unit 2.4*

taŋ ตังค์ n. money (shortened from สตางค์ /sa-taŋ/) *Unit 3.4*

tâŋ ตั้ง v. to set, place, set up, erect, establish *Unit 5.4*

tâŋ-tɛ̀ɛ ตั้งแต่ prep. from (a time or starting point), since *Unit 10.1*

tàt ตัด v. to cut, sever *Unit 6.2*

tàt-ŋən ตัดเงิน v. debit (from an account) *Unit 9.2*

tàt-phǒm ตัดผม to have one's hair cut *Unit 8.1*

taw เตา n. stove *Unit 5.4*

taw-rîit เตารีด n. iron *Unit 5.4*

tâw-hûu เต้าหู้ n. tofu, bean curd *Unit 3.3*

tên เต้น v. to jump, spring, dance (with feet, Western style) *Unit 4.2*

tên ram เต้นรำ v. to dance (ballroom dancing) *Unit 4.2*

tɛ̀ɛ แต่ conj. but *Unit 1.4*

tɛ̀ɛk แตก v. to break (of itself), split *Unit 3.1*

tɛ̀ɛk-ŋɔɔn แตกเงิน v. to change (small money) *Unit 3.1*

tɛɛŋ-moo แตงโม n. watermelon *Unit 6.3*

tɛ̀ŋ แต่ง v. to ornament, decorate, adorn *Unit 6.1*

tɛ̀ŋ-kaay แต่งกาย v. to dress *Unit 6.1*

tɛ̀ŋ-ŋaan แต่งงาน v. to get married, be married *Unit 2.3*

tɛ̀ŋ-tua แต่งตัว v. to dress, get dressed, be dressed *Unit 6.1*

tîa เตี้ย v. to be short, low (in height) *Unit 2.1*

tii ตี v. to hit, beat, strike *Unit 8.2*

tii ตี n. (time) an hour of the morning between midnight and 6 A.M. *Unit 4.1*

tìt ติด v. to be adjacent to *Unit 5.2*

tìt sǎay ติดสาย v. to be on the phone, to be on another line *Unit 7.2*

tìt-tɔ̀ɔ ติดต่อ v. to get in touch (with) *Unit 9.1*

tòk ตก v. to drop, fall; to fall down (from, into, onto) *Unit 4.4*

tòk-loŋ ตกลง v. to agree (to something) *Unit 3.1*

tôm ต้ม v. to boil *Unit 3.3*

tôm-yam ต้มยำ n. spicy soup *Unit 3.3*

tôn ต้น n. beginning, source *Unit 4.4*

tôn-máay ต้นไม้ n. plant, tree *Unit 5.4*

tóʔ โต๊ะ n. table, desk *Unit 1.3*

too โต v. to be big, large, mature *Unit 2.1*

tôo โต้ v. to counter, resist, withstand *Unit 7.1*

tôo-khlûun โต้คลื่น n. surfing, v. to surf, ride the waves *Unit 7.1*

tòp ตบ v. to slap, clap, pat *Unit 8.1*

tɔ̂ŋ ต้อง aux. have to, must, is to be *Unit 3.4*

tɔ̂ŋ-kaan ต้องการ v. to want, need, require (formal) *Unit 10.2*

tɔ̀ɔ ต่อ v. to join, connect, put together, construct *Unit 2.4*

tɔ̀ɔ ต่อ v. to continue, extend, add (on) *Unit 3.2*

tɔ̀ɔ-maa ต่อมา conj. later on (in time), afterwards *Unit 9.1*

tɔ̀ɔ-pay-níi ต่อไปนี้ conj. from now on, as follow *Unit 10.2*

tɔ̀ɔ thoo-ra-sàp ต่อโทรศัพท์ v. to dial a number *Unit 7.2*

tɔɔn ตอน conj. when *Unit 2.4*

tɔɔn ตอน clf. part, section (of space or time) *Unit 3.4*

tɔɔn ตอน prep. at (time), part, section (of space or time) *Unit 4.1*

tɔɔn-níi ตอนนี้ adv. now, at present; at this time *Unit 1.2*

tɔ̂ɔn-ráp ต้อนรับ v. to welcome, receive (e.g. guests) *Unit 2.4*

tɔ̀ɔp ตอบ v. to reply, answer *Unit 10.2*

traa ตรา n. trademark, seal, logo *Unit 9.2*

trii ตรี num. three (Indic loan) *Unit 2.4*

troŋ ตรง adv. punctually, exactly *Unit 4.1*

troŋ ตรง v. to move straight *Unit 5.2*

troŋ khâam ตรงข้าม v. to be opposite, the opposite of *Unit 5.2* truat ตรวจ v. to inspect, examine, check *Unit 8.2*

tua ตัว n. self, body *Unit 1.2*

tua ตัว clf. for animals and objects with arms or legs such as furniture, some clothing items *Unit 3.1*

tǔa ตั๋ว n. ticket *Unit 5.3*

tǔn ตุ๋น v. to stew, to braise *Unit 3.3*

tûu ตู้ n. cabinet *Unit 5.4*

tûu pray-sa-nii ตู้ไปรษณีย์ n. postbox *Unit 9.2*

tûu-yen ตู้เย็น n. refrigerator *Unit 5.4*

tɨ̀ɨn ตื่น v. to wake (of oneself) *Unit 4.2*

tɨ̀ɨn nɔɔn ตื่นนอน v. wake up, be awake; get up *Unit 4.2*

tɨ̀ɨn saay ตื่นสาย v. to wake up late *Unit 4.2*

th

tha-hǎan ทหาร n. soldier *Unit 2.4*

tha-lee ทะเล n. sea *Unit 3.3*

tha-na-bàt ธนบัตร n. banknote *Unit 3.1*

tha-naa-kaan ธนาคาร n. bank *Unit 2.4*

tha-nǒn ถนน n. street, road *Unit 2.2*

tha-wîip ทวีป n. continent *Unit 1.4*

thaa ทา v. to coat, spread (on) *Unit 8.1*

thaa-pàak ทาปาก to put on lipstick *Unit 8.1*

thâa ถ้า conj. if *Unit 3.1*

thâa-rɨa ท่าเรือ n. pier *Unit 5.1*

thâa-yaŋ-ŋán ถ้ายังงั้น conj. if that is so, in that case *Unit 2.3*

thaaŋ ทาง prep. in the direction of *Unit 5.1*

thaaŋ-kaan ทางการ n. government, authorities *Unit 10.2*

tháaw เท้า n. foot *Unit 6.1*

tham ทำ v. to do *Unit 1.3*

tham khwaam-sa-ʔàat ทำความสะอาด v. to clean *Unit 4.2*

tham thú-rá ทำธุระ v. to have business to do *Unit 9.1*

tham-ma-daa ธรรมดา v. to be ordinary, natural, common, usual *Unit 4.1*

tham-ŋaan ทำงาน v. to work *Unit 1.2*

tham-phǒm ทำผม v. to style a hairdo *Unit 8.1*

than ทัน v. to be on time, in time *Unit 8.1*

than-day ทันใด adv. suddenly, immediately (formal) *Unit 10.2*

than-thii ทันที adv. promptly, immediately, at once *Unit 10.2*

tháŋ ทั้ง quant. whole, entire *Unit 4.4*

tháŋ mòt ทั้งหมด quant. all (of it, of them), the whole lot *Unit 3.4*

tháŋ-nán ทั้งนั้น quant. all or any of them, everything and anything *Unit 7.1*

tháp ทับ v. to put on top of, overlay, superimpose *Unit 6.1*

thâw เท่า v. to be equal, the same (in size orquantity) *Unit 3.1*

thâw-nán เท่านั้น adv. only, only that, just that *Unit 2.1*

thâw-ray, thâw-rày เท่าไร q. how much, how many *Unit 2.1*

thay ไทย n. Thai *Unit 1.3*

thêet-sa-kaan เทศกาล n. festival, festival season *Unit 10.1*

then-nít, then-nís เทนนิส n. tennis *Unit 7.1*

thɛ̌ɛw แถว n. section, district (of a town, place) *Unit 2.2*

thɛ̌ɛw-thɛ̌ɛw แถว ๆ n. area, neighborhood; region; zone; vicinity *Unit 7.1*

thɛ̂ŋ แท่ง clf. for small tube-shaped items, e.g. pencils, lipstick *Unit 3.1*

thîaŋ เที่ยง n. noon *Unit 4.1*

thîaŋ-khɨɨn เที่ยงคืน n. midnight *Unit 4.1*

thîaŋ-wan เที่ยงวัน n. midday, noon *Unit 4.1*

thîaw เที่ยว v. to go out (for fun), go (from place to place) *Unit 1.3*

thîaw เที่ยว clf. classifier for a trip. *Unit 10.1*

thîaw diaw เที่ยวเดียว n. one way (Lit. a single trip) *Unit 10.2*

thii ที clf. for counting event *Unit 1.3*

thii-wii ทีวี n. television, from English "TV" *Unit 4.2*

thîi ที่ 1. n. place; space, room, 2. clf. for an order of a dish *Unit 3.3*

thîi khìa-bu-rìi ที่เขี่ยบุหรี่ n. ashtray *Unit 3.4*

thîi tham-kaan ที่ทำการ n. office *Unit 9.2*

thîi-lɛ́ɛw ที่แล้ว n. the previous, preceding *Unit 4.3*

thîi-nân ที่นั่น n. there *Unit 4.4*

thîi-nǎy ที่ไหน n., q. Where? *Unit 1.1*

thîi-nîi ที่นี่ n. here *Unit 1.2*

thîi-sùt ที่สุด adv. most, -est *Unit 4.4*

thíŋ ทิ้ง v. to abandon, discard *Unit 7.2*

thít ทิศ n. direction, point of compass *Unit 5.1*

thoŋ ธง n. flag, banner, pennant *Unit 4.1*

thoŋ-châat ธงชาติ n. national flag *Unit 4.1*

thoo-ra-sǎan โทรสาร n. telefax (formal) *Unit 5.4*

thoo-ra-sàp โทรศัพท์ n. telephone *Unit 2.2*

thoo-ra-thát โทรทัศน์ n. television *Unit 4.1*

thɔ̂ŋ-thîaw ท่องเที่ยว v. to tour, travel *Unit 2.4*

thɔɔn ทอน v. to give change (money) *Unit 3.1*

thɔ̌ɔn ŋən ถอนเงิน v. withdraw money *Unit 9.2*

thɔ́ɔŋ ท้อง abdomen, stomach *Unit 8.1*

thɔ̀ɔt ถอด v. to remove, take off (as an article of clothing) *Unit 6.1*

thɔ̂ɔt ทอด v. to pan fry, to deep fry *Unit 3.3*

thɔ̌y ถอย v. to retreat, draw back *Unit 5.2*

thú-rá ธุระ n. business, affairs, errands *Unit 3.2*

thú-rá-kìt ธุรกิจ n. business, trade; commerce *Unit 2.4*

thú-rian ทุเรียน n. durian *Unit 6.3*

thûa ทั่ว v. to be all over, to be general *Unit 7.2*

thúam ท้วม v. to be plump, be fat *Unit 2.1*

thûay ถ้วย n., clf. cup *Unit 3.1*

thûay-bɛ̀ŋ ถ้วยแบ่ง n. small bowl for an individual serving *Unit 3.4*

thûay-chaam ถ้วยชาม n. dishware *Unit 5.4*

thúk ทุก quant. every, each *Unit 4.3*

thúk ทุกข์ v. to suffer, to be unhappy, to be in trouble *Unit 7.2*

thûm ทุ่ม n. an hour of the night counting from 7 P.M. to midnight *Unit 4.1*

thǔŋ ถุง n., clf. bag, sack *Unit 3.1*

thǔŋ-tháaw ถุงเท้า n. socks, stockings, hose *Unit 6.1*

thùuk ถูก aux. element used in making passive constructions *Unit 9.1*

thùuk ถูก v. to be correct *Unit 1.3*

thùuk-cay ถูกใจ v. to please; to be satisfactory, pleasing; appealing *Unit 7.2*

thəəm เทอม clf. term, especially school term or semester *Unit 4.4*

thʉ̌ŋ ถึง v. to reach, arrive *Unit 4.2*

thʉ̌ŋ ถึง prep. until *Unit 4.3*

thʉ̌ʉ ถือ v. to hold, carry (in the hands) *Unit 3.4*

thʉ̌ʉ-sǎay ถือสาย v. to hold the line *Unit 7.2*

thə̀ʔ เถอะ prt. used to indicate an urging *Unit 3.2*

thəə เธอ pron. you (familiar) *Unit 1.1*

thəəm เทอม clf. term, especially school term or semester *Unit 4.4*

W

waa-ra-sǎan วารสาร n. magazine *Unit 7.1*

waa-ray-tîi วาไรตี้ n. variety show (from English) *Unit 7.1*

wâa ว่า v. to say *Unit 3.1*

waaŋ วาง v. to place, lay *Unit 7.2*

waaŋ-hǔu วางหู v. to hang up (the phone) *Unit 7.2*

waaŋ-sǎay วางสาย v. to hang up (the phone) *Unit 7.2*

wâaŋ ว่าง v. to be free, unoccupied *Unit 4.2*

wâay náam ว่ายน้ำ v. to swim *Unit 4.2*

wan วัน n. day *Unit 2.2*

wan-kɔ̀ɔn วันก่อน n. the other day *Unit 4.3*

wan-lǎŋ วันหลัง n. future, following day; later *Unit 4.3*

wan-níi วันนี้ adv. time. today *Unit 1.3*

wan-phrá วันพระ n. Buddhist day of worship *Unit 4.1*

waŋ วัง n. palace *Unit 6.1*

wát วัด n. temple *Unit 5.1*

wàt **หวัด** n. common cold *Unit 8.2*

wáy **ไว้** v. to keep, leave, place, put (something somewhere) for future use *Unit 7.2*

wee-laa **เวลา** conj. while; at the time when *Unit 3.4*

wee-laa **เวลา** n. time *Unit 4.1*

wɛ́ʔ **แวะ** v. to stop in, drop in (to see someone) *Unit 3.2*

wɛ̂n **แว่น** n. glasses, spectacles *Unit 6.2*

wí-chaa **วิชา** n. subject (of study) *Unit 7.2*

wí-naa-thii **วินาที** n. second *Unit 4.3*

wí-thii **วิธี** n. method, way, means *Unit 3.3*

wǐi **หวี** n. comb *Unit 6.2*

wîŋ **วิ่ง** v. to run *Unit 3.2*

wít-tha-yaa-sàat **วิทยาศาสตร์** n. science, the sciences *Unit 7.1*

wít-tha-yú **วิทยุ** n. radio, wireless *Unit 4.1*

wiw **วิว** n. view (from English "view") *Unit 10.1*

woŋ **วง** n. circle, ring, group *Unit 6.3*

woŋ-klom **วงกลม** n. circle, v. to be circle-shaped *Unit 6.3*

woŋ-rii **วงรี** n. oval, v. to be oval-shaped *Unit 6.3*

wua **วัว** n. ox, cow, cattle *Unit 3.3*

yaa **ยา** n. medicine, drug *Unit 8.1*

yaa-mɔ̀ɔŋ **ยาหม่อง** n. mentholated ointment, balm *Unit 8.2*

yaa-sà-phǒm **ยาสระผม** n. shampoo *Unit 8.1*

yaa-sǐi-fan **ยาสีฟัน** n. toothpaste *Unit 8.1*

yàa **หย่า** v. to divorce *Unit 2.3*

yàa **อย่า** aux. do not, don't *Unit 3.3*

yâa **ย่า** n. paternal grandmother *Unit 2.3*

yàak **อยาก** v. to want to, desire to *Unit 2.4*

yaam **ยาม** n. one of three periods into which the day was traditionally divided *Unit 4.1*

yaaŋ-lóp **ยางลบ** n. eraser *Unit 1.3*

yàaŋ **อย่าง** adv. like, the way, in the manner of *Unit 5.1*

yàaŋ **อย่าง** clf. kind, type, variety *Unit 5.3*

yàaŋ **อย่าง** conj. for instance, such as, like *Unit 7.1*

yàaŋ-ray **อย่างไร** q. How? What? In what way? (citation form) *Unit 1.1*

yâaŋ **ย่าง** v. to roast, to barbeque *Unit 3.3*

yâat **ญาติ** n. relative, kin *Unit 2.3*

yâat-phîi-nɔ́ɔŋ **ญาติพี่น้อง** n. relatives *Unit 2.3*

yaaw **ยาว** v. to be long (of objects) *Unit 2.1*

yaay **ยาย** n. maternal grandmother *Unit 2.3*

yák **ยักษ์** n. giant, ogre *Unit 2.1*

yam **ยำ** v. to toss/dress a salad, n. spicy salad *Unit 3.3*

yaŋ-ŋay **ยังไง** q. How? (spoken form) *Unit 1.1*

yày **ใหญ่** v. to be big, large *Unit 3.3*

yen **เย็น** v. to be cool *Unit 3.3*

yen **เย็น** n. evening *Unit 4.2*

yɛ̂ɛ **แย่** v. to be in trouble, in a bad way *Unit 8.1*

yɛ̂ɛk **แยก** n. a junction, v. to split *Unit 5.2*

yɛ̂ɛ-lɛ́ɛw **แย่แล้ว** excl. I'm in trouble. There's trouble. *Unit 8.1*

yîam **เยี่ยม** v. to visit *Unit 4.4*

yîaw **เยี่ยว** v. to urinate *Unit 3.2*

yím **ยิ้ม** v. to smile *Unit 8.1*

yin-dii **ยินดี** v. to be glad, to be happy *Unit 1.2*

yin-dii ráp-cháy **ยินดีรับใช้** At your service. *Unit 10.1*

yiŋ **ยิง** v. to shoot, shoot at *Unit 2.3*

yǐŋ **หญิง** n. woman, female *Unit 3.2*

yók **ยก** v. to lift, raise *Unit 10.1*

yɔ̂y **ย่อย** v. to break up into small particles *Unit 3.1*

yùt **หยุด** v. to pause, take a break, take a vacation, be absent *Unit 4.2*

yùu **อยู่** v. to live, stay, dwell *Unit 2.2*

yɨɨm **ยืม** v. to borrow *Unit 8.2*

yɨɨn **ยืน** v. to stand *Unit 4.1*

yɨ̂ɨt **ยืด** v. to stretch, extend, lengthen *Unit 6.1*

yə́ʔ **เยอะ** v. to be a whole lot, a great deal, plenty *Unit 3.1*

yə́ʔ-yɛ́ʔ **เยอะแยะ** v. to be a whole lot, a great deal, plenty *Unit 3.1*

a

abandon, discard thíŋ ทิ้ง *Unit 7.2*

abdomen, stomach thɔ́ɔŋ ท้อง *Unit 8.1*

able to, know how to pen เป็น *Unit 7.1*

about to kam-laŋ-ca กำลังจะ *Unit 2.4*

about, regarding; concerning kìaw-kàp เกี่ยวกับ *Unit 2.4*

about; approximately pra-maan ประมาณ *Unit 4.2*

above, over nʉ̌a **เหนือ** *Unit 5.4*

absent-minded cay-lɔɔy **ใจลอย** *Unit 7.2*

accident ʔù-bàt-tì-hèet, ʔu-bàt-ti-hèet อุบัติเหตุ *Unit 9.1*

according to, following taam-thîi ตามที่ *Unit 10.1*

account ban-chii บัญชี *Unit 9.2*

ache, to be in (aching) pain pùat ปวด *Unit 8.1*

acquainted with rúu-càk รู้จัก *Unit 1.2*

add, increase, augment phə̂əm เพิ่ม *Unit 9.2*

adjacent to tìt ติด *Unit 5.2*

admire, to be popular ní-yom นิยม *Unit 10.1*

adolescent boy; guy nùm หนุ่ม *Unit 2.1*

adolescent girl, young woman sǎaw **สาว** *Unit 2.1*

adopted bun-tham บุญธรรม *Unit 2.3*

after lǎŋ-càak หลังจาก *Unit 4.2*

afternoon bàay บ่าย *Unit 4.1*

afterwards tɔ̀ɔ-maa ต่อมา *Unit 9.1*

age ʔaa-yúʔ อายุ *Unit 2.1*

agree (to something) tòk-loŋ ตกลง *Unit 3.1*

air ʔaa-kàat อากาศ *Unit 4.4*

air-conditioner ʔɛɛ **แอร์** *Unit 3.2*

air-conditioner (formal) khrʉ̂aŋ pràp ʔaa-kàat เครื่องปรับอากาศ *Unit 5.4*

airline sǎay kaan-bin สายการบิน *Unit 10.2*

airplane (formal) khrʉ̂aŋ-bin เครื่องบิน *Unit 5.3*

airplane (informal) rʉa-bin เรือบิน *Unit 5.3*

airport sa-nǎam bin สนามบิน *Unit 5.1*

all (of it, of them) tháŋ mòt ทั้งหมด *Unit 3.4*

all or any of them, everything and anything tháŋ nán ทั้งนั้น *Unit 7.1*

all over, to be general thûa ทั่ว *Unit 7.2*

allergic to phɛ́ɛ แพ้ *Unit 8.2*

almost, nearly, about kʉ̀ap เกือบ *Unit 2.3*

aloha shirt sʉ̂a haa-waay เสื้อฮาวาย *Unit 6.1*

alone, by oneself ʔeeŋ เอง *Unit 5.4*

also, as well; too; likewise chên-kan เช่นกัน *Unit 4.1*

also, too dûay ด้วย *Unit 3.4*

ambulance rót pha-yaa-baan รถพยาบาล *Unit 9.1*

among, between ra-wàaŋ ระหว่าง *Unit 5.4*

and lɛ́ และ *Unit 1.2*

angular lìam **เหลี่ยม** *Unit 6.3*

announce pra-kàat ประกาศ *Unit 9.1*

another ʔìik อีก *Unit 1.3*

answer tɔ̀ɔp ตอบ *Unit 10.2*

answer the phone ráp sǎay รับสาย *Unit 7.2*

answer the phone, pick up the phone ráp thoo-ra-sàp รับโทรศัพท์ *Unit 7.2*

antibiotic pa-tì-chii-wa-ná ปฏิชีวนะ *Unit 8.2*

Anything will do. Anything is acceptable. dâay tháŋ-nán ได้ทั้งนั้น *Unit 7.1*

Anything will do. Anything whatever. ʔa-ray-kɔ̂-dâay อะไรก็ได้ *Unit 6.1*

apartment ʔa-pháat-mén อพาร์ตเมนต์ *Unit 2.2*

appearance nâa-taa หน้าตา *Unit 2.1*

appearance, form, shape rûup-râaŋ รูปร่าง *Unit 2.1*

appliances khrʉ̂aŋ เครื่อง *Unit 3.1*

appointment, make an appointment nát นัด *Unit 4.2*

approximately raaw-raaw ราวๆ *Unit 2.1*

area bɔɔ-ri-ween บริเวณ *Unit 2.2*

area, neighborhood, vicinity thɛ̌ɛw-thɛ̌ɛw แถวๆ *Unit 7.1*

arm khɛ̌ɛn แขน *Unit 6.1*

arrive thʉ̌ŋ ถึง *Unit 4.2*

as for, regarding sǎm-ràp สำหรับ *Unit 9.2*

ashtray thîi khìa-bu-rìi ที่เขี่ยบุหรี่ *Unit 3.4*

aside khâaŋ ข้าง *Unit 5.4*

associate with khóp คบ *Unit 7.2*

asterisk dɔ̀ɔk-can ดอกจัน *Unit 7.2*

at (time) tɔɔn ตอน *Unit 4.1*

at once, promptly than-thii ทันที *Unit 10.2*

At your service. yin-dii ráp-cháy ยินดีรับใช้ *Unit 10.1*

ATM card bàt ʔee-thii-ʔem บัตรเอทีเอ็ม *Unit 9.1*

aunt or uncle (younger maternal) náa น้า *Unit 2.3*

aunt or uncle (younger paternal) ʔaa อา *Unit 2.3*

awake (of oneself) tʉ̀ʉn ตื่น *Unit 4.2*

b

bachelor's degree pa-rin-yaa-trii ปริญญาตรี *Unit 2.4*

badminton bɛ̀t-min-tân แบดมินตัน *Unit 7.1*

bag, pocket kra-pǎw กระเป๋า *Unit 9.1*

bag, sack thǔŋ ถุง *Unit 3.1*

bake ʔòp อบ *Unit 3.3*

bald-headed hǔa láan หัวล้าน *Unit 6.2*

banana klûay กล้วย *Unit 6.3*

bandage (adhesive) phláas-tə̂ə พลาสเตอร์ *Unit 8.1*

bank tha-naa-kaan ธนาคาร *Unit 2.4*

banknote (formal) tha-na-bàt ธนบัตร *Unit 3.1*

banknote (spoken) bɛ́ŋ แบงค์ *Unit 3.1*

basil (Thai) ka-phraw กะเพรา *Unit 3.3*

basketball báas-kêt-bɔn **บาสเก็ตบอล** *Unit 7.1*

bath ʔàap náam อาบน้ำ *Unit 4.2*

bathroom hɔ̂ŋ-náam ห้องน้ำ *Unit 3.2*

bay ʔàaw อ่าว *Unit 10.1*

be khʉʉ คือ *Unit 2.1*

beach chaay-hàat ชายหาด *Unit 5.1*

beach hàat หาด *Unit 5.1*

beautiful ŋaam งาม *Unit 6.1*

because phrɔ́ʔ เพราะ *Unit 5.3*

bedroom hɔ̂ŋ nɔɔn ห้องนอน *Unit 5.4*

beer bia เบียร์ *Unit 3.4*

before kɔ̀ɔn ก่อน *Unit 2.4*

begin rə̂əm เริ่ม *Unit 10.1*

beginning tôn ต้น *Unit 4.4*

below lâaŋ ล่าง *Unit 5.2*

belt khěm-khàt เข็มขัด *Unit 6.1*

bench máa ม้า *Unit 5.4*

better than dii-kwàa ดีกว่า *Unit 1.4*

between, among ra-wàaŋ ระหว่าง *Unit 5.4*

bicycle càk-kra-yaan, càk-ka-yaan จักรยาน *Unit 4.2*

big, large too โต *Unit 2.1*

big, large yày ใหญ่ *Unit 3.3*

bill bin บิล *Unit 3.4*

bird nók นก *Unit 2.3*

black dam ดำ *Unit 2.1*

bland cʉ̀ʉt จืด *Unit 3.3*

blind taa bɔ̀ɔt ตาบอด *Unit 6.2*

blood lʉ̂at เลือด *Unit 3.3*

blow phát พัด *Unit 10.1*

board kra-daan กระดาน *Unit 1.3*

boat, ship rʉa เรือ *Unit 5.1*

body râaŋ-kaay ร่างกาย *Unit 8.1*

body tua ตัว *Unit 1.2*

boil tôm ต้ม *Unit 3.3*

bomb lûuk ra-bə̀ət ลูกระเบิด *Unit 6.3*

book nǎŋ-sʉ̌ʉ, naŋ-sʉ̌ʉ หนังสือ *Unit 1.2*

bookstore ráan khǎay-nǎŋ-sʉ̌ʉ ร้านขายหนังสือ *Unit 5.1*

born kə̀ət เกิด *Unit 2.1*

borrow yʉʉm ยืม *Unit 8.2*

bother, disturb kuan กวน *Unit 7.2*

bottle khùat ขวด *Unit 3.1*

bottom (of anything) kôn ก้น *Unit 3.3*

bowl chaam ชาม *Unit 3.1*

box, carton klɔ̀ŋ กล่อง *Unit 3.1*

boyfriend (slang) fɛɛn แฟน *Unit 2.3*

branch; subdivision sǎa-khǎa สาขา *Unit 9.2*

break (of itself), split tɛ̀ɛk แตก *Unit 3.1*

break up, end (an event) lə̂ək-raa เลิกรา *Unit 7.2*

breathe hǎay-cay หายใจ *Unit 8.2*

briefcase kra-pǎw ʔèek-ka-sǎan กระเป๋าเอกสาร *Unit 9.1*

bright (of hue) sa-wàaŋ สว่าง *Unit 6.2*

bright (of hue) sòt สด *Unit 6.2*

brother (older) phîi-chaay พี่ชาย *Unit 2.3*

brother (younger) nɔ́ɔŋ-chaay น้องชาย *Unit 2.3*

brothers and sisters phîi-nɔ́ɔŋ พี่น้อง *Unit 2.3*

brown nám-taan น้ำตาล *Unit 6.1*

brown rice khâaw klɔ̂ŋ ข้าวกล้อง *Unit 3.3*

brush prɛɛŋ แปรง *Unit 8.1*

brush one's teeth prɛɛŋ-fan แปรงฟัน *Unit 8.1*

brush one's teeth (informal) sǐi-fan สีฟัน *Unit 8.1*

Buddha image phrá พระ *Unit 4.1*

Buddhist Era phɔɔ-sɔ̌ɔ พ.ศ. *Unit 2.1*

burn, burned, charred mây ไหม้ *Unit 9.1*

bus (city bus) rót-mee รถเมล์ *Unit 5.1*

bus stop pâay-rót-mee ป้ายรถเมล์ *Unit 5.1*

bus terminal sa-thǎa-nii khǒn-sòŋ สถานีขนส่ง *Unit 5.1*

business thú-rá-kìt ธุรกิจ *Unit 2.4*

busy, occupied mii thú-rá มีธุระ *Unit 3.2*

but tɛ̀ɛ แต่ *Unit 1.4*

buy sʉ́ʉ ซื้อ *Unit 3.1*

cabinet tûu ตู้ *Unit 5.4*

cafeteria rooŋ-ʔaa-hǎan โรงอาหาร *Unit 5.1*

cake khéek เค้ก *Unit 3.1*

call rîak เรียก *Unit 1.3*

called, named rîak-wâa เรียกว่า *Unit 1.3*

can (container) kra-pɔ̌ŋ กระป๋อง *Unit 3.1*

can, could dâay, dây ได้ *Unit 1.3*

canal khlɔɔŋ คลอง *Unit 5.2*

canvas (material) phâa bay ผ้าใบ *Unit 6.1*

capital (of a country or state) mʉaŋ-lǔaŋ เมืองหลวง *Unit 5.1*

car rót-yon รถยนต์ *Unit 5.3*

carbonated beverage náam ʔàt-lom น้ำอัดลม *Unit 3.3*

card bàt บัตร *Unit 3.4*

carpet, rug phrom พรม *Unit 5.4*

carry (in the hands) thʉ̌ʉ ถือ *Unit 3.4*

cartoon kaa-tuun การ์ตูน *Unit 7.1*

cash ŋən-sòt เงินสด *Unit 3.4*

catch càp จับ *Unit 1.2*

ceiling phee-daan เพดาน *Unit 5.4*

cellular phone mʉʉ-thʉ̌ʉ มือถือ *Unit 2.2*

center (of activity) sǔun ศูนย์ *Unit 5.1*

centimeter sen-ti-méet เซนติเมตร *Unit 2.1*

certified mail pray-sa-nii ráp pra-kan ไปรษณีย์รับประกัน *Unit 9.2*

certify, guarantee, vouch ráp-rɔɔŋ รับรอง *Unit 9.2*

chair kâw-ʔîi เก้าอี้ *Unit 1.3*

chairman naa-yók นายก *Unit 2.4*

challenge, to put to the test lɔɔŋ-dii ลองดี *Unit 3.4*

change (money returned) ŋən-thɔɔn เงินทอน *Unit 3.1*

change, vary plìan เปลี่ยน *Unit 6.1*

channel chɔ̂ŋ ช่อง *Unit 7.1*

charge khít-raa-khaa คิดราคา *Unit 3.1*

chat khuy คุย *Unit 2.3*

check chék เช็ค *Unit 3.4*

chemical solution (non-technical term) nám-yaa น้ำยา *Unit 8.1*

chest (of body) ʔòk อก *Unit 8.1*

chest of drawers, a dresser lín-chák ลิ้นชัก *Unit 5.4*

chicken kày ไก่ *Unit 3.3*

child (offspring) lûuk ลูก *Unit 2.3*

child (young person) dèk เด็ก *Unit 2.1*

chili pepper phrík พริก *Unit 3.3*

chin khaaŋ คาง *Unit 8.1*

choose, elect, select lʉ̂ak เลือก *Unit 6.3*

chopsticks ta-kìap ตะเกียบ *Unit 3.4*

Christian era khɔɔ-sɔ̌ɔ ค.ศ. *Unit 2.1*

cigarette bu-rìi บุหรี่ *Unit 3.4*

circle woŋ วง *Unit 6.3*

circle, circle-shaped woŋ-klom วงกลม *Unit 6.3*

clean sa-ʔàat สะอาด *Unit 4.2*

clean tham khwaam-sa-ʔàat ทำความสะอาด *Unit 4.2*

climate din fáa ʔaa-kàat ดินฟ้าอากาศ *Unit 10.1*

day after tomorrow ma-rʉʉn มะรืน *Unit 4.3*

day before yesterday mʉ̂a-waan-sʉʉn เมื่อวานซืน *Unit 4.3*

daytime klaaŋ-wan กลางวัน *Unit 4.1*

debit (from an account) tàt ŋən ตัดเงิน *Unit 9.2*

decorate, adorn tɛ̀ŋ แต่ง *Unit 6.1*

defecate khîi ขี้ *Unit 3.2*

degree (academic), diploma pa-rin-yaa ปริญญา *Unit 2.4*

delicious, tasty (as food) ʔa-rɔ̀y อร่อย *Unit 3.4*

dental floss mǎy-khàt-fan ไหมขัดฟัน *Unit 8.1*

depend on (for help), rely on phʉ̂ŋ พึ่ง *Unit 10.1*

depend on, contingent on khʉ̂n-yùu-kàp ขึ้นอยู่กับ *Unit 9.2*

deposit money fàak ŋən ฝากเงิน *Unit 9.2*

desk tóʔ โต๊ะ *Unit 1.3*

dessert, candy kha-nǒm ขนม *Unit 1.3*

dessert, sweetstuffs khɔ̌ɔŋ-wǎan ของหวาน *Unit 3.4*

detain ʔaa-yát อายัด *Unit 9.1*

diagonal chǐaŋ เฉียง *Unit 5.1*

dial a number mǔn thoo-ra-sàp หมุนโทรศัพท์ *Unit 7.2*

dial a number tɔ̀ɔ thoo-ra-sàp ต่อโทรศัพท์ *Unit 7.2*

die taay ตาย *Unit 8.1*

different, various tàaŋ-tàaŋ ต่างๆ *Unit 8.2*

dining room hɔ̂ŋ kin-khâaw ห้องกินข้าว *Unit 5.4*

dining room (formal) hɔ̂ŋ ráp-pra-thaan ʔaa-hǎan ห้องรับประทานอาหาร *Unit 5.4*

direction, point of compass thít ทิศ *Unit 5.1*

dishware thûay-chaam ถ้วยชาม *Unit 5.4*

disturb, bother kuan-cay กวนใจ *Unit 7.2*

divide bɛ̀ŋ แบ่ง *Unit 3.4*

divorce yàa หย่า *Unit 2.3*

do tham ทำ *Unit 1.3*

do errand tham thú-rá ทำธุระ *Unit 9.1*

do not, don't yàa อย่า *Unit 3.3*

doctor mɔ̌ɔ หมอ *Unit 2.4*

document ʔèek-ka-sǎan เอกสาร *Unit 9.1*

documentary sǎa-rá-kha-dii สารคดี *Unit 7.1*

door pra-tuu ประตู *Unit 2.2*

dormitory hɔ̌ɔ-phák หอพัก *Unit 2.2*

down, downward loŋ ลง *Unit 4.1*

downstairs khâaŋ-lâaŋ, khâŋ-lâaŋ ข้างล่าง *Unit 5.2*

draw (a picture) khǐan เขียน *Unit 1.3*

draw back thɔ̌y ถอย *Unit 5.2*

drawing room hɔ̂ŋ ráp-khɛ̀ɛk ห้องรับแขก *Unit 5.4*

dress kra-prooŋ chút กระโปรงชุด *Unit 6.1*

drink dʉ̀ʉm ดื่ม *Unit 3.2*

drink; refreshment khrʉ̂aŋ-dʉ̀ʉm เครื่องดื่ม *Unit 3.3*

drive khàp rót ขับรถ *Unit 5.3*

drop off sòŋ ส่ง *Unit 5.3*

drum klɔɔŋ กลอง *Unit 10.2*

dry (as of the season), arid lɛ́ɛŋ แล้ง *Unit 4.4*

dry, dried hɛ̂ɛŋ แห้ง *Unit 3.3*

duck (animal and meat) pèt เป็ด *Unit 3.3*

durian thú-rian ทุเรียน *Unit 6.3*

each tàaŋ ต่าง *Unit 10.2*

each other, one another, mutually kan กัน *Unit 3.2*

ear hǔu หู *Unit 2.1*

east ta-wan-ʔɔ̀ɔk ตะวันออก *Unit 5.1*

eat kin กิน *Unit 3.2*

eat (one's meal) kin khâaw กินข้าว *Unit 3.2*

eat (something) (formal) ráp-pra-thaan รับประทาน *Unit 5.4*

economics (as a science) sèet-tha-sàat เศรษฐ-ศาสตร์ *Unit 7.2*

economize, thrifty pra-yàt ประหยัด *Unit 7.2*

edge, border, rim chaay ชาย *Unit 5.1*

edge, rim rim ริม *Unit 5.4*

egg khày ไข่ *Unit 3.3*

egg noodles ba-mìi บะหมี่ *Unit 3.3*

egg-shaped (vertical) rûup khày รูปไข่ *Unit 6.3*

elbow khɔ̂ɔ-sɔ̀ɔk ข้อศอก *Unit 8.1*

electricity fay-fáa ไฟฟ้า *Unit 5.2*
elephant cháaŋ ช้าง *Unit 2.1*
embassy sa-thǎan-thûut สถานทูต *Unit 2.4*
emergency chùk-chə̌ən ฉุกเฉิน *Unit 9.1*
empty, blank plàaw เปล่า *Unit 3.3*
encounter danger, face danger pha-con phay ผจญภัย *Unit 7.1*
encounter, meet, face, fight pha-con ผจญ *Unit 7.1*
end còp จบ *Unit 2.4*
end (of anything); tip plaay ปลาย *Unit 4.4*
enough, sufficient phɔɔ พอ *Unit 2.4*
enter khâw เข้า *Unit 3.2*
entertainment ban-thəəŋ บันเทิง *Unit 7.1*
envelope sɔɔŋ ซอง *Unit 9.2*
equal, the same (in size or quantity) thâw เท่า *Unit 3.1*
eraser yaaŋ-lóp ยางลบ *Unit 1.3*
errands thú-rá ธุระ *Unit 3.2*
escape nǐi หนี *Unit 9.1*
even though, even if mɛ́ɛ แม้ *Unit 7.2*
evening yen เย็น *Unit 4.2*
every thúk ทุก *Unit 4.3*
evil chûa ชั่ว *Unit 1.3*
exceed, be in excess of kəən เกิน *Unit 9.2*
exchange lɛ̂ɛk-plìan แลกเปลี่ยน *Unit 1.2*
exchange money lɛ̂ɛk ŋən แลกเงิน *Unit 9.2*
exchange rate ʔàt-traa lɛ̂ɛk-plìan อัตราแลกเปลี่ยน *Unit 9.2*
exclusively cha-phɔ́ʔ เฉพาะ *Unit 6.3*
excrement khîi ขี้ *Unit 3.2*
exercise ʔɔ̀ɔk kam-laŋ-kaay ออกกำลังกาย *Unit 4.2*
exit ʔɔ̀ɔk ออก *Unit 4.2*
expensive phɛɛŋ แพง *Unit 2.2*
explode, burst, blast ra-bə̀ət ระเบิด *Unit 6.3*
express mail pray-sa-nii dùan ไปรษณีย์ด่วน *Unit 9.2*
extra phí-sèet พิเศษ *Unit 3.4*
eye taa ตา *Unit 2.1*
eye-brow khíw คิ้ว *Unit 8.1*

faint pen-lom เป็นลม *Unit 8.2*
fair (of complexion) khǎaw ขาว *Unit 2.1*
fall; to fall down (from, into, onto) tòk ตก *Unit 4.4*
family khrɔ̂ɔp-khrua ครอบครัว *Unit 2.2*
family name; surnamed naam-sa-kun นามสกุล *Unit 1.2*
famous, famed mii chɨ̂ɨ-sǐaŋ มีชื่อเสียง *Unit 2.4*
fan (electric) phát-lom พัดลม *Unit 5.4*
fang khîaw เขี้ยว *Unit 2.1*
far klay ไกล *Unit 5.1*
far hàaŋ ห่าง *Unit 5.1*
fare khâa dooy-sǎan ค่าโดยสาร *Unit 5.3*
fare khâa rót ค่ารถ *Unit 5.3*
fat ʔûan อ้วน *Unit 2.1*
father phɔ̂ɔ พ่อ *Unit 2.3*
father-in-law (man's) phɔ̂ɔ-taa พ่อตา *Unit 2.3*
fax (informal) khrɨ̂aŋ-fɛ̀k เครื่องแฟ็กซ์ *Unit 5.4*
fee khâa tham-niam ค่าธรรมเนียม *Unit 10.2*
festival, festival season thêet-sa-kaan เทศกาล *Unit 10.1*
fever khây ไข้ *Unit 8.2*
feverish khrân-nɨ́a khrân-tua ครั่นเนื้อครั่นตัว *Unit 8.2*
field, lawn sa-nǎam สนาม *Unit 5.1*
fight búu บู๊ *Unit 7.1*
fill, fill out, fill in krɔ̀ɔk กรอก *Unit 9.2*
finger níw นิ้ว *Unit 8.1*
finished sèt เสร็จ *Unit 4.2*
fire fay ไฟ *Unit 9.1*
Fire! fay mây ไฟไหม้ *Unit 9.1*
first rɛ̂ɛk แรก *Unit 2.3*
fish plaa ปลา *Unit 1.2*
fish sauce nám-plaa น้ำปลา *Unit 3.3*
fitting room hɔ̂ŋ-lɔɔŋ ห้องลอง *Unit 6.2*
fixed account ban-chii fàak pra-cam บัญชีฝากประจำ *Unit 9.2*
flag thoŋ ธง *Unit 4.1*
flash (as lightning) lɛ̂p แลบ *Unit 10.1*

flat bɛɛn แบน *Unit 6.3*

flat rate, all inclusive price raa-khaa mǎw ราคาเหมา *Unit 9.2*

flood; floodwaters náam thûam น้ำท่วม *Unit 9.1*

floor phɨ́ɨn พื้น *Unit 5.4*

floor (of building) chán ชั้น *Unit 5.2*

flour pɛ̂ɛŋ แป้ง *Unit 8.1*

flow lǎy ไหล *Unit 8.2*

flower-pot kra-thǎaŋ กระถาง *Unit 5.4*

fluent khlɔ̂ŋ คล่อง *Unit 7.1*

fly bin บิน *Unit 5.1*

fog, mist mɔ̀ɔk หมอก *Unit 10.1*

follow taam ตาม *Unit 3.2*

food ʔaa-hǎan, ʔa-hǎan อาหาร *Unit 2.4*

foot tháaw เท้า *Unit 6.1*

foot (length measurement) fút ฟุต *Unit 2.1*

footware rɔɔŋ-tháaw, rɔŋ-tháaw รองเท้า *Unit 6.1*

for sǎm-ràp สำหรับ *Unit 4.4*

for example chên เช่น *Unit 1.2*

forbid, prohibit; forbidden (to) hâam ห้าม *Unit 5.4*

force oneself (to do something) against one's will fɨ̂ɨn-cay ฝืนใจ *Unit 7.2*

forehead nâa-phàak หน้าผาก *Unit 8.1*

forest, woods pàa ป่า *Unit 10.1*

forget lɨɨm ลืม *Unit 9.1*

fork sɔ̂m ส้อม *Unit 3.4*

form bɛ̀ɛp-fɔɔm แบบฟอร์ม *Unit 9.2*

form, shape rûup รูป *Unit 6.3*

frame krɔ̀ɔp กรอบ *Unit 6.3*

free, unoccupied wâaŋ ว่าง *Unit 4.2*

fresh, raw, uncooked sòt สด *Unit 3.4*

fried egg khày-daaw ไข่ดาว *Unit 3.3*

fried rice khâaw phàt ข้าวผัด *Unit 3.3*

frog kòp กบ *Unit 2.1*

from càak จาก *Unit 1.2*

from (a time or starting point), since tâŋ-tɛ̀ɛ ตั้งแต่ *Unit 10.1*

from now on, as follows tɔ̀ɔ-pay-níi ต่อไปนี้ *Unit 10.2*

front nâa หน้า *Unit 4.3*

fruit phǒn-la-máay ผลไม้ *Unit 3.3*

fry thɔ̂ɔt ทอด *Unit 3.3*

full (from eating) ʔìm อิ่ม *Unit 3.2*

funny ta-lòk ตลก *Unit 7.1*

furniture fɔɔ-ni-cɔ̂ɔ เฟอร์นิเจอร์ *Unit 5.4*

furniture khrɨ̂aŋ-rɨan เครื่องเรือน *Unit 5.4*

game show keem-choo เกมโชว์ *Unit 7.1*

garage rooŋ-rót โรงรถ *Unit 5.4*

garden sǔan สวน *Unit 5.4*

gather together, congregate chum-num ชุมนุม *Unit 10.2*

generous cay-kwâaŋ ใจกว้าง *Unit 7.2*

germ, bacteria chɨ́a เชื้อ *Unit 8.2*

get better khɔ̂y-yaŋ-chûa ค่อยยังชั่ว *Unit 8.2*

get dressed tɛ̀ŋ-kaay แต่งกาย *Unit 6.1*

get dressed, be dressed tɛ̀ŋ-tua แต่งตัว *Unit 6.1*

get up, to get to one's feet lúk ลุก *Unit 10.2*

get well hǎay หาย *Unit 8.2*

get, obtain dâay ได้ *Unit 2.3*

ghost, spirit phǐi ผี *Unit 7.1*

giant, ogre yák ยักษ์ *Unit 2.1*

gift, present khɔ̌ɔŋ-khwǎn ของขวัญ *Unit 9.2*

girlfriend (slang) fɛɛn แฟน *Unit 2.3*

give change (money) thɔɔn ทอน *Unit 3.1*

glad, to be happy yin-dii ยินดี *Unit 1.2*

glass kɛ̂ɛw แก้ว *Unit 3.1*

glasses, spectacles wɛ̂n แว่น *Unit 6.2*

go pay ไป *Unit 1.1*

go around (here and there for pleasure); to go out (as for an evening) pay thîaw ไปเที่ยว *Unit 4.2*

go back klàp กลับ *Unit 4.2*

go beyond, to pass ləəy เลย *Unit 5.2*

go out (for fun), go (from place to place) thîaw เที่ยว *Unit 1.3*

go to bed khâw nɔɔn เข้านอน *Unit 4.2*

good dii ดี *Unit 1.1*

government official khâa-râat-cha-kaan ข้าราช-

i

I chǎn, chán ฉัน *Unit 1.2*

I (for female) di-chǎn, di-chán ดิฉัน *Unit 1.2*

I (for male) phǒm ผม *Unit 1.2*

I apologize. I'm sorry. khɔ̌ɔ-thôot, khɔ̌-thôot ขอโทษ *Unit 1.1*

I'm fine. sa-baay dii สบายดี *Unit 1.1*

I'm in trouble. There's trouble. yɛ̂ɛ-lɛ́ɛw แย่แล้ว *Unit 8.1*

ice nám-khɛ̌ŋ น้ำแข็ง *Unit 3.3*

ice cream ʔay-sa-khriim, ʔay-sa-kriim ไอศกรีม *Unit 3.4*

if thâa ถ้า *Unit 3.1*

if that is so, in that case thâa-yaŋ-ŋán ถ้ายังงั้น *Unit 2.3*

if, in case, provided that hàak หาก *Unit 7.2*

impatient cay-rɔ́ɔn ใจร้อน *Unit 7.2*

in nay ใน *Unit 1.2*

in front khâaŋ-nâa, khâŋ-nâa ข้างหน้า *Unit 5.2*

in order to cʉŋ-ca จึงจะ *Unit 9.2*

in order to, in order that phʉ̂a ca-dâay เพื่อจะได้ *Unit 7.1*

in the back khâaŋ-lǎŋ, khâŋ-lǎŋ ข้างหลัง *Unit 5.2*

in the direction of thaaŋ ทาง *Unit 5.1*

in time than ทัน *Unit 8.1*

inch níw นิ้ว *Unit 2.1*

include ruam รวม *Unit 3.4*

including ruam-tháŋ รวมทั้ง *Unit 9.2*

inflamed, infected ʔàk-sèep อักเสบ *Unit 8.2*

inflated fɔ́ɔ เฟ้อ *Unit 8.2*

inform cɛ̂ɛŋ แจ้ง *Unit 9.1*

inform (to a superior) rian เรียน *Unit 7.2*

ingredient khrʉ̂aŋ-pruŋ เครื่องปรุง *Unit 3.3*

inject, inoculate chìit ฉีด *Unit 8.2*

injured, wounded bàat-cèp บาดเจ็บ *Unit 9.1*

in-law (female) sa-pháy สะใภ้ *Unit 2.3*

in-law (male) khɔ̌ɔy เขย *Unit 2.3*

inside khâaŋ-nay, khâŋ-nay ข้างใน *Unit 5.2*

inspect, examine, check trùat ตรวจ *Unit 8.2*

instant khrûu ครู่ *Unit 7.2*

institution sa-thǎa-ban สถาบัน *Unit 6.1*

interested (in) sǒn-cay สนใจ *Unit 6.1*

interesting nâa-sǒn-cay น่าสนใจ *Unit 7.1*

Internet ʔin-thəə-nèt อินเทอร์เน็ต *Unit 7.1*

interview sǎm-phâat สัมภาษณ์ *Unit 7.1*

introduce nɛ́ʔ-nam แนะนำ *Unit 1.2*

investigate sʉ̀ʉp-sǔan สืบสวน *Unit 7.1*

invite chəən เชิญ *Unit 4.1*

iron taw-rîit เตารีด *Unit 5.4*

iron (metal) lèk เหล็ก *Unit 6.3*

iron, press rîit รีด *Unit 5.4*

island kɔ̀ʔ เกาะ *Unit 10.1*

it man มัน *Unit 2.1*

It's true. I agree. ciŋ-dûay จริงด้วย *Unit 3.4*

itch, to be itchy khan คัน *Unit 8.2*

It's raining. It rains. fǒn tòk ฝนตก *Unit 4.4*

jackfruit kha-nǔn ขนุน *Unit 3.1*

jar khùat ขวด *Unit 3.1*

jeans kaŋ-keeŋ yiin กางเกงยีน *Unit 6.1*

join, connect tɔ̀ɔ ต่อ *Unit 2.4*

juice náam phǒn-la-máay น้ำผลไม้ *Unit 3.3*

junction yɛ̂ɛk แยก *Unit 5.2*

just now phɔ̂ŋ เพิ่ง *Unit 9.1*

just right (in size, amount) kam-laŋ-dii กำลังดี *Unit 6.2*

just right (in size, amount) phɔɔ-dii พอดี *Unit 6.2*

just, approximately; only sàk, sák สัก *Unit 3.4*

keep kèp เก็บ *Unit 5.4*

keep company with khóp-hǎa คบหา *Unit 7.2*

kill khâa ฆ่า *Unit 8.2*

kilogram ki-loo-kram กิโลกรัม *Unit 2.1*

kind cay-dii ใจดี *Unit 7.2*

kitchen hɔ̂ŋ khrua ห้องครัว *Unit 5.4*

knee khàw เข่า *Unit 8.1*

knick-knacks khɔ̌ɔŋ kra-cùk-kra-cìk ของ

กระจุกกระจิก *Unit 7.1*

knife mîit มีด *Unit 3.4*

know, acquainted with rúu-càk รู้จัก *Unit 1.2*

know; learn of (formal) sâap ทราบ *Unit 7.2*

l

lab lɛ̀p แล็บ *Unit 4.3*

lamp, lighting fixture khoom-fay โคมไฟ *Unit 5.4*

lanai, balcony ra-biaŋ ระเบียง *Unit 5.4*

lane leen เลน *Unit 9.1*

language phaa-sǎa, pha-sǎa ภาษา *Unit 1.3*

late sǎay สาย *Unit 4.2*

late at night dʉ̀k ดึก *Unit 4.2*

late evening khâm ค่ำ *Unit 4.2*

late morning sǎay สาย *Unit 4.2*

later wan-lǎŋ วันหลัง *Unit 4.3*

laugh hǔa-rɔ́ʔ หัวเราะ *Unit 8.1*

launder sák phâa ซักผ้า *Unit 4.2*

law kòt-mǎay กฎหมาย *Unit 2.4*

layer chán ชั้น *Unit 6.1*

learn, study (formal) sʉ̀k-sǎa ศึกษา *Unit 4.3*

leather nǎŋ หนัง *Unit 6.2*

leave (something) (with someone) fàak ฝาก *Unit 7.2*

leave a message fàak khɔ̂ɔ-khwaam ฝากข้อความ *Unit 7.2*

left (direction) sáay ซ้าย *Unit 2.1*

leg khǎa ขา *Unit 6.1*

lemon ma-naaw มะนาว *Unit 3.3*

letter còt-mǎay จดหมาย *Unit 9.2*

level chán ชั้น *Unit 5.2*

library hɔ̂ŋ-sa-mùt ห้องสมุด *Unit 2.4*

life chii-wít ชีวิต *Unit 7.1*

lift, raise yók ยก *Unit 10.1*

light (of color) ʔɔ̀ɔn อ่อน *Unit 6.2*

light, electricity fay ไฟ *Unit 5.2*

lightning fáa lɛ̂p ฟ้าแลบ *Unit 10.1*

like, be fond of chɔ̂ɔp ชอบ *Unit 2.4*

likewise mʉ̌an-kan เหมือนกัน *Unit 1.2*

lime ma-naaw มะนาว *Unit 3.3*

line, route sǎay สาย *Unit 5.1*

lineage, descendants chʉ́a-sǎay เชื้อสาย *Unit 1.4*

list, list of items raay-kaan รายการ *Unit 7.1*

listen faŋ ฟัง *Unit 1.3*

little, small (in quantity) nɔ́ɔy น้อย *Unit 3.4*

live, stay, dwell yùu อยู่ *Unit 2.2*

living room hɔ̂ŋ nâŋ-lên ห้องนั่งเล่น *Unit 5.4*

lobster kûŋ กุ้ง *Unit 3.3*

logo traa ตรา *Unit 9.2*

long (of objects) yaaw ยาว *Unit 2.1*

long time naan นาน *Unit 5.3*

longan (fruit) lam-yay ลำไย *Unit 3.1*

long-sleeved top sʉ̂a khɛ̌ɛn yaaw เสื้อแขนยาว *Unit 6.1*

look duu ดู *Unit 4.2*

look for, search for hǎa หา *Unit 2.2*

loose (of clothing) lǔam หลวม *Unit 6.2*

lose sǐa เสีย *Unit 5.3*

loud daŋ ดัง *Unit 1.3*

lovable, lovely, cute nâa-rák น่ารัก *Unit 2.1*

love rák รัก *Unit 7.1*

lychee lín-cìi ลิ้นจี่ *Unit 6.3*

magazine mɛ́k-kaa-siin แมกกาซีน *Unit 7.1*

magazine nít-ta-yá-sǎan นิตยสาร *Unit 7.1*

magazine, journal waa-ra-sǎan วารสาร *Unit 7.1*

mango ma-mûaŋ มะม่วง *Unit 6.3*

mangosteen maŋ-khút มังคุด *Unit 6.3*

many, several lǎay หลาย *Unit 6.2*

map phɛ̌ɛn-thîi แผนที่ *Unit 1.3*

mark with line khìit ขีด *Unit 3.1*

mark, symbol khrʉ̂aŋ-mǎay เครื่องหมาย *Unit 7.2*

market ta-làat ตลาด *Unit 1.3*

marry, married tɛ̀ŋ-ŋaan แต่งงาน *Unit 2.3*

meal ʔaa-hǎan, ʔa-hǎan อาหาร *Unit 2.4*

mean, unkind cay-dam ใจดำ *Unit 7.2*

meat, flesh nʉ́a เนื้อ *Unit 3.3*

meatball lûuk-chín ลูกชิ้น *Unit 3.3*

medicine, drug yaa ยา *Unit 8.1*
medium (of size) klaaŋ กลาง *Unit 6.2*
meet (in a group), assemble; to hold a meeting pra-chum ประชุม *Unit 10.2*
meet (spoken) cəə เจอ *Unit 1.1*
menu mee-nuu เมนู *Unit 3.3*
method, way, means wí-thii วิธี *Unit 3.3*
microwave may-khroo-wéep ไมโครเวฟ *Unit 5.4*
midday, noon thîaŋ-wan เที่ยงวัน *Unit 4.1*
middle, center klaaŋ กลาง *Unit 2.2*
midnight thîaŋ-khʉʉn เที่ยงคืน *Unit 4.1*
million láan ล้าน *Unit 2.2*
mind cay ใจ *Unit 4.2*
minibus taxi rót sɔ̌ɔŋ-thɛ̌ɛw รถสองแถว *Unit 5.3*
minister (of the government) rát-tha-mon-trii รัฐมนตรี *Unit 2.4*
minute (of time) naa-thii นาที *Unit 4.1*
model (female) naaŋ-bɛ̀ɛp นางแบบ *Unit 2.1*
mold (e.g. things of clay, plaster, etc.) pân ปั้น *Unit 10.1*
money ŋən เงิน *Unit 2.4*
money (spoken) taŋ ตังค์ *Unit 3.4*
monsoon mɔɔ-ra-sǔm มรสุม *Unit 10.1*
month dʉan เดือน *Unit 2.2*
more (to a greater degree) kwàa กว่า *Unit 2.1*
morning (time) cháaw เช้า *Unit 4.2*
mosquito net múŋ มุ้ง *Unit 5.4*
most, -est thîi-sùt ที่สุด *Unit 4.4*
mostly, the greater part sùan-mâak ส่วนมาก *Unit 6.1*
mother mɛ̂ɛ แม่ *Unit 2.3*
mother-in-law, wife's mother mɛ̂ɛ-yaay แม่ยาย *Unit 2.3*
motorcycle càk-ka-yaan-yon จักรยานยนต์ *Unit 5.3*
motorcycle mɔɔ-təə-say มอเตอร์ไซค์ *Unit 5.3*
mountain phuu-khǎw ภูเขา *Unit 7.1*
mountain, hill khǎw เขา *Unit 10.1*
mouse nǔu หนู *Unit 3.4*
moustache nùat หนวด *Unit 8.1*
mouth pàak ปาก *Unit 5.4*
mouthwash nám-yaa bûan-pàak น้ำยาบ้วนปาก *Unit 8.1*
movie nǎŋ หนัง *Unit 4.2*
movie theater rooŋ-nǎŋ โรงหนัง *Unit 5.1*
MSG, monosodium glutamate phǒŋ chuu rót ผงชูรส *Unit 3.3*
muscle klâam กล้าม *Unit 6.1*
music don-trii ดนตรี *Unit 4.2*
must, have to tɔ̂ŋ ต้อง *Unit 3.4*
mysterious lʉ́k-láp ลึกลับ *Unit 7.1*

n

nail (of a finger) lép เล็บ *Unit 8.1*
name, named chʉ̂ʉ ชื่อ *Unit 1.2*
narrow-minded cay-khɛ̂ɛp ใจแคบ *Unit 7.2*
nasal mucus, nasal discharge nám-mûuk น้ำมูก *Unit 8.2*
nation châat ชาติ *Unit 4.1*
national flag thoŋ-châat ธงชาติ *Unit 4.1*
navy blue krom-ma-thâa กรมท่า *Unit 6.1*
near klây ใกล้ *Unit 2.1*
neck khɔɔ คอ *Unit 8.1*
necktie nék-thay เนคไท *Unit 6.1*
neighbor phʉ̂an-bâan เพื่อนบ้าน *Unit 1.4*
news khàaw ข่าว *Unit 7.1*
nickname, nicknamed chʉ̂ʉ-lên ชื่อเล่น *Unit 1.2*
night khʉʉn คืน *Unit 4.1*
nighttime klaaŋ-khʉʉn กลางคืน *Unit 4.1*
No, it's not! No! mây-chây ไม่ใช่ *Unit 1.3*
no, not mây ไม่ *Unit 1.1*
non colorfast sǐi tòk สีตก *Unit 6.2*
noodles kǔay-tǐaw ก๋วยเตี๋ยว *Unit 3.3*
noon thîaŋ เที่ยง *Unit 4.1*
normal, usual pòk-ka-tì, pà-ka-tì ปกติ *Unit 3.4*
north, northern nʉ̌a เหนือ *Unit 2.2*
northeast ʔii-sǎan อีสาน *Unit 2.2*
northeast ta-wan-ʔɔ̀ɔk-chǐaŋ-nʉ̌a ตะวันออกเฉียงเหนือ *Unit 5.1*
northwest ta-wan-tòk-chǐaŋ-nʉ̌a ตะวันตกเฉียงเหนือ *Unit 5.1*

o

pick a pocket, to put one's hand in a pocket or bag lúaŋ kra-pǎw ล้วงกระเป๋า *Unit 9.1*

pick up ráp รับ *Unit 5.3*

picture rûup รูป *Unit 5.4*

pier thâa-rʉa ท่าเรือ *Unit 5.1*

pig, pork mǔu หมู *Unit 2.1*

pineapple sàp-pa-rót สับปะรด *Unit 3.1*

pink chom-phuu ชมพู *Unit 6.1*

place thîi ที่ *Unit 3.3*

place, site sa-thǎan-thîi สถานที่ *Unit 4.1*

plain (white) rice khâaw plàaw ข้าวเปล่า *Unit 3.3*

platform (rail station) chaan chaa-laa ชานชาลา *Unit 10.2*

play lên เล่น *Unit 4.2*

play, soap opera la-khɔɔn ละคร *Unit 7.1*

playing cards phây ไพ่ *Unit 7.1*

please (do such and such) kà-rú-naa, ka-ru-naa กรุณา *Unit 6.1*

please (do such and such) pròot โปรด *Unit 6.1*

Please do. Go ahead. chəən เชิญ *Unit 1.1*

pleased, to be satisfactory doon-cay โดนใจ *Unit 7.2*

pleasing, satisfactory thùuk-cay ถูกใจ *Unit 7.2*

plenty yə́ʔ เยอะ *Unit 3.1*

plenty yə́ʔ-yɛ́ʔ เยอะแยะ *Unit 3.1*

plump, be fat thúam ท้วม *Unit 2.1*

pocket kra-pǎw กระเป๋า *Unit 9.1*

poet ka-wii กวี *Unit 2.4*

point cùt จุด *Unit 6.1*

police station sa-thǎa-nii tam-rùat สถานีตำรวจ *Unit 5.1*

policeman tam-rùat ตำรวจ *Unit 2.4*

polite sù-phâap สุภาพ *Unit 6.1*

politics; political affairs kaan-mʉaŋ การเมือง *Unit 2.4*

polo shirt sʉ̂a poo-loo เสื้อโปโล *Unit 6.1*

pomelo sôm-ʔoo ส้มโอ *Unit 6.3*

porch, terrace cha-lǐaŋ เฉลียง *Unit 5.4*

porch, terrace nɔ̂ɔk-chaan นอกชาน *Unit 5.4*

post office pray-sa-nii ไปรษณีย์ *Unit 9.2*

postbox tûu pray-sa-nii ตู้ไปรษณีย์ *Unit 9.2*

postcard póos-káat โปสการ์ด *Unit 9.2*

pound (weight) pɔɔn ปอนด์ *Unit 2.1*

power, energy, force kam-laŋ กำลัง *Unit 4.2*

practice fʉ̀k ฝึก *Unit 4.3*

prawn kûŋ กุ้ง *Unit 3.3*

press on (something), push kòt กด *Unit 7.2*

pretty (of things that are seen) sǔay สวย *Unit 2.1*

previous day wan-kɔ̀ɔn วันก่อน *Unit 4.3*

previous, preceding thîi-lɛ́ɛw ที่แล้ว *Unit 4.3*

price raa-khaa ราคา *Unit 3.1*

priest phrá พระ *Unit 4.1*

prime minister; premier naa-yók rát-tha-mon-trii นายกรัฐมนตรี *Unit 2.4*

prize, reward, award raaŋ-wan รางวัล *Unit 9.1*

probably khoŋ-ca คงจะ *Unit 2.1*

profession ʔaa-chîip อาชีพ *Unit 2.4*

professor ʔaa-caan, ʔa-caan อาจารย์ *Unit 1.1*

proficiently, skillfully kèŋ เก่ง *Unit 1.3*

program proo-krɛm โปรแกรม *Unit 4.4*

pub; bar; tavern phàp ผับ *Unit 7.1*

purple mûaŋ ม่วง *Unit 6.1*

purse, wallet kra-pǎw sa-taaŋ กระเป๋าสตางค์ *Unit 9.1*

put on lipstick thaa-pàak ทาปาก *Unit 8.1*

put on, to put in sày ใส่ *Unit 6.1*

put on, wear sǔam สวม *Unit 6.1*

put, lay waaŋ วาง *Unit 7.2*

q

quit, be over, give up lə̂ək เลิก *Unit 7.2*

r

radio, wireless wít-tha-yú วิทยุ *Unit 4.1*

rain fǒn ฝน *Unit 4.4*

rainbow rúŋ รุ้ง *Unit 10.1*

raise, breed líaŋ เลี้ยง *Unit 10.2*

rambutan ŋɔ́ʔ เงาะ *Unit 6.3*

rash phɨɨn ผื่น *Unit 8.2*
rash (heat), prickly heat phòt ผด *Unit 8.2*
rate ʔàt-traa อัตรา *Unit 9.2*
reach into (e.g. a pocket, deep drawer, hole) lúaŋ ล้วง *Unit 9.1*
read ʔàan อ่าน *Unit 1.3*
ready phrɔ́ɔm พร้อม *Unit 10.1*
ready, all set rîap-rɔ́ɔy เรียบร้อย *Unit 10.2*
really, very ciŋ-ciŋ จริงๆ *Unit 6.1*
receive, accept ráp รับ *Unit 3.1*
recline nɔɔn นอน *Unit 3.2*
recommendation letter còt-mǎay ráp-rɔɔŋ จดหมายรับรอง *Unit 9.2*
recover from sickness hǎay-pùay หายป่วย *Unit 8.2*
rectangle, rectangular sìi-lìam สี่เหลี่ยม *Unit 6.3*
red dɛɛŋ แดง *Unit 5.2*
reduce the price, discount lót-raa-khaa ลดราคา *Unit 3.1*
reduce, decrease lót ลด *Unit 3.1*
refrigerator tûu-yen ตู้เย็น *Unit 5.4*
region (an administrative unit) phâak ภาค *Unit 2.2*
registered mail pray-sa-nii loŋ tha-bian ไปรษณีย์ลงทะเบียน *Unit 9.2*
regret (about a lost opportunity) sǐa-daay เสียดาย *Unit 7.2*
regularly, habitually pra-cam ประจำ *Unit 6.1*
relative, kin yâat ญาติ *Unit 2.3*
relatives yâat-phîi-nɔ́ɔŋ ญาติพี่น้อง *Unit 2.3*
remedy, relieve (an illness) kɛ̂ɛ แก้ *Unit 8.2*
rental fee khâa châw ค่าเช่า *Unit 2.2*
report to police cɛ̂ɛŋ-khwaam แจ้งความ *Unit 9.1*
reputation chɨ̂ɨ-sǐaŋ ชื่อเสียง *Unit 2.4*
request khɔ̌ɔ ขอ *Unit 3.3*
research khón-khwáa ค้นคว้า *Unit 2.4*
reserve, make a reservation cɔɔŋ จอง *Unit 10.2*
respect khaw-róp เคารพ *Unit 4.1*
rest, take a rest phák-phɔ̀n พักผ่อน *Unit 5.4*
restaurant ráan ʔaa-hǎan ร้านอาหาร *Unit 5.1*
return (something) khɨɨn คืน *Unit 4.1*
return trip khǎa-klàp ขากลับ *Unit 10.1*
rice khâaw ข้าว *Unit 3.2*
rice soup khâaw tôm ข้าวต้ม *Unit 3.3*
ride, straddle khìi ขี่ *Unit 4.2*
right (direction) khwǎa ขวา *Unit 2.1*
rinse one's mouth bûan-pàak บ้วนปาก *Unit 8.1*
river mɛ̂ɛ-náam แม่น้ำ *Unit 5.2*
roast, to barbeque yâaŋ ย่าง *Unit 3.3*
rob plôn ปล้น *Unit 9.1*
room hɔ̂ŋ ห้อง *Unit 1.3*
rose apple chom-phûu ชมพู่ *Unit 6.3*
round klom กลม *Unit 6.3*
round trip pay klàp ไปกลับ *Unit 10.2*
routine kìt-ca-wát กิจวัตร *Unit 8.1*
run wîŋ วิ่ง *Unit 3.2*

S

safe, out of danger plɔ̀ɔt-phay ปลอดภัย *Unit 10.1*
sailboat rɨa-bay เรือใบ *Unit 7.1*
salary, monthly salary ŋən-dɨan เงินเดือน *Unit 2.4*
salt klɨa เกลือ *Unit 3.3*
salty khem เค็ม *Unit 3.3*
same (in size or quantity) thâw เท่า *Unit 3.1*
savings (account) ʔɔɔm-sáp ออมทรัพย์ *Unit 9.2*
savings account ban-chii ʔɔɔm-sáp บัญชีออมทรัพย์ *Unit 9.1*
say phûut พูด *Unit 1.3*
scald, to blanch (vegetables), to parboil lûak ลวก *Unit 3.3*
school rooŋ-rian โรงเรียน *Unit 5.1*
science, sciences wít-tha-yaa-sàat วิทยาศาสตร์ *Unit 7.1*
Scotch, Scottish, Scotland sa-kɔ́t สก็อต *Unit 6.1*
sea tha-lee ทะเล *Unit 3.3*
seaside chaay-tha-lee ชายทะเล *Unit 7.1*
season nâa หน้า *Unit 4.4*
season rɨ́-duu ฤดู *Unit 4.4*

season, flavor pruŋ ปรุง *Unit 3.3*
seasoning khrʉ̂aŋ-pruŋ เครื่องปรุง *Unit 3.3*
second wí-naa-thii วินาที *Unit 4.3*
secretary lee-khǎa-nú-kaan เลขานุการ *Unit 2.4*
section (of a town, place) thɛ̌ɛw แถว *Unit 2.2*
section (of space or time) tɔɔn ตอน *Unit 3.4*
sedan (car, automobile) rót-kěŋ รถเก๋ง *Unit 10.2*
see hěn เห็น *Unit 2.1*
seed, grain mét เม็ด *Unit 6.3*
sell khǎay ขาย *Unit 3.1*
sell (formal) cam-nàay จำหน่าย *Unit 9.2*
semester (of school) phâak kaan-sʉ̀k-sǎa ภาคการศึกษา *Unit 4.3*
send sòŋ ส่ง *Unit 3.3*
serve bɔɔ-ri-kaan บริการ *Unit 4.3*
serve, be in service of ráp-cháy รับใช้ *Unit 10.1*
serve, wait on a table sə̀əp เสิร์ฟ *Unit 2.4*
service bɔɔ-ri-kaan บริการ *Unit 4.3*
serving spoon chɔ́ɔn-klaaŋ ช้อนกลาง *Unit 3.4*
set up, establish tâŋ ตั้ง *Unit 5.4*
shampoo chɛm-phuu แชมพู *Unit 8.1*
shampoo yaa-sà-phǒm ยาสระผม *Unit 8.1*
shave koon โกน *Unit 8.1*
shaving cream khriim koon-nùat ครีมโกนหนวด *Unit 8.1*
she kháw เขา *Unit 1.2*
shelf chán ชั้น *Unit 5.4*
shell (of egg, nut) plʉ̀ak เปลือก *Unit 6.3*
shellfish hɔ̌y หอย *Unit 3.3*
shirt sʉ̂a-chə́ət เสื้อเชิ้ต *Unit 6.1*
shirt, blouse sʉ̂a เสื้อ *Unit 3.1*
shit, defecate ʔʉ̀ʔ อึ, ขี้ *Unit 3.2*
shoot, shoot at yiŋ ยิง *Unit 2.3*
shop sʉ́ʉ-khɔ̌ɔŋ ซื้อของ *Unit 3.2*
shopping chɔ́p-pîŋ ช็อปปิ้ง *Unit 7.1*
shopping center sǔun-kaan-kháa ศูนย์การค้า *Unit 5.1*
short (in length) sân สั้น *Unit 2.1*
short story rʉ̂aŋ-sân เรื่องสั้น *Unit 7.1*
short, low (in height) tîa เตี้ย *Unit 2.1*
shorts, short pants kaŋ-keeŋ khǎa-sân กางเกงขาสั้น *Unit 6.1*
short-sleeved top sʉ̂a khɛ̌ɛn sân เสื้อแขนสั้น *Unit 6.1*
should khuan-ca ควรจะ *Unit 6.3*
shrimp kûŋ กุ้ง *Unit 3.3*
shrink hòt หด *Unit 6.2*
sibling (older), i.e. older brother or sister phîi พี่ *Unit 2.3*
sibling (younger), i.e. younger brother or sister nɔ́ɔŋ น้อง *Unit 2.1*
sick (in the stomach), to feel nauseated khlʉ̂ʉn-sây คลื่นไส้ *Unit 8.2*
sick, ill, unwell pùay ป่วย *Unit 8.2*
side khâaŋ ข้าง *Unit 5.2*
side dâan ด้าน *Unit 5.4*
sign sen เซ็น *Unit 9.2*
sign, placard pâay ป้าย *Unit 5.1*
silk mǎy ไหม *Unit 6.2*
sincere ciŋ-cay จริงใจ *Unit 7.2*
sing rɔ́ɔŋ-phleeŋ ร้องเพลง *Unit 2.4*
single (quantity) dìaw เดี่ยว *Unit 6.1*
single, unmarried state sòot โสด *Unit 2.3*
sister (older) phîi-sǎaw พี่สาว *Unit 2.3*
sister (younger) nɔ́ɔŋ-sǎaw น้องสาว *Unit 2.3*
sit nâŋ นั่ง *Unit 3.2*
size kha-nàat ขนาด *Unit 6.2*
skiing, ski sa-kii สกี *Unit 7.1*
skirt krà-prooŋ, kra-prooŋ กระโปรง *Unit 6.1*
sky fáa ฟ้า *Unit 7.2*
sky blue (color) fáa ฟ้า *Unit 6.1*
slap, clap tòp ตบ *Unit 8.1*
sleeping car, sleeper (of a train) rót nɔɔn รถนอน *Unit 10.2*
sleepy, drowsy ŋûaŋ-nɔɔn ง่วงนอน *Unit 3.2*
sleeve khɛ̌ɛn แขน *Unit 6.1*
sleeveless blouse sʉ̂a khɛ̌ɛn kùt เสื้อแขนกุด *Unit 6.1*
slippers, sandals rɔŋ-tháaw-tɛ̀ รองเท้าแตะ *Unit 6.1*
slow cháa ช้า *Unit 1.3*

small (in size) lék เล็ก *Unit 3.3*
smile yím ยิ้ม *Unit 8.1*
snake ŋuu งู *Unit 5.1*
sneeze caam จาม *Unit 8.2*
snow hi-má หิมะ *Unit 4.4*
soap sa-bùu สบู่ *Unit 8.1*
socks thǔŋ-tháaw ถุงเท้า *Unit 6.1*
sofa kâw-ʔîi-yaaw เก้าอี้ยาว *Unit 5.4*
sofa soo-faa โซฟา *Unit 5.4*
soil din ดิน *Unit 10.1*
soldier tha-hǎan ทหาร *Unit 2.4*
sole; only one diaw เดียว *Unit 2.3*
some baaŋ บาง *Unit 4.4*
sometimes, at times baaŋ-thii บางที *Unit 4.4*
son lûuk-chaay ลูกชาย *Unit 2.3*
sopadilla la-mút ละมุด *Unit 6.3*
sorry, feel sorry, regret sǐa-cay เสียใจ *Unit 7.2*
soup kɛɛŋ-cʉ̀ʉt แกงจืด *Unit 3.3*
soup/curry dish kɛɛŋ แกง *Unit 3.3*
south, southern tâay ใต้ *Unit 2.2*
southeast ta-wan-ʔɔ̀ɔk-chǐaŋ-tâay ตะวันออกเฉียงใต้ *Unit 5.1*
southwest ta-wan-tòk-chǐaŋ-tâay ตะวันตกเฉียงใต้ *Unit 5.1*
spaghetti strap tank top sʉ̂a sǎay-dìaw เสื้อสายเดี่ยว *Unit 6.1*
speak phûut พูด *Unit 1.3*
special phí-sèet พิเศษ *Unit 3.4*
spend càay จ่าย *Unit 3.2*
spicy curry kɛɛŋ-phèt แกงเผ็ด *Unit 3.3*
spicy salad yam ยำ *Unit 3.3*
spicy soup tôm-yam ต้มยำ *Unit 3.3*
spicy; peppery phèt เผ็ด *Unit 3.3*
spirits, morale khwǎn ขวัญ *Unit 7.1*
spoon chɔ́ɔn ช้อน *Unit 3.4*
sports kii-laa กีฬา *Unit 7.1*
sports shoes rɔɔŋ-tháaw kii-laa รองเท้ากีฬา *Unit 6.1*
sprinkle rooy โรย *Unit 3.4*
squid, cuttlefish plaa mʉ̀k ปลาหมึก *Unit 3.3*
stadium sa-nǎam kii-laa สนามกีฬา *Unit 5.1*
stair, staircase ban-day บันได *Unit 5.4*
stamp sa-tɛm แสตมป์ *Unit 9.2*
stand yʉʉn ยืน *Unit 4.1*
star fruit ma-fʉaŋ มะเฟือง *Unit 6.3*
state rát รัฐ *Unit 1.4*
statement, message khɔ̂ɔ-khwaam ข้อความ *Unit 7.2*
station sa-thǎa-nii สถานี *Unit 4.1*
stay over (as at someone's home, at a hotel) phák พัก *Unit 2.2*
steal kha-mooy ขโมย *Unit 9.1*
steam nʉ̂ŋ นึ่ง *Unit 3.3*
stepfather; foster father phɔ̂ɔ-líaŋ พ่อเลี้ยง *Unit 2.3*
stew, to braise tǔn ตุ๋น *Unit 3.3*
sticky rice khâaw nǐaw ข้าวเหนียว *Unit 3.3*
sticky, viscous nǐaw เหนียว *Unit 3.3*
stomach thɔ́ɔŋ ท้อง *Unit 8.1*
stop in, drop in (to see someone) wɛ́ʔ แวะ *Unit 3.2*
stop, take a break yùt หยุด *Unit 4.2*
storage room, closet hɔ̂ŋ kèp-khɔ̌ɔŋ ห้องเก็บของ *Unit 5.4*
store, shop ráan ร้าน *Unit 2.4*
storm phaa-yúʔ พายุ *Unit 10.1*
story, subject, subject matter rʉ̂aŋ เรื่อง *Unit 6.3*
stove taw เตา *Unit 5.4*
straight troŋ ตรง *Unit 5.2*
strange, unusual plɛ̀ɛk แปลก *Unit 7.2*
street, road tha-nǒn ถนน *Unit 2.2*
stretch, extend, lengthen yʉ̂ʉt ยืด *Unit 6.1*
stroke, pat, wipe lûup ลูบ *Unit 8.1*
student nák-sʉ̀k-sǎa นักศึกษา *Unit 1.2*
study (in a class) rian เรียน *Unit 1.2*
study further, continue to study rian-tɔ̀ɔ เรียนต่อ *Unit 2.4*
study room, office hɔ̂ŋ tham-ŋaan ห้องทำงาน *Unit 5.4*
style a hairdo tham-phǒm ทำผม *Unit 8.1*
subject (of study) wí-chaa วิชา *Unit 7.2*

subway, underground train rót-fay tâay-din รถไฟใต้ดิน *Unit 5.3*

such as, like yàaŋ อย่าง *Unit 7.1*

suffer, to be unhappy thúk ทุกข์ *Unit 7.2*

sugar nám-taan น้ำตาล *Unit 3.3*

sugarcane ʔɔ̂ɔy อ้อย *Unit 3.3*

suit sùut สูท *Unit 6.1*

suitcoat, jacket sɯ̂a-nɔ̂ɔk เสื้อนอก *Unit 6.1*

sunlight dɛ̀ɛt แดด *Unit 10.1*

surfing, surf, ride the waves tôo-khlɯ̂ɯn โต้คลื่น *Unit 7.1*

surprised, amazed plɛ̀ɛk-cay แปลกใจ *Unit 7.2*

surround, encircle lɔ́ɔm ล้อม *Unit 10.2*

swim wâay náam ว่ายน้ำ *Unit 4.2*

symbol sǎn-ya-lák สัญลักษณ์ *Unit 5.2*

symptom ʔaa-kaan อาการ *Unit 8.1*

table tóʔ โต๊ะ *Unit 1.3*

tail haaŋ หาง *Unit 2.1*

take ʔaw เอา *Unit 2.4*

take along, bring along phaa พา *Unit 4.3*

take off (an article of clothing) thɔ̀ɔt ถอด *Unit 6.1*

tall sǔuŋ สูง *Unit 2.1*

taste rót รส *Unit 3.3*

taxi rót thɛ́k-sîi รถแท็กซี่ *Unit 5.3*

tea chaa ชา *Unit 3.1*

teach sɔ̌ɔn สอน *Unit 2.4*

teacher khruu ครู *Unit 2.4*

teeth fan ฟัน *Unit 8.1*

telefax (formal) thoo-ra-sǎan โทรสาร *Unit 5.4*

telephone thoo-ra-sàp โทรศัพท์ *Unit 2.2*

to telephone, to speak (with) phûut sǎay พูดสาย *Unit 7.2*

television thoo-ra-thát โทรทัศน์ *Unit 4.1*

television (informal) thii-wii ทีวี *Unit 4.2*

tell bɔ̀ɔk บอก *Unit 3.2*

temperature ʔun-ha-phuum อุณหภูมิ *Unit 10.1*

temple wát วัด *Unit 5.1*

tennis then-nít, then-nís เทนนิส *Unit 7.1*

term (school term or semester) thəəm เทอม *Unit 4.4*

terrified, frightened sa-yɔ̌ɔŋ khwǎn สยองขวัญ *Unit 7.1*

Thai thay ไทย *Unit 1.3*

thank; Thank you. khɔ̀ɔp-khun ขอบคุณ *Unit 1.1*

thank; Thank you. (informal) khɔ̀ɔp-cay ขอบใจ *Unit 6.1*

That's alright. It doesn't matter. mây-pen-ray ไม่เป็นไร *Unit 1.1*

there thîi-nân ที่นั่น *Unit 4.4*

there is, there are mii มี *Unit 5.4*

There it is. nân-ŋay นั่นไง *Unit 9.2*

therefore, as a consequence cɯŋ จึง *Unit 9.1*

thick nǎa หนา *Unit 6.2*

thief kha-mooy ขโมย *Unit 9.1*

thin baaŋ บาง *Unit 6.2*

thin (not fat), lean phɔ̌ɔm ผอม *Unit 2.1*

think khít คิด *Unit 2.1*

think of, miss khít-thɯ̌ŋ คิดถึง *Unit 2.3*

throughout ta-lɔ̀ɔt ตลอด *Unit 6.3*

thunder fáa rɔ́ɔŋ ฟ้าร้อง *Unit 10.1*

thunderbolt fáa phàa ฟ้าผ่า *Unit 10.1*

ticket bàt บัตร *Unit 3.4*

ticket tǔa ตั๋ว *Unit 5.3*

tie, bind, fasten phùuk ผูก *Unit 6.1*

tiger sɯ̌a เสือ *Unit 9.1*

tight-fitting fít ฟิต *Unit 6.2*

tight-fitting kháp คับ *Unit 6.2*

time wee-laa เวลา *Unit 4.1*

tired, fatigued nɯ̀ay เหนื่อย *Unit 3.2*

tired, stiff (of muscles) mɯ̂ay เมื่อย *Unit 3.2*

today wan-níi วันนี้ *Unit 1.3*

tofu, bean curd tâw-hûu เต้าหู้ *Unit 3.3*

toilet hɔ̂ŋ sûam ห้องส้วม *Unit 5.4*

toilet, lavatory (formal) sù-khǎa สุขา *Unit 3.2*

tomorrow phrûŋ-níi พรุ่งนี้ *Unit 4.3*

too, excessively kəən-pay เกินไป *Unit 6.1*

toothbrush prɛɛŋ-sǐi-fan แปรงสีฟัน *Unit 8.1*

toothpaste yaa-sǐi-fan ยาสีฟัน *Unit 8.1*

tour thɔ̂ŋ-thîaw ท่องเที่ยว *Unit 2.4*
tour bus, motor coach rót-thua รถทัวร์ *Unit 10.1*
township caŋ-wàt จังหวัด *Unit 2.1*
trade kaan-kháa การค้า *Unit 5.1*
traffic ca-raa-cɔɔn จราจร *Unit 5.2*
traffic jam rót tìt รถติด *Unit 5.3*
traffic light fay-dɛɛŋ ไฟแดง *Unit 5.2*
train rót-fay รถไฟ *Unit 5.1*
train station sa-thǎa-nii rót-fay สถานีรถไฟ *Unit 5.1*
transfer money ʔoon ŋən โอนเงิน *Unit 9.2*
translate plɛɛ แปล *Unit 2.4*
transport khǒn-sòŋ ขนส่ง *Unit 5.1*
travel dəən-thaaŋ เดินทาง *Unit 5.3*
travel by a vehicle (as a passenger) dooy-sǎan โดยสาร *Unit 5.3*
treat (i.e. provide a treat for) líaŋ เลี้ยง *Unit 3.4*
tree, plant tôn-máay ต้นไม้ *Unit 5.4*
trek through the montains dəən-khǎw เดินเขา *Unit 10.1*
triangle, triangular sǎam-lìam สามเหลี่ยม *Unit 6.3*
trousers, long pants kaŋ-keeŋ khǎa-yaaw กางเกงขายาว *Unit 6.1*
true, real ciŋ จริง *Unit 3.4*
trunk (of elephant) ŋuaŋ งวง *Unit 2.1*
try, try out, try on lɔɔŋ ลอง *Unit 3.4*
T-shirt, tee-shirt sɨ̂a-yɨ̂ɨt เสื้อยืด *Unit 6.1*
tube top sɨ̂a kɔ̀-ʔòk เสื้อเกาะอก *Unit 6.1*
turn (and proceed in another direction); to veer líaw เลี้ยว *Unit 5.2*
turn, rotate, spin mǔn หมุน *Unit 7.2*
tusk, ivory ŋaa งา *Unit 2.1*
twin fǎa-fɛ̀ɛt ฝาแฝด Unit 2.3
type, variety yàaŋ อย่าง *Unit 5.3*

u

ugly nâa-klìat น่าเกลียด *Unit 2.1*
ugly (of person's appearance) khîi-rèe ขี้เหร่ *Unit 2.1*
uncle (older brother of father or mother) luŋ ลุง *Unit 2.3*
uncle or aunt (younger, maternal) náa น้า *Unit 2.3*
uncle or aunt (younger, paternal) ʔaa อา *Unit 2.3*
under, below tâay ใต้ *Unit 2.1*
undershirt (men's) sɨ̂a klâam เสื้อกล้าม *Unit 6.1*
understand khâw-cay เข้าใจ *Unit 1.3*
understand rúu-rɨ̂aŋ รู้เรื่อง *Unit 7.1*
undo (an error), correct kɛ̂ɛ แก้ *Unit 6.2*
uniform khrɨ̂aŋ-bɛ̀ɛp เครื่องแบบ *Unit 6.1*
university ma-hǎa-wít-tha-yaa-lay มหาวิทยาลัย *Unit 1.2*
until thɨ̌ŋ ถึง *Unit 4.3*
upstairs khâaŋ-bon, khâŋ-bon ข้างบน *Unit 5.2*
upward khɨ̂n ขึ้น *Unit 5.2*
urgent dùan ด่วน *Unit 9.1*
urinate (informal) chìi ฉี่ *Unit 3.2*
urinate (vulgar) yîaw เยี่ยว *Unit 3.2*
use cháy ใช้ *Unit 2.4*
used to khəəy เคย *Unit 2.1*
used up, exhausted (in supply) mòt หมด *Unit 8.2*
usually, ordinarily taam tham-ma-daa ตามธรรมดา *Unit 4.1*
utensils, appliances khrɨ̂aŋ-cháy เครื่องใช้ *Unit 3.4*

van rót-tûu รถตู้ *Unit 10.2*
variety show waa-ray-tîi วาไรตี้ *Unit 7.1*
vegetable phàk ผัก *Unit 3.3*
vegetarian food cee เจ *Unit 3.3*
vegetarian food maŋ-sa-wí-rát มังสวิรัติ *Unit 3.3*
vehicle rót รถ *Unit 5.1*
vendor (female) mɛ̂ɛ-kháa แม่ค้า *Unit 2.4*
vendor (male), merchant phɔ̂ɔ-kháa พ่อค้า *Unit 2.4*

vertical nεεw tâŋ แนวตั้ง *Unit 6.3*

very much (colloquial) caŋ จัง *Unit 3.1*

very, extremely (colloquial) mây-baw ไม่เบา *Unit 2.1*

view wiw วิว *Unit 10.1*

village mùu-bâan หมู่บ้าน *Unit 10.1*

villager chaaw-bâan ชาวบ้าน *Unit 10.2*

vinegar nám-sôm sǎay-chuu น้ำส้ม (สายชู) *Unit 3.3*

visit yîam เยี่ยม *Unit 4.4*

vomit ʔaa-cian อาเจียน *Unit 8.2*

vomit (informal) ʔûak อ้วก *Unit 8.2*

waist ʔeew เอว *Unit 8.1*

wait, wait for, await rɔɔ รอ *Unit 7.2*

wake up, get up tɯ̀ɯn nɔɔn ตื่นนอน *Unit 4.2*

walk dəən เดิน *Unit 3.2*

wall pha-nǎŋ ผนัง *Unit 5.4*

wall, partition fǎa ฝา *Unit 5.4*

want to, desire to yàak อยาก *Unit 2.4*

want, need, require (formal) tɔ̂ŋ-kaan ต้องการ *Unit 10.2*

wash (clothes) sák ซัก *Unit 4.2*

wash one's hair sà phǒm สระผม *Unit 8.1*

watch naa-li-kaa นาฬิกา *Unit 1.3*

Watch out! Be careful! ra-waŋ ระวัง *Unit 9.1*

waterfall nám-tòk น้ำตก *Unit 7.1*

watermelon tεεŋ-moo แตงโม *Unit 6.3*

wave khlɯ̂ɯn คลื่น *Unit 7.1*

we raw เรา *Unit 1.1*

wear (lower garment) nûŋ นุ่ง *Unit 6.1*

wear, put on, put in sày ใส่ *Unit 6.1*

weather ʔaa-kàat อากาศ *Unit 4.4*

week ʔaa-thít อาทิตย์ *Unit 4.3*

week sàp-daa สัปดาห์ *Unit 4.3*

weep, cry rɔ́ɔŋ-hâay ร้องไห้ *Unit 8.1*

weight nám-nàk น้ำหนัก *Unit 9.2*

welcome, receive (e.g. guests) tɔ̂ɔn-ráp ต้อนรับ *Unit 2.4*

west ta-wan-tòk ตะวันตก *Unit 5.1*

Westerner (Caucasian) fa-ràŋ ฝรั่ง *Unit 1.4*

what ʔa-ray อะไร *Unit 1.*

wheel lɔ́ɔ ล้อ *Unit 5.3*

when mɯ̂a เมื่อ *Unit 4.1*

when tɔɔn ตอน *Unit 2.4*

When? At what time? mɯ̂a-ray เมื่อไร *Unit 2.1*

Where are you going? pay-nǎy ไปไหน *Unit 1.1*

Where have you been? pay-nǎy-maa ไปไหนมา *Unit 1.1*

Where? thîi-nǎy ที่ไหน *Unit 1.1*

while; at the time when wee-laa เวลา *Unit 3.4*

white (color) khǎaw ขาว *Unit 6.1*

who khray ใคร *Unit 1.2*

whole, entire tháŋ ทั้ง *Unit 4.4*

wide kwâaŋ กว้าง *Unit 8.2*

wife mia เมีย *Unit 2.3*

wife (formal) phan-ra-yaa, phan-yaa ภรรยา *Unit 2.3*

wind lom ลม *Unit 10.1*

window nâa-tàaŋ หน้าต่าง *Unit 2.2*

withdraw money thɔ̌ɔn ŋən ถอนเงิน *Unit 9.2*

woman, female yǐŋ หญิง *Unit 3.2*

wonton kíaw เกี๊ยว *Unit 3.3*

work tham-ŋaan ทำงาน *Unit 1.2*

work, task, job ŋaan งาน *Unit 2.4*

wound, cut phlɛ̌ɛ แผล *Unit 8.1*

wrap hɔ̀ɔ ห่อ *Unit 9.2*

write, draw khǐan เขียน *Unit 1.3*

year pii ปี *Unit 1.2*

yellow lɯ̌aŋ เหลือง *Unit 6.1*

Yes. chây ใช่ *Unit 1.3*

yesterday mɯ̂a-waan เมื่อวาน *Unit 4.3*

yonder nóon โน้น *Unit 6.2*

you khun คุณ *Unit 1.2*

you (familiar) thəə เธอ *Unit 1.1*